LOST FOR WORDS?

PITT LATIN AMERICAN SERIES

George Reid Andrews, General Editor

GOETZ FRANK OTTMANN

LOST FOR WORDS?

Brazilian Liberationism in the 1990s

UNIVERSITY OF PITTSBURGH PRESS

Published by the University of Pittsburgh Press, Pittsburgh, Pa., 15260

Copyright © 2002, University of Pittsburgh Press

Manufactured in the United States of America

Printed on acid-free paper

10 9 8 7 6 5 4 3 2 1

Library of Congress Cataloging-in-Publication Data

Ottmann, Goetz Frank.

  Lost for words? : Brazilian liberationism in the 1990s / Goetz Frank
Ottmann.

    p. cm. — (Pitt Latin American series)
Includes bibliographical references and index.

  ISBN 0-8229-4181-3 (alk. paper)

  1. Liberation theology—Brazil—São Paulo—History—20th century. 2.
Catholic Church—Brazil—São Paulo—History—20th century. 3. São
Paulo (Brazil)—Church history—20th century. I. Title. II. Series.

  BX1467.S3 O88 2002

  230'.0464'098161—dc21

                                                    2002003128

CONTENTS

Acknowledgments   *vii*

1. Introduction   *1*

2. The Voice of the Voiceless: The People, the Struggle, Authenticity, and Popular Culture   *25*

3. Genesis and Crisis of the Liberationist Struggle: 1968–1985   *48*

4. Institutionalization and Death of the Liberationist Struggle: Mid-1980s to Mid-1990s   *84*

5. Dogmatic Liberationism and Pragmatist Responses to Everyday Needs   *109*

6. Resurrecting the Liberationist Spirit   *134*

7. Liberationism at the End of the Millennium   *159*

Appendix   *181*

Notes   *185*

References   *215*

Index   *223*

ACKNOWLEDGMENTS

The production of this volume was made possible by a great many people to whom I wish to express my sincerest gratitude. The book would not have been possible if the people interviewed for the study—who are in danger of disappearing behind terms such as interviews and methodology—had refused to extend their trust and friendship. I am deeply indebted to all those who opened their homes, workplaces, and headquarters to me and my intrusive camera. I hope that, in spite of the innumerable mistakes that I made while enjoying the hospitality of my objects of study, we convinced each other that ethnographic research can be useful to both parties.

Above all, I would like to thank Jardim Damasceno, Jardim Princesa, Jardim Vista Alegre, and Jardim Recanto for their support, hospitality, and patience. I am grateful to Maria de Lourdes Beldi de Alcântara, Maria Regina Toledo Sader, and Helenilda Cavalcanti for their support, intellectual inspiration, and friendship. The early stages of my work benefited greatly from the critical input of Teresa Pires do Rio Caldeira and Pedro Jacobi. Furthermore, I would like to express my gratitude to Alastair Greig and Patrick Guinness and to the members and staff of the Sociology Department at the Australian National University. Elisabeth McCormack deserves special mention for her excellent work as a proofreader. For some, however, like Rowan Ireland and Mary Aitken, thanks are not sufficient. Moreover, I am indebted to the Institute of Latin American Studies at LaTrobe University for the resources they furnished.

LOST FOR WORDS?

INTRODUCTION

Edilene, Cleide, and Maria da Glória are veteran Catholic community activists and administrators of the day-care centers in Jardim[1] (Jd.) Vista Alegre, a *bairro* (neighborhood) at the northern fringe of São Paulo. In the neoliberal environment of the mid-1990s, these day-care and youth centers underwent severe funding cuts. Faced with the seemingly impossible task of adjusting to the new political climate, their project is in profound crisis. Adriana, a veteran political activist in the same region, complains about the political apathy she encounters in the groups she is trying to mobilize. Her eleventh land occupation, which she initiated during 1996, shows ominous signs of a lack of unity that seems to stem from an ambivalence surrounding the collective identities of participants. Padre Pedro, one of the *liberationist* Catholic priests who have been working in the region since the early 1990s, has lost his faith in the revolution from the bottom up. He sums this up in one of his more polemical statements: "The masses here won't rise up at the best of times." In the words of Julie, an Irish Catholic activist who has been in the region for more than thirty years, the trouble with these local activists is their attachment to a discourse that "is really a discourse of the 1980s. Today something else is happening. What, then, is the discourse of the '90s?" she asks, immediately answering her own question with yet another one: "Maybe we don't need a discourse of the '90s?"

Activists and members of militant Catholic communities in one of the few regions that have enjoyed the unabated support of São Paulo's progressive ecclesiastical hierarchy made these comments in 1996. They reveal the depth of the liberationist crisis. The symbolism that inspired hundreds of thousands of citizens to take to the streets just a decade earlier now seems to lack mobilizing power, and the procession (*caminhada*) of the people (*o povo*) into a better future has come to a halt. Political achievements of the past two decades, such as the establishment of day- and health-care centers, are evanescing as rapidly as the centers are deteriorating. The extraordinary communitarian spirit that, according to many academic observers, defined the (authentic) culture of popular[2] neighborhoods (*bairros populares*) during the 1970s and 1980s has disappeared, and drugs, gang warfare, and domestic violence appear to have undermined the last vestiges of collective action (Doimo 1995). Militants who try to reignite the vigor of *the struggle* (*a luta*) complain about movement participants' fighting predominantly for individual gains. All these factors point toward a complete implosion of the liberationist struggle. Terms like *fragmentation* or *individualism* have been used, perhaps justly, by authors like Roberto Mangabeira Unger and Gómes (1996) to describe the state of Brazilian popular politics in the 1990s.

AIMS AND FOCUS

Despite such evidence, on the basis of which many academic commentators discarded the liberationist struggle, my field work in four low-income *bairros* at the northern fringe of São Paulo, Brazil, cemented my conviction that this academic retreat was in many ways premature. Abandoning militant Catholic communities during an admittedly spectacular instance of crisis precludes any possibility of gaining important insights into the remaking of liberationism. In fact, the information gathered between 1995 and 1998 suggests that such a remaking is actually taking place. Liberationist pastoral practice inspired by liberationist thought continues to give rise to new initiatives that transform and renovate the symbolic universe of the struggle.

In the *bairros*, local conditions, conflicts, and experiences continue to be reworked in liberationist terms to form a frame of reference that contains "the specific metaphors, symbolic representations, and cognitive cues used to render or cast behavior and events in an evaluative mode and to suggest alternative modes of action" (Zald 1996, 262), called here a Catholic liberationist symbolic universe. However, the significant changes within this universe can be fathomed only if the religious symbolic sphere is reconsidered as a dynamic factor. Largely overlooked by authors who deal with Brazilian popular politics, the religious imagery and faith that underpin the struggle have been explained predominantly in secular terms. As a consequence, concepts such as pragmatist responses to everyday experiences have come to replace catechist reflection and spiritual guidance. Such a secular reading of popular politics, however, is inevitably incomplete because it neglects the fact that in the liberationist struggle religious imagery and politics are fused together and mutually inform one another. The course of Brazilian politics gains an explanatory dimension when the contested nature of this religious symbolic universe is taken into account.

Focusing on the symbolic dimension of the struggle brings to light the contestation that occurs within this realm, a contestation that has encouraged as well as obstructed the development of a new political and religious *bairro* culture. This book documents the struggle over representation and meaning involving three groups: local residents, Catholic and secular militants, and the progressive Catholic Church. In this struggle individual interest groups try to impose their frame of reference on the political and spiritual outlook of other group members. They semantically rearticulate, assimilate, or colonize the symbolic universe of other actors. The book is also an account of an endeavor to stem or undermine such colonization efforts.

Following Stephen Greenblatt in *Possessões maravilhosas*, I see the *bairros* as a sphere of various conflicting symbolic universes shaped and reinterpreted by assimilative processes (Greenblatt 1996, 20). Through these assimilative processes, webs of meaning are attached to symbols that previously conjured up different images.[3] These webs of meaning, alongside stories, rituals, and world views, form part of a cultural repository people may draw on to solve problems encountered in everyday life. In this sense, "culture, with religion as one of its central components, offers a repertoire of discursive and nondiscursive resources from which individuals may draw to articulate identities and to construct alternative strategies of action to deal with the particular existential predicament they confront" (Vásquez 1998, 11). Hence, rather than conceiving the symbolic universe as merely discursive, as text that has no bearing on the decisions of actors, the following pages will demonstrate, time and time again, the linear connection between meaning and action.

In order to render visible this reelaboration of symbolic meaning and its effect on decisions and, consequently, practice, I will concentrate on concepts such as *the people, authenticity, the struggle,* and *popular culture,* key symbols that have been of enormous importance in popular politics during the 1970s and 1980s. These concepts form a recurrent feature in the work of authors who have been studying the role of the progressive Catholic Church in Brazil (see, for instance, Assies 1999; Burdick 1993; Drogus 1997; Lehmann 1996; Mariz 1994; Nagle 1997; Vásquez 1998). Despite the centrality of these concepts, only David Lehmann's (1996) contribution attempts to delineate the cultural universe of what he terms the culture of *basismo* and unravels some of the contradictions embedded in the currents of *basismo. Basista* Catholicism, as defined by Lehmann, "depicts an idealized image of popular culture in the face of which its activists and theorists prostrate themselves in an almost reverential manner: the result is that they try very hard to take up the habits and idioms of this popular culture in order to bring the Catholic religion, as they see it, nearer to the people and also in order to reform Catholicism itself in the direction of the point of view of the poor" (1996, 18). As the term *basismo* has turned into a catch-all phrase for any intellectual current or movement that claims to take seriously the concerns of poor people, I use it only sparingly. Moreover, as nuances and marked differences within the current of *basismo* are important to my argument, I will stick with terms such as liberationist theology, liberationist thought, and vanguardism, using the term *basismo* only if the occasion invites a rendering reminiscent of Lehmann's.

The following pages reveal the story of the genesis, death, and resurrection of liberationist projects in four popular neighborhoods in São Paulo that enjoyed the support of a progressive diocese for the time of the study. As the neighborhoods were, by and large, shielded from the conservative currents emanating from the Vatican during the 1980s and 1990s, they offer an opportunity to study the liberationist project under conditions unfettered by institutional constraints, often cited as one of the main impediments to liberationism in Brazil. By tracing the shifts in the symbolic sphere of *bairro* politics, this volume provides new insights into how local militancy is constructed, undermined, and reconstructed within a liberationist institutional space. In this way, I hope that my work will enrich our understanding of currents in Brazilian popular politics beyond the realm of the *bairros* studied.

THEORETICAL CONSIDERATIONS

Many academic commentaries dealing with collective mobilization in the Brazil of the 1970s and 1980s focus on pragmatism as the driving force in a transformative process that culminates in the birth of a new and independent secular *subject*.[4] Somehow, during a process that has remained largely unexplained, this emerging subject adjusts the learned discourse to her everyday experiences, giving rise to a new political language.

In his noted work *Quando novos personagens entram em cena*, Eder Sader tells the story of the Brazilian social movements of the 1970s and 1980s in the poorer neighborhoods and identifies the emergence of new subjects "from where nobody had dared to hope. . . ." (Sader 1988, 36). These subjects surfaced as a result of a concurrence of everyday experiences and a discursive matrix. Sader outlines the three most important discourses contributing to this matrix: the progressive Catholic Church, the Left, and the union movements. The pragmatic rearrangement of these discourses, stimulated by everyday experiences, shaped the voices of these new subjects. Notably absent from Sader's matrix were the actual voices of the new subjects. Instead, Sader gives us a collective voice that, he believes, gave rise to *social movements, new social movements,* or even *popular movements.* Interestingly, in the overwhelming majority of contributions to the debate around popular movements, collective subjects are constructed by way of this barely explained transformation process.

For many academic observers who understand Brazilian social movements as predominantly secular phenomena, popular subjects emerged as the result of an enigmatic metamorphosis. Actors who during the mid-1970s were still represented as insecure and subdued political clients (Perlman, quoted in Assies 1992, 9) were suddenly transformed into independent democratic subjects. How this transformation took place, though, was not easy to distinguish from these accounts. Foweraker (1995, 90), for instance, identifies a three-step procedure used by many authors to explain the generation of democratic actors. According to this formula, actors are seen as "processing inexorably from (1) daily resistance to (2) political protest to (3) democratic project." Such simplicity prompts Foweraker to note that the proposed process successfully avoids a more concrete analysis of the dynamics of a transformation process in real actors. Subjectivity or agency is taken largely as a precondition on which collective mobilization comes to rest (Slater 1996). What is often left implicit in such analysis, according to Daniel Levine, is the influence of institutions such as the progressive Catholic Church and their associated militants (Levine 1995, 112).

In fact, the form of movement politics that emerged in São Paulo during the 1970s and 1980s is inextricably linked to the activities of the progressive Catholic Church. During the 1970s, the Church functioned as an umbrella for opposition groups, offering minimal protection against the attempts of the military dictatorship (1964–85) to silence such groups. However, more than offering a protected political space in which an opposition could emerge, the militant clergy and laity, together with secular activists, stimulated the construction of a political-moral culture that became encapsulated in slogans such as "Preferential option for the poor," "Don't oppress your brother," and, more recently, "The cry of the excluded" (*o grito dos excluídos*) and "Social debt" (*dívida social*). A secular commentary on these themes describes them as "opposition to military," "democracy" and later "citizenship" couched in a language of "inclusion" and "exclusion" (Hochstetler 2000, 166). Militants of the progressive Church not only left strong imprints on the culture and posture of a popular Left that would consolidate in the formation of the Workers Party (PT) in 1980, but also contributed fundamentally to the construction of a new critical consciousness among the poorer classes. Much of their work was institutionalized in militant Catholic communities, increasingly represented during the late 1970s as Ecclesiastical Base Communities (CEBs).[5] These small, progressive, Church-sponsored community groups prepared the ground for the rise of what came to be known as popular movements.

Sader argues that during the 1970s most popular political groups in São Paulo were influenced by the progressive Catholic Church (1988, 198). My interviews with former members of such groups in the *bairros* largely confirm his claim. In these *bairros*, community mobilization and development activities drew almost exclusively on the capacity of Catholic militants.[6] In contrast to the impact of the secular Left during the 1970s, the symbolic imprint of the progressive Church is powerful and lasting. Even today, political groupings in these *bairros* use key concepts such as the people, the struggle, and the journey (or procession) that tie them inextricably to the symbolic universe of the liberationist Catholic Church. Furthermore, the overwhelming majority of these groups maintain direct links with this Church.

At the same time, the secular Left before the 1980s had only an indirect effect.[7] Physically distant from the "new" or "authentic" unionism that emerged in the 1970s in the south of greater São Paulo, this Left became a significant force in *bairro* politics only after the consolidation of the PT in the 1980s. Furthermore, with some exceptions, pockets of secular Left militants involved in the mobilization of the *bairros* had only limited impact, almost completely erased from the memory of interviewed local residents.[8] Hence, in the *bairros* the activities of Catholic radicals were indispensable to the formation of local political activism. Any analysis focusing on the construction of collective subjects in these *bairros* must take into account the role of the progressive Catholic Church. A failure to do so produces empty categories.[9]

Despite the strong liberationist influence underpinning *bairro* politics during the 1970s and 1980s,[10] many authors tried to give these "new" phenomena a secular reading. Optimistically, observers commented on the birth of new independent subjects in popular neighborhoods. According to this view, the people, assisted by a popular Church that valorized popular wisdom and knowledge, were able to develop their own voice, driving local politics to a point where truth could no longer be predetermined by certain actors but was derived through discussion (Barreira 1986, 139). These observations led Sader and others to adopt the following position: while acknowledging the importance of the radical Catholics, they were confident about the emergence of a new secular Left voice from the grassroots. They saw the emerging subjectivity as an amalgam of ideologies that slowly started to condense.

The Construction of a Secular Civil Society

This secularization of essentially religious mobilization attempts in low-income neighborhoods formed part of a project to construct a civil society in a democratic wasteland marked by more than two decades of military dictatorship. Something of the urgency of this project reverberates in Francisco Weffort's often quoted passage:

> We would have liked to have a civil society, felt the need for it in order to defend us against a monstrous state. So, as this civil society did not exist, we had to invent it. If it were small, we would have to nurture it (engrandecê-la). . . . It is obvious that, if I talk here of invention or nurturing, I am not tak-

ing these words in the sense of artificial propaganda. I take them as signs of values present in political action. These values lend meaning to political action because action intended to turn them into reality (Weffort 1984, 95).

For authors like Sader, actively engaged within the emerging Left's project in São Paulo, it was important to purge the strong Catholic religious/moral influences contained within this Left in order to construct the desired political force. They felt that this endeavor to construct the voice of the people outside the religious/moral realm of the progressive Catholic Church should no longer rely on the transformative force of the liberationist clergy and laity, but needed a concept that could deliver these new subjects from the influence of the Church. Consequently these authors endowed local activists with the ability to pragmatically adjust discourses to everyday experiences as though there were no possibility that the very moment of experience might not be constituted out of religious symbolic elements.

For Sader, the everyday experience of exploitation and injustice of the poorer classes formed the preconditions for the emergence of these social movements, the locus of the new "collective subjects." These subjects were able to cast everyday experiences into a new language—that of social movements (Sader 1988, 142). In other words, the raw, lived experience of collective subjects initiates a reconstruction of discourses, so that they approximate more closely true representations of the lived reality of the popular classes. These subjects forged their own voices by acting on their everyday experiences and pragmatically adapted and tailored the available discourses according to their needs. With this notion, Sader's elaboration epitomizes a thinking that became dominant in Brazil during the mid-1980s.

This approach views the Church as contributing to the construction of a new critical but ultimately conservative consciousness, but dismisses the religious content of this consciousness. Insistence on a political analysis loses sight of the symbolic fabric that informs local Catholic communities.[11] Pedro Jacobi and others who try to read the project of the progressive Church in secular political terms see the influence of the progressive Church, if it exists at all, in terms of creating pre–social movement conditions, such as providing an umbrella for collective action (Foweraker 1995, 4; Jacobi 1993). This assumption neatly separates political and religious universes, leaving the academic observer to interpret religious, moral, and spiritual tendencies within *bairro* politics in secular terms. This explanation is predicated largely on the notion of pragmatic response to everyday experiences. Hence, during the early 1980s, analysts were able to represent social movements as authentic popular responses to state repression and economic austerity (Foweraker 1995, 5).

By the mid-1980s, as it became obvious that such an explanation was less than compelling, the inventors of new social movements began to represent the spiritual and religious content of *bairro* politics in terms of identity and culture. It became increasingly accepted that political activism involved a "search for different identities" (Jellin in Foweraker 1995, 45) that were never entirely negotiable (Melucci 1989, 343) and always dependent on context. This identity-forming context, however, was rendered opaque by the majority of academic reflections on Brazilian social movements. Hence, religion and spirituality remained confined to an institutionalized space, removed from politics.[12] CEBs were allowed to enter the political debate only as long as the political content of their discourse and action was self-evident,[13] effectively barring access to the politics of religion.[14] As a result, much of the academic commentary on militant, Catholic community–inspired, Latin American social movements or, more recently, popular movements, reads like a secular restatement and reduction of a religious theme.[15]

Liberationist Currents in Academic Writing

Accounts acknowledging the central role of the progressive Church are few compared with the wealth of published material dealing with *bairro* politics in predominantly secular terms. Virtually all contributions that do focus on the role of the progressive Church in Brazil during the 1970s and 1980s strongly favor the project of liberation theology (Sader 1988, 156).[16] Consequently, this area has been dominated by authors whose work reflects the symbolic framework of liberationism and the influence of liberationist militants (Lehmann 1996, 14).

The influence of the progressive Catholic Church is hard to escape. The Church's proposal for a new, just, and more harmonious world, by emphasizing social and economic justice, proved seductive, especially against the backdrop of a violent military dictatorship. In conjunction with the—at times —heroic stance of members of the progressive Church against the authoritarian government during the 1970s, it created an immense moral legitimation. As a result, even authors like Eder Sader, who would prefer to tell the story of the new Left in Brazil without the Church, find themselves fighting the spell of Catholic liberationism on a number of pages.[17]

Liberationist thought colored many of the debates in Brazil between the mid-1970s and the late 1980s. The doctrine was so dominant among intellectuals in representation of what was going on at the grass roots that it is difficult to discern its real engagement and impact. Some of its moral importance may have been exposed by a paradigmatic break in this discourse that occurred during the late 1980s. This rupture reduced the previous academic outlook to a kind of "ingenuous optimism of those who let themselves be seduced by their object or who took for reality things only happening in the interior of their own imagination" (Telles, quoted in Assies 1992, 12). While this explanation cannot be excluded, many observers lived an instance of profound liberationist mobilization that tended to invest poor communities with aspects of an authentic purity.[18] With the fading dominance of the progressive Catholic symbolic universe over academic representation, scholars began to focus increasingly on "the 'other face' of the movements, dismantling the hope vested in them or, at least, making it necessary to rethink their political significance" (Assies 1992, 11).

Debating the Role of the Progressive Church

Authors who take account of the impact of the Brazilian progressive Catholic Church differ in the degree to which they endow CEBs and respective militants with transformative capacity. Hewitt (1991) identifies three positions within this debate: a liberationist position favoring a renovation from the grass roots; an institutionalist position, asserting that the hierarchy holds a crucial control over this project; and a position that holds that the liberationist project unleashes its transformative potential principally within the cultural sphere. More recently, the focus shifted to shortcomings of liberationism itself, as academics became disenchanted with liberation theology.

Following a liberationist framework that uses a Gramscian Marxism interpretation of social change, authors like Enrique Dussel, Gustavo Gutierrez, Leonardo Boff, and Otto Maduro have argued strongly for the potential of the grass roots to renovate religious as well as social structures (Hewitt 1991, 21). For authors following this trajectory, the potential for structural change rests with the popular classes, which are endowed with a prophetic role in effecting this transformation. Dussel believes that the Church's reorientation in Latin America toward the poor and its adoption of a sometimes radical social mission comes from a "people-rooted Christianity." For Gutierrez and Boff, the oppressed masses, having successfully appealed to their Church for assistance, transform themselves into the people, make their presence felt, and engage in a struggle in which power and autonomy are wrested from the dominant classes (Hewitt 1991, 21; Lehmann 1996, 64–72). From this viewpoint, institutional or structural constraints that could potentially impede this transformative process are less important.

The institutionalists oppose this view, arguing that the symbolic space of subjects is always constrained by the Church hierarchy. In principle, Ralph Della Cava (1986) and Thomas Bruneau (1979) are positively disposed toward liberationism and especially its aim of democratizing the Church hierarchy, but they are equally skeptical about the success of this venture. They claim that the Church hierarchy has always controlled and directed the development of liberationist social doctrine. Explaining the motives of the Church hierarchy's policy shift toward social justice, Della Cava focuses on events: the advent of positivism, Protestantism, socialism, communism, and Afro spiritism. Other contributing factors were hierarchical changes, the chronic lack of clergy in conjunction with a rapidly expanding population, a mass religiosity that needed no institutional structures, and the success of the political Left within the context of deteriorating living conditions (Della Cava 1986, 15, 19). Within this analytical tradition, institutional interests, by and large, subsume agency.

For these authors, the liberationist claim that the progressive Church represents the "voice of the voiceless" contains a fallacy. As changes within the Church are controlled by the hierarchy, and as the dogma and symbolic power of the Church always shapes initiatives that arise from within its ranks, it is not possible for CEB agents to embody effectively the interests of local communities. CEB practices will always contain elements of the project of the Catholic Church that may conflict with local interests (Bruneau 1979, 70, 174). For CEBs to really constitute the basis for popular movements, Della Cava claims, their activities most certainly must take on an independent character (1986, 21). Such independence, however, would endanger the survival of the Church as an institution. This academic orientation, then, allows for only limited autonomy at the grass roots. The political autonomy of *bairro* residents is largely undermined in the long run by the successful attempt of the hierarchy to imprint its agenda on the project of the nascent subjects.

Most contemporary commentators acknowledge the importance of institutional power in the decline of the liberationist Church (Berryman 1996, 14–15; Drogus 1999, 41; Hewitt 1998, 183; Levy 2000, 168; Vásquez 1998). Hewitt, for instance, endorses the position of the institutionalists when he argues that CEBs became depoliticized in much the same manner that they and other Catholic groups became politicized during the 1970s and early 1980s. Hewitt says that Dom Paulo Evaristo Arns, archbishop of São Paulo between 1970 and 1998, initiated a "chain of activists" by surrounding himself with institutional leaders interested in a politicized Church. This "chain of activism," Hewitt claims, disintegrated with the increasing opposition of the Vatican, culminating in the division of the archdiocese in 1989. The breakup of the archdiocese spelled dramatic changes for regions that were subsequently under the control of conservative bishops. "As new bishops assumed command of their domains, more radical pastoral agents either were removed from positions of influence within the CEBs or voluntarily left to work in areas —within the Church or elsewhere—where the social justice cause [was] still valued" (Hewitt 1998, 183).

Faced by this rolling back of institutional support for the popular Church, the liberationists struck a strong antiestablishment tone. Comblin (1990) and Benedetti (1988), for instance, deplore the loss of hegemony of the social doctrine within the Church. For these authors, the liberationist pledge facilitated the emergence of a new and authentic form of Catholicism, whose disseminated political message and values are directly transforming social and religious structures. Due to a paradox encapsulated in liberation theory, however, liberationism is under pressure. Vásquez sums this up: "By working to renovate the Catholic Church from the grass roots and by decentralizing power within it, the progressive clergy and laity undermine the positions of those who have been vital for its establishment. This, in turn, weakens progressive pastoral initiatives" (Vásquez 1998, 108). In order to safeguard some of the CEBs' achievements, Comblin proposes to disentangle the CEBs from the institutional web by turning them into a national lay movement (Vásquez 1998, 108). Hence institutional concerns seem to play a larger role than initially anticipated.

Critical of liberationist as well as institutionalist viewpoints, Daniel Levine

(1992), W. E. Hewitt (1991), Scott Mainwaring (1986b), and Rowan Ireland (1986), for instance, relegate the thrust of the liberationist transformative potential to the cultural sphere. Rather than producing social change by means of revolutionary political activity, *bairro* residents affect society through their everyday activities, potentially altering the cultural makeup of Brazilian society. By participating in CEB groups, some of these authors would argue, people learn a new outlook on society and realize that they have the possibility to participate in it. This learning process strengthens the voices of CEB participants and enhances their capacity to make their presence felt. CEBs are seen to produce a more aware citizen who is able to participate more actively in society (Hewitt 1991, 90). By stimulating new social practices that further communitarianism and democratization, CEBs have a substantial effect on political life (Mainwaring 1986b, 204). Even the more skeptical writings emanating from this position represent CEBs as inspiring cultural change. Their presence is seen to generate a space that encourages an antihegemonic sensibility whose wider impact on society remains ambiguous (Ireland 1986, 180). From this point of view, CEBs exert a certain empowering influence, potentially adding to the options of participants and the wider community.

Thus a wide variety of intellectuals representing popular struggles endorse liberationism. While the discourse on social movements recasts liberationist values and morals in the terms of a postindustrialist analysis, authors who address the strong influence of the progressive Church tend to openly embrace liberationism. Levine, Mainwaring, Ireland, and Hewitt believe that the progressive Church fulfils at least three functions that have a liberating effect. Progressive Catholicism provides the institutional space in which an antihegemonic sensibility can flourish; it fulfils a strong educative role that transforms the local residents into a community of citizens; and it strengthens a community-centered cultural framework that is conducive to democratic processes.

More recently, however, even cautiously optimistic writers, such as Rowan Ireland (1991), are increasingly concerned about the shortcomings of the liberationist movement. Criticism of the movement by authors who have detected problems in the very project of liberation theology has gained in ardor. Church militants, these authors argue, never managed to overcome the gap that divided them from the people for whom they claimed to speak. Cultural studies exponents, such as John Burdick (1993) and David Lehmann (1996), corroborate these claims by arguing that the liberationist movement is essentially an elite position vying for leverage in a political and spiritual struggle for a new constituency.

Moreover, observers have become aware that liberationism has ceased to resonate within Brazilian working class neighborhoods. Factors leading to this decline in mobilizing power include changing material, political, physical, and spiritual needs (Lehmann 1996; Vasquez 1998; Drogus 1999; Burdick 1993; Mariz 1994; Nagle 1997).

MATERIAL NEEDS

Manuel Vásquez, for instance, contends that it is the liberationists' teleological view of history, "in which human actions point to the realization of the reign of God on earth" increasingly in conflict with the deteriorating living conditions of the poor that has led to a disenchantment with liberationist Catholicism (1998, 125). Lehmann phrases this in slightly different terms, claiming that *basismo*, the language of opposition to the gruesome abuses of the military dictatorship, is powerless against the dispersed and subtle, but no less devastating than the influences of neoliberal reforms and economic globalization (1996, 114). Drogus, adding a gendered account, claims that the economic crisis of the 1980s reduced the ability of women to participate in CEBs (1999, 39). At the same time, she notes that the fulfillment of material demands alongside other factors often led women to return to their households (1999, 40).

POLITICAL NEEDS

Underscoring political themes that led to the decline of liberationism, Drogus notes that women in positions of leadership were often put off by the corrupt and masculinist world of politics they encountered after the reinstatement of democracy in 1985 (1999, 39). In Drogus's account, this effect is exacerbated by the faltering Church support for structures that allowed women to organize (1999, 41).

PHYSICAL NEEDS

For some authors, CEBs do inspire an involvement of participants in the public sphere, though only at the expense of a lack of concern for issues involving the family or the individual. Mariz, for instance, contrasts CEBs with groups formed by Pentecostal churches and concludes that CEBs do not offer avenues for social and economic self-advancement of the kind offered by the Pentecostal groups (1994, 79, 100, 143, 150). Focusing on a similar point, Drogus and Burdick note that the popular Church has not taken seriously women's issues and intrafamily gender roles. Marital problems and domestic violence remain beyond the focus of reflection (Drogus 1997, 156; Burdick 1993).

SPIRITUAL NEEDS

Moreover, the architects of the popular Church are charged with building an excessively rational religious edifice whose spiritual foundation has been largely neglected. Nagle notes that the shift from spiritual to political matters has provoked a disenchantment with the liberationist project per se as politics is perceived as intrinsically soiled and corrupt. "Devout Brazilians of many traditions," she claims, "are willing to work to change social structures that oppress them, but not by neglecting the rituals, mysteries, and histories that inform their religious practice" (Nagle 1997, 159).

This and similar accounts led during the 1990s to a fundamental pessimism. Observers began to abandon interest in liberation theology. The stubborn rejection of a cooperative dialogue with institutions, Lehmann observed, "has the effect of restricting *basismo* to little more than endless cascading expressions of localistic frustration, anger, and immediate demands whose potential for achieving structural change in the long term is grossly exaggerated by overenthusiastic intellectuals in search of a new revolutionary paradigm—or perhaps merely of new rhetorical devices in which to dress an old paradigm" (Lehmann 1996, 29).[19] Increasingly, liberation theology was—prematurely in Daniel Levine's eyes (Levine 1995, 107)—reported to be dead.[20]

Why, then, should one focus on CEB-like communities in the late 1990s? The case studies presented in this book indicate that it is too soon to narrate the demise of liberationist communities. Over the course of the 1990s, CEB-like communities have changed profoundly, adapting themselves to a new institutional and cultural context. Although most of the revolutionary zeal of the 1970s has evaporated, progressive Catholic communities at the turn of the millennium continue a liberationist struggle for a more just society. Daniel Levine has it right when he claims that liberation theology is not static (Levine 1995, 105–6). I believe, however, that it is of great importance to differentiate between liberation *theology*, consolidated by the progressive Catholic Church, and liberationist *thought*, a rather heterogeneous body of beliefs and practices closely interwoven with this theology. Indeed, as will emerge from the following chapters, liberationist thought has evolved substantially over the past two decades, and it still accounts for much of the construction of a critical and political *bairro* culture. Levine has it only partially right because the evolution of institutionalized liberationist theology has been limited during the 1980s and 1990s (Drogus 1997, 157).[21] This institutionalization process has given rise to structural constraints, recently documented by Vàsquez (1997). While Vàsquez's account manages to document many of the tensions that have emerged between local militants and clerics, he tends to ignore the symbolic backdrop to this conflict.

The following pages will reveal the way in which the liberationist symbolic universe represents a further dynamic factor (albeit ambiguous) in *bairro* politics. While the liberationist imagery certainly encouraged local residents to acquire a critical outlook, this process was truncated not only by the local liberationist clergy and hierarchy, but also by a dogmatic reading of the liberationist framework per se. The ensuing incapacity of local leaders to deconstruct, investigate, and reconstruct their symbolic frame of reference undermined their ability to adjust their strategies to a rapidly changing context. In other words, the dogmatic reading of the by now liberationist doctrine promoted by the progressive Catholic Church introduced a certain static quality to the liberationist project. This significantly undermined the development of a new liberationist synthesis. However, to sum up these events as "the death of liberation theology"—thus giving them an absolute finality—would be certainly premature. On the contrary, the enduring presence of liberationist faith ensures a radical rethinking of past representations and enhances the possibility of resurrection. In the *bairros* this has led to the construction of a new popular liberationist synthesis.[22]

Construction of new liberationist projects is an extremely intricate and challenging process, a process that is shaped and often undermined by institutional and symbolic factors. Daniel Levine underemphasizes the complexities involved in this symbolic reelaboration when he claims, "Throughout Latin America popular groups have taken those ideas [the doctrine of the Church and liberationist ideas] and *reworked them in the context of urgent everyday needs and conflicts*" (Levine 1992, 18; emphasis added). In fact, as the quotation above shows, Levine's optimism seems to flow from an often unwarranted trust in the pragmatic responses of the poorer classes to everyday experiences. This position appears in the works of a host of authors dealing with Brazilian popular politics.

Given the centrality of pragmatism in accounts dealing with popular politics in Brazil, it is worth referring to Roberto Mangabeira Unger (1975, 1987), a Brazilian philosopher, a member of the Democratic Workers Party (*Partido Democrático Trabalhista*, PDT), and founder of the legal studies movement in the United States. He gives concepts such as pragmatism and everyday life experiences a philosophical basis and follows the liberationist Catholics down to the grass roots, where he constructs his key concept around "alternative spiritual responses to a shared experience" (Unger 1987, 75).[23] Unger's work of the 1980s is strongly colored by the liberationist prophecy, calling for the creation of a "new man," who seems to issue from the sources that gave rise to progressive Catholic activism (see chapter 2). Unger recasts this Brazilian vision of a renewed society, which emerged in the 1960s and 1970s, to create his notion of "practical reason" (Unger 1975, 97). With this radical pragmatist rereading of liberationist ideas, Unger attempts to reinvigorate the "bleak defensiveness and resignation" of tragic liberals like Richard Rorty.[24] Unger's philosophy tends to epitomize, if in different terms, the project of liberationists and academic commentators who too uncritically locate the motor of transformation in the pragmatic response of the popular classes to the experiences and constraints of their lives.

SYMBOLIC CONTESTATION

During the 1970s, the political culture of the *bairros* was significantly shaped by the progressive Church's institutionalized commitment to molding the popular masses into subjects whose consciousness has been awakened. CEBs were located at the center of this transformative policy, endorsed by a modest majority of members of the high clergy and aimed at political and spiritual empowerment of the popular classes. Embracing liberation theology, the Brazilian Catholic Church transformed itself into an agent of empowerment.

The term empowerment is often used to denote the practices of the progressive Church per se. As a consequence, it tends to disguise potential tensions arising from an imposition of individual or institutional interests. In other words, the term empowerment is used as a semantic device, conjuring up the image of an organic alliance between the progressive Church and the popular classes. Nonetheless, within the progressive and popular Catholic Church there are significant differences about its interpretation. In *bairro* communities, Catholic militants no longer endorse the empowerment project proposed by a progressive hierarchy. Hence, in order to elucidate fundamental shifts in *bairro* politics, the term empowerment needs to be rolled back and read within a historical context of symbolic contestation.

In this book, I reintroduce the religious symbolic dimension as a dynamic factor, by describing the symbolic universe of *bairro* politics as a contested space in which political and religious militancy is often assimilated by institutional interests. However, this institutional assimilation process is far from all consuming, and the rips in its symbolic fabric stimulate a radical semantic reelaboration that renovates the liberationist project.

THE CASE STUDY

The case study on which this work is based focuses on events in four low-income neighborhoods in Brasilândia. This region, located at the northern fringe of São Paulo, came to fame for its grass-roots activism during the late 1970s and early 1980s. Organized residents of Jd. Damasceno, Jd. Princesa, Jd. Vista Alegre, and Jd. Recanto—the *bairros* that are the focus of this study—participated in a struggle that united innumerable grass-roots organizations in this region.[25] Brasilândia has become an enclave of the progressive Catholic Church. In 1989 the progressive archdiocese of São Paulo was carved up by a conservative Vatican. Brasilândia, still within the domain of the progressive archbishop Dom Paulo Evaristo Arns, was placed within the hands of a charismatic figure within the liberationist movement, Dom Angélico Sândalo Bernardino. Under his leadership, Brasilândia became a refuge for liberationist pastoral agents, priests and nuns who left the newly created, increasingly conservative episcopates (Hewitt 1998). Given the level of documented political activity in the area (for instance, Jacobi 1993, Hewitt 1998, and Levy 2000), a study of religious, political, cultural, and economic factors in these four *bairros* can shed light on historical changes in the contested liberationist symbolic universe and trace the reframing of key symbols underpinning popular activism since the mid-1960s.[26]

In popular politics, the neighborhoods were—together with Jd. Guaraní, one of the neighboring *bairros*—an important locus of radicalism (Jacobi 1993). Much of the driving force of the popular struggle for urban infrastructure during the late 1970s emanated from these *bairros*. Jd. Damasceno and Jd. Vista Alegre are particularly renowned for their radical Catholic priests who stood at the forefront of the nascent struggle. Hence, radical Catholicism may have had a stronger impact on these *bairros* than on the wider region. Furthermore, the *bairros* attracted foreign Catholic radicals who were active in them for many years. During the 1970s, these foreigners certainly played a decisive role in local politics. In this regard also, the *bairros* may differ from the wider region. As a result of this intense political involvement of militants and radicals, the *bairros* were propelled toward the forefront of the struggle. They are thus ideal for an inquiry into the development of popular politics in the region since the late 1960s.

Despite these specific differences, the *bairros* are in many ways representative of the area. Socioeconomically they are a cross-section of low-income *bairros*. While Jd. Recanto and Jd. Vista Alegre are locally viewed as more affluent, Jd. Damasceno has the reputation of being one of the poorest neighborhoods in the region. Jd. Damasceno and Jd. Vista Alegre distinguish themselves from other *bairros* as violent places. Extensive media coverage of homicides, resulting from drug trade disputes in the *bairros*, has contributed effectively to a label that may or may not be justified.

METHODOLOGY

Searching for a term that could encompass the methodology for my fieldwork, I lean toward "empathetic social intervention." Gathering information represents an intrusion that affects locals as well as the ethnographer. Rather than pitching my tent in a Malinowskian fashion outside communities, I tried to stimulate exchanges that clarified cultural differences by directly engaging with local residents. In this exchange, I believe, knowledge is communicated in both directions. This may facilitate a kind of pragmatism on both sides that enhances the ability to act strategically. During this process, I may have culturally polluted the local realm. The fact that I was a white male foreigner with an elite education affected my interaction with local residents. I may have imposed a male logic on local projects and defiled the authentic local culture with fragments of a bourgeois world view. I certainly caused some serious conflicts. In any case, my intrusion into the *bairros* was largely welcomed by most local residents, who were eager to contract my skills to make their projects more viable. In this sense I was invited to work as a consultant with local projects, and my presence was more often requested than my time allowed. At the same time, I was faced with an incredible array of expectations, some of which were bound to be disappointed in the course of my stay.

While critics inspired by a neo-Nietzschean revisionism have been addressing their concern about the impact of action or intervention research (see, for instance, Papadakis 1989), I would like to remind these observers of the specificity of these *bairros*. The *bairros* are distinguished from most locations in developed countries by their limited access to elite information flows. This trend has been accentuated by recent shifts in job markets. As a result, contact points between the formal economy and *bairro* residents have been diminishing. This limited access to information and to a certain extent an inability to translate this information into local discourses militates strongly against the ability of local residents to adjust to changes in the political and economic landscape. In the past, middle-class interventions in the four *bairros* were most important in providing this exchange of information and the development of citizenship, subjectivity, and autonomy. In this book I argue that the muffling of voices in the late 1980s and 1990s has to do very much with the absence of an interventionist extra-ecclesial force committed to social change. To be sure, the impact of interventionist practices is always equivocal and may cause some impediments to local developments. In the *bairros*, this was predominantly the case when strategies were institutionalized and locked into formal Left populist politics, as a result skewing attempts to create a more pragmatic and flexible mode of action.

When the aim is to observe changes and to trace the causes that might militate against such changes in the behavior of popular activists, a pragmatic mixture of methodologies is needed. The methodology should be able to assist in establishing a link between discourse, action, and milieu. Much of the discursive sequences recorded were of a rhetorical nature and did not necessarily lead to action. To fathom links between discourses and action, the only reliable methodology, I found, was a form of interventionist participant observation. Only by participating actively in the local environment was I able to fathom certain relationships between discourses and action. Hence, my intervention in a local cooperative and in a land occupation formed an invaluable experience. Furthermore, through engagement I found the need to contextualize my experiences and discourse analysis in order to see how local discourses and action responded to changes within the wider environment. This led to the use of other research methods. Lacking reliable statistical material documenting the area's demographic and socioeconomic shifts, I was not able to draw on existing quantitative material. Hence, I saw the need to establish a quantitative basis that could help to elucidate the collected interview and experiential material.

By the time I arrived in the *bairros*, most historical sources, such as press releases, pamphlets, and photos about local political activity, had been thrown away. As a result, the reconstruction of local events came to rely heavily on interviews with key individuals. These interviews were, wherever possible, cross-referenced with newspaper articles and, whenever available, with visual documents of the era. The chapters dealing with the struggle, a historical period now almost twenty years in the past, rely on the accounts of only a few residents and community organizers active in the *bairros* at the time. This is because the area was barely settled during the mid 1970s and the residential flux has been enormous. Consequently, only a few *bairro* residents have been living in the area longer than fifteen years. Events in the more recent past are reconstructed on the basis of interviews with group leaders and participants, newspaper articles, and extensive participant observation. In order to contextualize this information, I conducted a survey.

Interviews were structured in two ways. During the first months in the *bairros*, at the beginning of 1996, I conducted mainly unstructured interviews with a broad focus. In an attempt to cross-reference the emerging themes, the interviews that followed had a more specific focus and concentrated on gender relations, violence, and economic changes, as well as strategies. Through in-depth interviews, I compared and tested the established perspectives. Local political interests, gossip, and myth slowly started to take shape. Some one hundred interviews were conducted in this manner. If possible, interviews were videotaped. Over the subsequent months, the individual stories changed substantially (alarmingly at first) and were adapted to the prevalent political climate and to the degree of trust extended toward me. At the end of my field-work period, I introduced local residents to the line of argument I had established. As *bairro* residents agreed, often enthusiastically, with my representation, I proceeded with the elaboration of this manuscript.

Throughout the interview process I experienced what then seemed substantial difficulties. Most important, the residents demanded something in return for their cooperation. This enticed me to become involved with various local, popular cooperatives active in the area. While this represented a great opportunity to get to know the *bairros* better, I also became associated with one particular group in the *bairro*, a group very closely aligned with the local Catholic Church and with the PT. As a result, the contacts that I was able to establish occurred within this specific realm. I am therefore not able to make any comments on local Pentecostal communities or groups associated with other political camps.

A further source of difficulty I encountered at times during the interview process issued from ethnic, cultural and class tensions. I do not want to exaggerate my 'otherness' in this instance, as local residents whom I employed as research assistants came up against similar barriers. In many ways I found it easier to open certain topics of conversation than did the local research assistants. Being an outsider, I was often able to ignore the sensitivity of issues and local codes of honor and morals, as well as the local sense of insecurity, and was thus able—at times even invited—to pose questions that locals would not dare to touch. Selectivity of memory, rhetorical answers, and carefully crafted responses that, at times, had not much to do with local events, produced obstacles known to other researchers in this and similar areas.[27] This made careful cross-referencing and follow-up interviews necessary. Fear certainly had an effect on the quality of the information gathered. For instance, some of the local research assistants and interviewees feared violent retribution. Feeling that they exposed themselves too much through the interview process, they started to boycott certain questions dealing with violence and drugs. This gives a vivid expression of the influence of local interests associated with the drug trade over the local population. I was able to overcome this obstacle only by conducting the interviews in small groups of close friends, where those involved could be certain that no word would reach those who formed the topic of conversation. Within these groups, locals would find strength and security in the presence of others, perceiving that others were in a very similar situation.

A host of other factors inhibited the gathering of information. To give an impression of the diversity of these inhibiting factors in my 'fact'-finding journey, I would like to cite an example reported by a seventeen-year-old interviewer. As he attempted to conduct his interviews, residents would often immediately close their doors on him. This was apparently because door-to-door salespeople often claim to work for research agencies and, once they are let into a house, are extremely difficult to get rid of.

Statistical material dealing with the economic and social background of the four *bairros* is difficult to obtain. Most surveys conducted by the statistic-producing bodies such as IBGE, SEADE, and EMPLASA deal with the Brasil-ândia region as a whole. Their output largely glosses over the social differences between individual *bairros*. Moreover, their statistics suffer from well-known idiosyncrasies, which I will not detail here, that render a time-line approach examining the period before the mid 1980s futile. In addition, available statistical data that rely on demographic forecasts suffer from the fact that, until the mid 1990s, these forecasts tended to overestimate substantially the population growth of greater São Paulo, distorting per capita data. Existing statistical data tended to produce a picture too general to serve as a cross-referencing tool for the often specific questions that emerged in interviews with local residents. Hence, the survey I conducted was geared toward getting a better idea of local demographics, income situations, education, and political activity. The survey was conducted in Jd. Damasceno between April and August 1996; it obtained a sample of around 8 percent (n=234) of the approximately 2,600 resident families.[28] To my knowledge, no such in-depth study had been conducted previously.[29] The interviews were conducted by six local residents —five female and one male—and myself. All the interviewers, whose ages, varied from fourteen to forty, had above-average education levels. Their backgrounds were similar—all were Catholic, all participated in local Catholic communities, and all had attained more than minimal economic stability, slightly enhanced by the minimal financial contribution they received for their participation. We held regular meetings, at which we discussed the suitability of the questions, the quality of the work, and the responses of the interviewees. The content of the questionnaire underwent some minor alterations as a result of these meetings. For instance, questions that did not apply to the *bairro* population were deleted and the wording of certain questions changed as interviewers experienced difficulties in getting their meaning across. The responses to one question in particular remained ambiguous. Asked if justice existed in their *bairro*, most residents replied negatively, assuming that the question was inquiring about the presence of *justiçeiros* (a mob of vigilantes). The questionnaire provides a material context and serves as a valuable cross-referencing tool for the interviews and participant observation that inform this work.[30] An abridged version of the survey's findings is in the appendix of this volume.

Parts of the book dealing with contemporary political formations in the *bairros* rely on my own observation. My observations often had an active quality. I developed a cooperative assistance project,[31] accompanied various local political groupings, became the official video scribe of the *movimento pela moradia da região Brasilândia* (housing movement of the Brasilândia area), and acted as a conflict mediator between warring political factions. Some of the impressions gathered during this involvement are recorded on nine hundred minutes of videotape. This participant observation, including four months of residency in Jd. Vista Alegre, made many of the political strategies used in the *bairros* more obvious. Working with *bairro* residents gave me insights into local creativity, constraints, and modes of operation that I would not have seen otherwise. Empathetic intervention allowed me to clarify issues that would otherwise have eluded my attention.

THE VOICE OF THE VOICELESS

The People, the Struggle, Authenticity, and Popular Culture

The symbolic fabric that lent shape to Catholic activism in São Paulo during the 1970s and 1980s was woven from various sources. Eventually these sources consolidated into a body of thought often referred to as liberation theology (Smith 1991). Within the Church hierarchy, the development of a sociopolitical outlook that allowed for an integration of these liberationist tendencies is often traced to the Catholic Action (*Ação Católica*, AC) movement (Soares 1988). Formed during the late nineteenth century with the aim of accommodating the new tendencies within modern society, the AC created the basis for its conservative Brazilian counterpart, *Ação Católica Brasileira* (ACB), formed during the 1920s by Cardinal Leme.[1] During the 1930s, ACB groups began to develop infrastructure projects following a "see, judge, act" methodology leading to more radical experiments such as Padre Helder Câmera's organization of factory workers in the northeast of Brazil during the mid 1940s (Nagle 1997, 41). In the 1950s and early 1960s, in a climate of social renewal, the ACB created various forums, encouraging groups that developed increasingly radical orientations. These groups were responsible for the creation of a vocabulary and imagery that shaped much of Brazil's social-critical political and moral culture during the 1970s and 1980s. This body of thought, consolidated by the progressive Catholic Church during the 1970s, had a tremendous influence on the shape of the Brazilian political landscape. Many of the elements that led to the current crisis of the liberationist movement are encoded in certain key symbols that lent shape to its overall orientation. Within this framework, predicated on certain basic assumptions about the nature of society and the transformative role of the poor within it, some of the central tensions inherent in the world view of the Catholic militants are already visible.

Catholic activism has been strongly influenced by militant Catholic and secular student movements, increasingly prolific during the late 1950s and early 1960s. The language, symbols, hopes, and desires of these student movements have, in turn, affected attempts to construct a critical consciousness in the *bairros*.

Some of the most important concepts that influenced Catholic militancy in the *bairros* emerged during the 1950s and 1960s but still resonate in the memory and practice of Catholic radicals and local residents. An etymology of symbols like the people, popular culture, authenticity, and the struggle manages to convey elements that both shaped and undermined local militancy during the 1970s and 1980s. These key symbols harbor major tensions that came to bear significantly on Catholic militants and residents of these *bairros*. Furthermore, these key terms delineate the parameters of the early liberationist project of empowerment as clearly as they reveal an implicitly elitist power dynamic. In fact, the continuing influence of these symbols has had a rather ambiguous effect on social, political, and economic developments within these neighborhoods. Many of the difficulties faced by local residents, such as their failure to adapt the liberationist struggle to the context of the 1990s, can be traced to concepts consolidated by liberation theology.[2]

THE PEOPLE

The concept of the people occupies a central place in the liberationist symbolic universe of the progressive Church. For nearly three decades, the symbol of *the people of God* added legitimacy to the struggle for a more just society and stood at the center of mobilization attempts by Catholic militants. As during the intensely populist era of the 1940s and 1950s, the concept of the people in Brazilian liberationism discursively concealed social and cultural differences and served as an impressive mobilization platform (Rowe and Schelling 1991).[3] Reinterpreted by liberationists, the term came to stand for the "bearers of the

Light of Faith," the "chosen ones," the oppressed, and the suffering. Within the Brazilian progressive Church, the preoccupation with the people as subjects emerged as a result of multiple influences. Most important was the development of a Catholic social doctrine that, once endorsed by the Vatican, began to replace purely moral and spiritual concerns. However, to insert the poor into the Church's cosmic theme as actors rather than as objects, the concept of the people needed a radical reinterpretation.

Until World War II, the popular classes were viewed by the Church hierarchy as an amorphous mass captured by the biblical term *ochlos*—"the little or simple people; the marginalized, mass, multitude, those who have neither voice nor power" (Soares 1988, 329n74). In order to encapsulate the central concern of the progressive Catholic Church, this mass with neither voice nor power had to be transformed into *laos*, "the chosen people, a theological concept always pointing at Israel" (Soares 1988, 329n74). The foundation for this conceptual transformation was, by and large, laid down by the conservative Pope Pius XII, who started to differentiate between the masses and the people. During World War II he appeared to have recognized the significance of human rights, and by the end of the war he had acknowledged the importance of an informed populus. Henceforth, the term the people came to denote "those who live and move for themselves." Thus, during the 1940s, the term the people had been invested with a substantial degree of subjectivity. From now on, the people were to be differentiated from the masses, whose amorphous apathy was moved only by external forces (Soares 1988, 74). However, only during the late 1950s was the term the people explicitly incorporated into the vocabulary of the Catholic Church.[4]

The shift toward a more sociopolitical direction in general and the preferential focus on the people in particular occurred under Pope John XXIII (1958–1963). Encyclicals such as *Mater et Magistra* (1961) and *Pacem in Terris* (1963), as well as *Inter Mirifica*, a document presented at the Vatican II Council (11 April 1963), changed official Catholic thought (Mainwaring 1986b, 43). Inspired by these writings, a new conception of the Church developed, allowing it to distance itself from an exclusively moralist discourse to create space for tendencies that were regarded as positive in a modern secular society. Wanting to promote human aspirations such as harmony and unity and progress and social justice under the reign of God, these writings planted the official seeds for a Christian humanism at the service of mankind. Pope Paul VI

(1963–1978) continued the Church's renewal (Mainwaring 1986b, 43). Within the context of the Vatican II Council and John's encyclicals, inspired theologians were able to fuse the concepts of the masses, the people of God, and the people. In the light of the sociopolitical opening offered by the Church during these years, the term the people not only referred to a collection of the popular classes, but soon began to stand for the oppressed and dominated in general (Macedo 1986, 47; Vásquez 1998, 118).

Most important, John's discourse lent official support to the voices of the progressive clergy and laity within the Brazilian Church who had been emphasizing Christian humanism and the Church's adopting a greater commitment toward the poor. When the impact of a reforming Vatican reached the Brazilian Catholic Church, it encouraged an important segment of ACB-inspired clergy, such as Dom Helder Câmera, whose social commitment had led them to reach out to the poor in the form of MEB literacy and consciousness-raising campaigns. Moreover, this call reverberated with some of the messianic and prophetic heritage that had existed for centuries in Brazilian Catholicism.[5] Working within popular communities that they often regarded as mystical and superstitious, many clerics at the bottom of the hierarchy were tempted to assume a posture that reflected local beliefs.[6] In general, however, even this section of the clergy was far from reading popular Catholicism as an authentic expression of faith (Bruneau 1979). Instead, these Church agents set out to construct their own synthesis of fragmented local Catholicism.[7]

AUTHENTICITY

Authenticity became one of the key concepts stimulating the imagery of many militants in the *bairros*. Authenticity, in its secular version, aimed at the intrinsically good elements in everything Brazilian and spelled out the promise that these elements could be uncovered and brought into the open, where they would contribute to a radical transformation of society. In this sense, the term framed the project of many Catholic and secular militants, attempting to reconstruct an authentic popular culture (Lehmann 1996, 79). It also clarified the role in the struggle of the educated Catholic elite, which aimed at the liberation of the oppressed and exploited. This elite assumed the role of a catalyst in a transformation that they visualized would bring about an authentic and just Brazilian society. For many militants, authenticity became bound up with estheticism and led to an iconographic rendering of the popular classes in terms of an authentic essence, intrinsically beautiful and good.[8] This belief was reinforced by a certain strand of Paulo Freire's methodology and facilitated the emergence of forms of *basismo* encountered in the *bairros* in the mid-1990s. In its more extreme—but by no means uncommon—form, the concept gave rise to something that could be compared with certain charismatic beliefs. By being touched by a superior force, the authentic subjectivity of the people would burst forth, unleashing their true revolutionary, cultural, or religious force.

During the late 1950s and 1960s, much of the preoccupation with authenticity within Catholic and secular Left circles issued from a debate over the construction of an authentic national Brazilian culture. Until the mid 1960s, this debate was strongly shaped by a Left developmentalist nationalism, propounded by academics of the Rio de Janeiro–based Higher Institute of Brazilian Studies (ISEB).[9] At stake was the construction of a "truthful," or authentic, national identity as opposed to the existing "false" one that was, it was argued, contaminated by dominant foreign and, especially, U.S. elements (Ortiz 1985, 63–68). The ISEB project was strongly tinged with the populism of the time. Guerreiro Ramos wrote at the end of the 1950s: "Today, finally, the people are beginning to be a political entity, mature because they are the carriers of desire and their own discernment. The people are substituting, in this manner, those groups and classes in their role as principal actors of the political process" (cf. Ortiz 1985, 63). Consequently, the ISEB generated a discourse that aimed to promote a national development project in which the popular classes would stand united behind the leading educated classes. To raise such an authentic national consciousness, the ISEB's national development ideology emphasized the need for mass education. Broader education, it was argued, would enable the masses to express their authenticity, defined as the natural emotional identification with the ISEB's national development project (Ortiz 1985, 63–68).[10]

For the ISEB, authenticity did not arise simply as a result of a nondirective educational process. The masses had to have their consciousness raised by selected educators in order to emerge as the people (Ortiz 1985, 65, 68). As a consequence, a segment of the educated elite was designated to function as catalyst as well as defining pole. From this position of omnipotence the ISEBians proposed to lead the nation into an era of flourishing prosperity, unhampered by foreign influences. In this populist endeavor, then, mass education was to disseminate a particular elite-designed popular culture endowed by the ISEB with a label of authenticity (Ortiz 1985, 63–68). Thenceforth, the concept became a central element for projects sponsored by the elite, trying to mold the masses to their vision for a new Brazil. During the 1950s, this discourse, with all its elitist and paternalist features, was a powerful influence not only within wider Brazilian society but also within movements of the Catholic and the secular Left (Ortiz 1985, 48–49).[11] Within these groupings of the Left, subjectivity became increasingly anchored in what came to be promoted as the authentic expression of the popular classes. In virtually all of the projects using this concept, elite groups assigned themselves a central task that allowed them to distinguish between authentic and inauthentic popular manifestations.

By the late 1950s, virtually all Catholic movements with more radical leanings and secular movements, such as the *Centro Popular de Cultura* (Popular Centre of Culture, CPCs) belonging to the *União National dos Estudantes* (National Student Union, UNE), had adopted elements of the ISEB discourse (Soares 1988, 324). All major Catholic lay movements that grew out of the ACB, such as Catholic University Youth (JUC),[12] Base Education Movement (MEB), Catholic Student Youth (JEC), Catholic Workers Youth (JOC), and Catholic Agrarian Workers Youth (JAC), posited authenticity at the core of their projects. Furthermore, national developmentalism had a strong influence on the stance of Paulo Freire and the Recife-based *Movimento da Cultura Popular* (Popular Culture Movement, MCP) (Ortiz 1985, 48).[13] During the 1960s, in a climate of growing polarization and violence, youth movements shifted to the left. The JOC, for instance, began to propagate a mix of Maoism and religious commitment that required its members to go to the "point of production as a rite of passage marking the baptism into a new religion" (Martins 1998; cf. Lehmann 1996, 64). From this point onward, Lehmann argues, the authenticity of the people takes on quasi-religious proportions (Lehmann 1996, 64).

The ISEB not only influenced young Catholic militants, but also had a direct influence on the Church hierarchy.[14] This emerges clearly in Dom Eugênio Sales's rhetoric during his involvement with a movement that came to embody this new social posture of the Catholic Church: the *Movimento de Natal* (Natal Movement) (Procópio 1971). In the Natal Movement, most active during the early 1960s, ISEB thought led to a redrawing of religious images. The image of God became a disfigured man dried out by underdevelopment (Procópio 1971, 84). This image tied Brazil's harsh modernization and development project to a cosmic theme, the extinguishing of the religious authenticity of the people.[15] Increasingly, however, the elite nationalism promoted by the ISEB attracted the critique of young socialists within the Catholic movements (Soares 1988, 324). This growing opposition created the impetus for an important reinterpretation, aligning student movements more closely with the people.

The work of Paulo Freire was most important for the emergence of this body of Catholic and secular thought, which emphasized a proximity to the poor (Mainwaring 1986b, 70). His teachings, enhanced by his personal charisma, are still attractive to Catholic and secular activists (Lehmann 1990, 96–101). Freire's influence was particularly strong at PUC (Catholic University), São Paulo, where he taught postgraduate courses during the 1980s. His thought is distinguished by its positive outlook but, according to Soares (1988), it is fundamentally critical of society, while never losing its compassion and modesty in the face of those whose consciousness is to be raised. Freire contrasts his Christian humanist position with the arrogant, dogmatic, anticommunicative sectarianism that is often characteristic of a Left incapable of loving, disrespectful of the outlook of others, and trying to impose its own direction on the people[16] (Soares 1988, 322). During the late 1970s, Freire's emphasis on nondirective practices was particularly appealing to those militants who followed what they perceived as a nonvanguardist methodology based on raising popular consciousness.[17] However, Paulo Freire's thought was equally important to, if slightly distorted by, groups with vanguardist tendencies, such as the CPCs of the UNE.

These varying interpretations of vanguardism carried over into the popular politics of the 1970s and 1980s. The ideological differences that emerged during the late 1950s and early 1960s persisted, accentuating the division between Catholic and secular Left projects in the *bairros*. Based on a differentiated reading of authenticity within the popular classes, this rift not only created a tension between the Catholic and the secular Left but also undermined the political alliance with local residents.

The Authentic Popular Culture of the Secular Left

At the beginning of the 1960s, an important secular[18] movement in search of a third path between capitalism and communism drew on Marxist and Christian humanist discourses developed by the ISEB and Paulo Freire: the CPCs of the UNE[19] (Ortiz 1985, 48; Martins Filho 1998, 157). Inspired by these discourses, the CPCs worked them into the context of secular Left student politics. This produced a discursive mélange, favoring an artistic vanguardist ideology based on the broad theme of consciousness raising (Ortiz 1985, 69). The CPCs perceived popular culture as intrinsically political and potentially revolutionary. This perception, however, necessitated refashioning the term "popular culture," which until then had described a conservative, reactionary populus favoring the established order (Ortiz 1985, 71). The CPCs, especially Ferreira Gullar, questioned this conservative notion of popular culture, noting that the term described a phenomenon that was new to Brazilian life. This break with old cultural practices, made explicit through definition, made room for the new, authentic popular culture of the CPCs (Ortiz 1985, 71).

The CPCs defined popular culture exclusively in terms of transformative potential. In this sense, the concept already entailed the notion of action, derived from a particular critical consciousness read into popular culture. The CPC perceived this consciousness as intrinsically political, capable of inciting popular political action (Ortiz 1985, 71). Thus the CPC leaders believed that they could incite political action by providing the proper stimulus. In order to awaken this authentic revolutionary popular culture, the CPCs used performing and visual arts, assuming that once the popular classes recognized their own position within society, they would be jolted into a revolutionary mode of action.

While acquiring the role of a catalyst, CPC activists made their own elite status discursively opaque by dissolving any class boundaries and, hence, by becoming the people. This emerges particularly clearly from an article published by the CPC leadership in 1962: "When talking to the people [about the problems of the people] the intellectual becomes part of the people and, as a result, turns into their voice as well as the intellectual of society: not only the intellectual of an anti-society."[20]

Hence, within the realm of the CPCs and the UNE, the difference between middle-class intellectuals and the people was extinguished. Consequently, the

CPCs effectively became the intellectual voice of the people. This again placed them in a position of power that entitled militants to shape and define popular culture. Deriving their legitimation from their organic link with the masses, CPC members saw themselves as able to differentiate between authentic popular manifestations and false ones (Ortiz 1985, 73, 74). CPC activists managed to redefine the term popular culture, emptying it of most of its earlier context.

This CPC elitism, which surfaced in the late 1950s and early 1960s, substantially influenced Left militants who graduated from PUC, São Paulo, during the 1970s. Traces of this approach were still highly visible in the initiative of secular Left militants active in the *bairros* between the mid-1970s and mid-1980s. During the mid-1980s, this CPC-inspired model of authenticity added greatly to the collapse of secular political initiatives in the *bairros*. CPC authenticity gave rise to a disillusionment that still flavored the political outlook of many secular militants I encountered during the mid-1990s.

Authenticity and Paulo Freire

Not unlike the CPCs, the JUC also made ample use of its self-ordained power to redefine concepts such as popular culture. The JUC intellectuals carried the notion of authenticity further. For the JUC, authenticity resided in the methodology or pedagogy as well as in the popular classes. The JUC was influenced primarily by the ACB, and it featured humanist as well as Christian personalist symbolism.[21] The movement also drew on an ISEB-inspired analysis of national development, as well as rudimentary Marxism. Furthermore, the JUC adopted the new official developmentalist discourse of the Church as outlined in *Mater et Magistra* (Soares 1988, 307). At the center of the JUC's approach stood the production of an active as well as critical subject in control of historical processes (Soares 1988, 305). Like the CPCs of the UNE, the JUC leadership assigned itself a vanguard status in popular education and embarked on a journey to socialize, structurally reform, raise consciousness, and increase political awareness. The goal was to produce an authentic popular culture, using the fashionable terminology of the time (Soares 1988, 307). JUC members also felt that an authentic popular culture did not always exist, but had to be delivered through education. To this end, JUC members argued for a mass education campaign featuring a Freireian pedagogy (Soares 1988, 307).[22] Authenticity played a central role in this pedagogy: "Popular culture is, by and large, the consequence of an authentic conscientization and politicization: It is the Brazilian people and all the conscientized and politicized people, freely creating their form of expression, their model of global development. . . ." (Soares 1988, 307). Thus authenticity was posited in the method that produced this new subject. This method transferred authenticity to the people, who were then released to engage with historical processes.

In other words, the ISEB and Freire, but also Marx and Gramsci, shaped the projects of these Catholic and secular Left groupings during the late 1950s and early 1960s, giving rise to similar proposals. The movements saw themselves as renovating catalysts, inducing structural change by raising the consciousness of the masses. Over the course of this process, the movements claimed, "object man" was transformed into "subject man/woman."[23] These fundamental notions, albeit conceptually transformed, informed *bairro* politics until the mid-1990s.

Cultural Revolutionarism vs. Vanguardism

In the 1960s, the progressive Catholics differed largely in their positioning within this process of mass mobilization and construction of a new authentic society. Catholic Left movements predominantly opted for an approach that was more inclined toward a nondirective *conscientização*—awakening through learning—a term that derived much weight from Freire's pedagogy stressing education as the authentic method that would make the oppressed aware of their social position, an awareness that would enable them to make their own political choices (de Kadt 1970, 107). At the same time, many militants of the secular Left, were less concerned with the philosophy of *conscientização* and "seemed to believe that mere awareness, mere 'de-alienation,' would suffice to bring about the necessary climate for a change of structures" (de Kadt 1970, 106). The Catholic Left believed that authentic popular culture would develop from the grass roots up in a process of *conscientização* (consciousness raising), while the secular Left regarded popular culture as a tool "to be forged by the political leadership, out of the latter's interpretation of how best to use a particular cultural phenomenon in the political struggle" (de Kadt 1970, 106). For the secular Left, the authentic content of popular culture was relative. Its main feature was its usefulness in the hands of a political elite. These differences in ideology created a rift in the radical populism—one with ecclesiastical and cultural aspirations, the other with exclusively political ones.[24] Fundamentally, however, both orientations held on to the concept of authenticity, in conjunction with the people, appending populist features to their militant projects.[25]

In fact, Freireian nondirective, nonvanguardist methodologies, forming the dominant methodology of the Ecclesiastical Base Communities (CEBs) during the late 1970s and 1980s, remained nondirective in theory only. This emerges clearly in the following statement of a militant:

> Everybody, including Paulo Freire, had during that era many illusions. We thought that the people were going to tell us what the aim of this mobilization was. At the same time we always had representative democracy as a model. In reality, it wasn't the people who were going to tell us what the best political regime was for them. The people were prepared in order to participate at an electoral level of decisionmaking. The people were valued up to the moment of voting, then it was the affair of the state. . . . Besides this, in application, everything was permeated by nationalism; we guided our forces trying to demonstrate how Brazil was exploited by foreigners. We started with a discussion about concrete hunger and ended in the U.S. . . . The curriculum was meticulously prepared by us in meetings. We always knew what we were going to explore during the classes, no matter if the students were willing or not. . . . Maybe in theory the method took recourse to spontaneity: in practice we worked like a vanguard (cf. Soares 1988, 330).

The Freireian cultural vanguardism of the Catholic Left was different in nature but not necessarily less elitist.[26] It issued from a dominance in which the power of religious symbols was bound up with the education process aiming at the construction of a politicized culture. The secular Left, meanwhile, displayed a vanguardism that, while taking cultural references into account, was more overtly political.

In the *bairros*, as in the rest of São Paulo, these differences in approach gave rise to tensions that would divide militant factions (Sader 1988, 148). In the context of the *bairros*, many of these tensions were eliminated by the consolidation of the progressive Church in the mid-1970s. In this consolidation, a Freire-inspired consciousness-raising process became the source of an authentic popular culture. It radically altered the terms of the debate surrounding the methodology of mass education.

At this stage, the debate shifted to the question of how much truth was embedded in popular culture and to what extent it and the people embodied authenticity before the process of consciousness raising. In other words, how much tutelage did the people require. At stake was the *basista* tendency encouraged by Paulo Freire's nondirective methodology. While some activists at times displayed a mystical veneration of popular practices, rejecting especially university-educated outsiders (Mainwaring 1986b, 215, 216; Lehmann 1996), others argued that such an orientation was detrimental to the struggle.[27] This tension embodies an ambiguity that is already detectable in Freire's teachings. While emphasizing a nondirective methodology, Freire was aware of the impossibility of a purely nondirective approach, a realization that actually led him to depart from the belief that national solutions had to be found with the poor who, according to the early Freire, were "truthful, authentic, connected with the real country and not with the lies of the elite" (Soares 1988, 330).

Never properly resolved within the space of the progressive Catholic Church, radical *basista* and anti-elite tendencies persisted among Catholic militants as well as in local activist circles and informed the Catholic faction of the Workers Party (PT) in São Paulo well into the 1990s.[28] *Basismo*, in this respect, represents a radical departure from Leftist assumptions of the elite status of militants, elevating the authentic local culture above the inauthentic position of the militant.[29] At the same time, *basistas* strongly reject the establishment and condemn its rationalistic and instrumentalist logic (see also Lehmann 1996, 29–30). Such *basista* tendencies have been undermining local attempts to adjust to rapidly changing contexts.

Student Movements and Militant Catholic Base Communities

The practices of the movements of the late 1950s and early 1960s directly and indirectly inspired the progressive Catholic Church in general and militant Catholic communities in particular. Because these movements constantly influenced each other, and because activists participated in various groups, it is difficult to discern one individual intellectual current that informed the outlook of these communities and inspired *bairro* politics. Academic observers generally acknowledge that ideas that were later taken up by the progressive Church, contributing directly to liberation theology (Soares 1988, 320), originated in the JUC. However, my interviews with Catholic militants active in the *bairros* during the 1970s and early 1980s indicate that this claim needs some qualification.

The JUC underwent rapid radicalization during the late 1950s and early 1960s. Toward the end of the 1950s, JUC members began to redefine their faith in terms of a social commitment. At a national conference in 1959, for example, the JUC explicitly endorsed responsibility for political action as part of an evangelical commitment. This growing evangelical commitment to political involvement turned the JUC into an integral part of the Left. By the early 1960s, the JUC had emerged as the most important force in student politics and was effectively competing with the two other major Left forces: the PCdoB (Communist Party of Brazil) and the PCB (Brazilian Communist Party)[30] (Mainwaring 1986b, 62). The JUC became the dominant force in student politics in 1961, when it captured the presidency of the UNE[31] (Mainwaring 1986b, 63). Its rapid radicalization and increasing national visibility led to a conflict with the Church hierarchy that escalated in late 1961. Two years after the military coup (1964), the JUC disbanded. Disenchanted with the lack of support from the Church hierarchy during a period of increasing repression, the movement's militants were searching for other avenues of political activism.[32]

From the early 1960s on, faced by increasing ecclesiastical pressure, many JUC members were searching for a less restrictive political environment. Becoming increasingly concerned with the theme of social justice, a theme not accommodated by the existing Church structures, JUC members cofounded and joined the Popular Action (AP) in May 1962. Formed outside the dominion of the Church hierarchy, the AP turned rapidly into a channel for radicalizing Catholic and secular voices. The AP, as opposed to the JUC, unanimously embraced a Catholic Marxist humanist discourse (Mainwaring 1986b, 64–66). In its general outlook and methods, the AP interpreted the ideas that emerged among the student movements in the 1950s and 1960s in a different manner and began to raise the consciousness of the masses by initiating a popular education campaign and working with the unions and peasant organizations. After the coup in 1964, the AP turned more radical and finally splintered into various increasingly radical and militant factions (Mainwaring 1986b, 64–66).

In order to continue their consciousness-raising work within the climate of growing state repression and persecution, many Catholic and secular radicals left the disbanding student movements and turned to progressive cells within the Catholic Church. These cells were increasingly the only forum that offered a space for the political mobilization attempts of the opposition during these years. Under the protective umbrella of the Catholic Church, many radicals contributed to the establishment of militant Catholic communities in São Paulo. In this sense, these communities carried much of the heritage of the progressive AC, ACB, MEB, JUC, JEC, AP, and later JOC and JAC as well as secular movements[33] (Mainwaring 1986b, 66). Mainwaring sums this up by claiming that the CEBs, often recognized and fostered by the bishops in the 1970s, created the institutional structure that allowed for a blending of the approaches espoused by the hierarchy, priests and nuns, seminarists, and former student activists (1986b, 110). This activity has underpinned *bairro* politics during the past three decades.

Furthermore, at least in the *bairros*, much of the political dynamic derived from yet another religious influence, that of radical Catholic foreigners. These foreigners, especially militants from Italy, brought with them the heritage of various streams of European political Catholic radicalism that flourished within the European social democratic context (Beozzo 1996; Rivière D'Arc 1999). As a consequence, they introduced a different dynamic to *bairro* mobilization. Departing from the charitable policies of the Catholic Church in the region, they introduced a radical antiassistentialism, arguing that it was the basic social responsibility of the modern state to supply urban infrastructure (see also Lehmann 1996, 81). Often their vanguardist activism, more determined than that of most Brazilian Catholic militants in the region, took on radical proportions. In fact, the first *bairro* movements of the 1970s were initiated almost exclusively by foreign Catholic radicals. The activism of these militants energized the region. Under their tutelage, local mobilization attempts, aimed at publicizing the lack of urban services in the region and taking corrective action, peaked during the mid- and late 1970s. These movements were—in a chronological sense—at the forefront of social or popular movements in Greater São Paulo.

THE STRUGGLE

The symbol of the struggle (*a luta*) remains central to the projects of militant Catholic communities. It derives in large part from the orientations that informed liberation theology. Elements of a Marxist class analysis were given a symbolic biblical context, connecting the profane with the sacred. The struggle of the people against the state, landowners, or capitalism was, henceforth, seen as a religious struggle aiming at the construction of God's Kingdom on earth (Levine 1995, 108). The film *Pé na Caminhada*, which can be roughly translated as "setting out on a journey,"[34] exemplifies the practices of the progressive Church during the 1970s. Shot in 1979, it attracted much attention as the first Catholic feature film and gained international acclaim at the Third International Film Festival in Mannheim in 1980. Moreover, the film has become one of the most important visual documents of the progressive Church and has been shown in countless Catholic base communities all over Brazil.

Pé na Caminhada is a modernized story of St. Francis. In transposing St. Francis to the Brazilian (liberationist) context, however, the filmmaker omits the rather opulent life the saint led before his renunciation of material goods; the allegory of the Brazilian people begins in sacred poverty.[35] The focus of the film is on the suffering of the oppressed popular classes, a suffering that is—not unlike the life of Christ—glorified and resolved in martyrdom and earthly death. The film is narrated by Leonardo Boff,[36] a prominent Brazilian liberation theologian. In each frame, he articulates the view of the progressive Catholic Church, fusing various contextual layers of faith and politics (*fé e política*).

With the political made divine, the boundaries distinguishing morals and politics are blurred. Beneath the veneer of class analysis lies a liberationist symbolic universe, evoking traditional Catholic images. Through it, some of the most important social tensions were captured and centralized by a supposedly ecumenical religious struggle for a more harmonious world created through adherence to Christian (Catholic) values. In this sense, liberationist thought effectively absorbed difference. Symbols and practices taken from popular culture or Catholicism were interpolated with academic or political discourses conceptually integrated to form the basis for an alliance of diverse interests and social status. In this sense, liberation theology provided an important canvas on which a meaningful collage of diverse social and cultural tendencies could be constructed. However, different parties read different meanings into the collage, and the collage as a whole was more meaningful to some of the parties than to others.

The basis for this synthesis rests on the liberationist insistence that sacred and human history are one. This symbolic fusion inextricably links the secular political struggle with a religious metaphysical struggle, and each step toward communal survival becomes a step toward a new person in a new society, closer to God. To struggle is to participate in the transformation of a community. By individual engagement with this liberationist community, object man becomes subject man. The transformed society consists of evangelical communities.

The symbolic reframing of elements from popular culture, from the progressive Catholic symbolic universe, and from new theoretical currents relocates the daily struggles of the popular classes onto a religious or cosmic platform. This principle of symbolic rereading is already spelled out in the title of the video. On the cover, "foot" (*pé*) is crossed out and replaced with "faith" (*fé*) *na caminhada*. In this sense, the setting out on a journey to a more just life turns into an invocation of faith in the face of the procession to the Promised Land. Superimposing a religious context onto a sociopolitical basis unites the spiritual and the social worlds. Henceforth, as illustrated by the film, what separates the oppressed, miserable, poor from this Promised Land are the barbed wire fences and physical violence, ensuring a state of social segregation. The social question is posed in terms of the individualist capitalist greed of the spiritually impoverished owning classes; a social question that can be resolved through the mobilization of the authenticized spirituality of the poor and humble: the people—who have joined/have been joined together in the progressive Church to embark on a journey that will lead to a new society that is the Kingdom of God. This leads to a struggle against the oppressors, resulting in the deaths of many who participated in the struggle. No doubt is left that the creation of the Kingdom of God on earth is a task that requires many sacrifices by the people. This reinterpretation inextricably ties the struggle of the humble (*humilde*)—so called because they occupy a humble role in society but are also humble before God—to the liberationist religious struggle.

Notably absent from the script is the personified evil opponent of God's people. He is simply referred to in some sequences featuring cattle on a pasture that is lined by barbed wire (oppression) and zealously protected by armed guards. The consequence of this spiritual poverty is depicted in long scenes featuring the abject misery of the dispossessed and the maimed. At this stage, the progressive Catholic Church emerges as the decisive force that is able to do away with this injustice. "In the face of this most extreme oppression," the progressive local hierarchy (the voice of the voiceless) asserts,

"Goods become common." In extreme hardship, the label theft no longer applies. Land invasions are no longer invasions but occupations, and the theft of consumer goods is no longer theft but sheer necessity. Private property, the most sacred aspect of capitalism, is attacked in order to establish a new harmony and communion between the people and God. The people become a prophetic force, capable of transforming society. Their force is revolutionary, not because of their ability to carry weaponry and to fight in the name of a new classless society, but because they are already living the ways of this new society. This transformation grows organically out of the moral renovation of society, issuing from the grass roots, but encouraged by the progressive Church. No development model is needed as actions are guided by a Christian moral purity. In fact, the morals contained within the symbolic universe of the progressive Church form the development model.[37] Justice, equality, harmony, and communion are spread throughout society by the everyday practice of the people of God.

Harmony and communion arise in the context of a direct connection of the people with the earth. Bare feet on red soil demonstrate this most primordial union, which gives birth to life; the honest work of those tilling the ground. This organic religiosity creates the basis for communal practices and harmonious cohabitation. The *voice of the voiceless* celebrates the humility of the worker and so becomes the most important virtue of the people of God. As a result of this humility, the people are able to experience the will of God and implement it. That this is by no means a purely organic affair emerges out of the frequent references to CEB leaders and priests who are in the process of reinforcing these Christian virtues. Hence, the local representative of the progressive Church acquires the role of a catalyst, mediator, and purifier of popular religiosity. The regular contact between him and the people ensures the purity of the struggle. Placards that spell "greed," "complacency," and "capitalism" are lowered, one by one, into the all-consuming flames. By means of this ritualistic burning of social ills, the political struggle of the people is inextricably fused with the religious sphere. Rather than simply fighting for social justice, the people—under the tutelage of the progressive Church—struggle for religious authenticity.

The film leaves no doubt that the position of the progressive Catholic Church is central in this supposedly ecumenical struggle. Throughout the film, bishops and priests lead the procession of the people. Situated always at the very front, protecting the people from the abuses of the oppressors, these bishops become carriers of the voice of the voiceless. From the pulpit they represent and politicize everyday life events of the poor, adding legitimacy to the struggle of the people; a struggle in which the earth, the worker, family, and community are the basic units. Through the tilling of the earth, man is able to construct a dignified existence and form a family. Within the realm of this family, life and faith are nurtured, ensuring the basis for a more harmonious, communal, and just Christian community. The humble worker acquires in this context a prophetic force, as he is implementing God's will under the guidance of the local pastoral agent. At this point, the film organically inserts the Church as the natural leader of this procession, uniting the Church hierarchy, clergy, pastoral workers, and the people—a unity that leads the people into the promised land.

The natural leadership of the Church depicted in the film was very much reinforced by the fact that during the post–military coup era (1964–1985), the progressive Catholic Church emerged as the most important moral and political force, filling the political vacuum left by the exterminated political opposition. This position was further cemented by the violent state repression of the late 1960s and early 1970s. When the Church began to embrace the people, by denouncing the plight of the oppressed, the hierarchy, borrowing from the discourse that had emerged at the local church level, assumed leadership of a movement and became its voice. As a result of this seemingly organic union, the Church hierarchy came to represent, symbolically, a major segment of a society that increasingly questioned the methods of the authoritarian state.

During this era of unity, the Church hierarchy initiated a process that tied many of the highly heterogeneous militant practices at the local level closer to its authority, expanding the concept of the struggle and its accompanying symbolic universe. By the late 1970s, the hierarchy had achieved the recommendations developed by CELAM, the Latin American bishops conference, during the early 1970s: The Church had successfully entered the social realm with a prophetic posture, denouncing the structures of domination, and had become the voice of the voiceless (Soares 1988, 350).

Henceforth, social issues raised in this liberationist realm are understood by the Church in moral and political terms. Carmen Cinira Macedo notes in her work on CEBs that despite the distancing of the progressive Church from an exclusively moral stance, the political and social world is very much read in terms of morals. For this reason, the progressive Church understands social questions as intrinsically political (Macedo 1986, 64). Morals contained in the voice of the voiceless effectively delineate the boundary of the political discourse of the people. This blending of the spiritual with the political reinforces political authenticity by tying it to religious truthfulness. Anything defined by the voice of the voiceless as outside that for which the people (of God) are struggling is not good (Telles 1986, 65). Benedetti highlights this political and religious fusion from another angle. CEBs are, beyond their religious mission, political. Evangelical politics strives toward the authenticity of the world of God (Benedetti 1988, 497). In this sense, the struggle of CEBs represents the struggle for Christian authenticity in an objective world. In the life of communities, it is hoped, discourses meet and merge; secular and religious authenticity become indistinguishable; the political and the evangelical become one. This fusion of secular and religious realms tends to limit local, pragmatic choices, as an essentially premodern frame of reference clashes with the exigencies of modern life.[38]

CEBs

CEBs played a most important part in renovating the progressive Catholic Church in Brazil. From an institutional perspective, CEBs tied the people to the Church by disseminating the symbolic universe of the progressive Catholic Church within the realm of the popular classes. At the same time, however, CEBs are regarded as the cradle of a new religious and political and, consequently, social subject. CEBs thus had a crucial catalytic and mediating role in the creation of the liberationist symbolic universe. They also embody a fundamental tension that arises from the often incompatible relationship of universal institutional interests and individual or local Christian humanist practices. This tension has often been neglected by authors such as Hewitt (1991), Mainwaring (1986b), and others.

Mainwaring says that the pastoral reforms of Archbishop Dom Carmelo Vasconcellos Motta had encouraged CEBs, and they existed throughout the 1960s (Mainwaring 1986b, 103). Even after the departure of the archbishop in 1964, a strong contingent of priests, nuns, and lay persons continued their work with the popular classes[39] (Mainwaring 1986b, 103). Hewitt adds to this that the succession of Dom Paulo Evaristo Arns as archbishop of São Paulo in 1971 added great impetus to the emergence of the CEBs. He claims that under the administration of Dom Paulo, CEBs in São Paulo received the moral as well as financial support of the local hierarchy[40] (Hewitt 1991, 36).

By attaching the label CEB to militant Catholic communities, these authors tend to dismiss a most important tension in the relationship between the Catholic hierarchy and its militant base. In the local Catholic communities that I studied, both the leaders and the members are extremely reluctant to identify their nucleus as a CEB. From the perspective of local residents and, in particular, Catholic militants, the term CEB is synonymous with an attempt of the progressive Catholic Church to homogenize the multifaceted Catholic radicalism of the grass roots. The contours of this strategy emerge from a statement of Dom Luis Fernandes, one of the main animators of CEBs, defining CEBs as "any solidary activity of small groups inspired by Evangelism" (Sader 1988, 157). Archbishop Dom Paulo Evaristo Arns asserted, "CEBs 'are the Church' and as such must stand 'always united with their priests and bishops'" (Hewitt 1991, 54). For Catholic militants, however, the term CEB forms part of a strategic vocabulary used by the hierarchy to maintain or at least to pressure for the appearance of clerical control.

As a result, militants answered my question whether their activities had constituted a CEB with "yes and no." Yes because they are, according to Sister Rachel, a community leader in Jd. Recando, "defined by the hierarchy in these terms"; and no because this would tie them too closely to the ecclesiastical structure. Hence, in the *bairros*, the label carries distinctly ambiguous qualities. Only during a short and decidedly progressive period during the 1970s did the term enjoy greater popularity. The term CEB, then, arose only with the attempt by local clerics and elite laity to consolidate the progressive Catholic Church. The rejection of this label by the rank and file very much reflects its ambivalent relationship with the hierarchy and foreshadows a tendency to claim a certain autonomy vis à vis the institution. At the same time, it reflects an ill-resolved tension at the core of liberation theology that has turned the economically oppressed into the "privileged subject of God's salvic work and the only valid locus of prophetic action and theological reflection"—a tension that potentially leads to a crack in the edifice of the Catholic Church (Vásquez 1998, 118). Nevertheless, applying the label CEB to militant Catholic communities would, by and large, endorse the hierarchy's attempt to interpret the diversity at the grass roots as a new, united, homogeneous evangelical movement. Dismissing this tension and representing the range of groups as homogeneous obscures one of the most important clues to the emergence and vitality of progressive Catholicism.

In fact, these Catholic communities, claimed by the hierarchy when represented as CEBs, are the locus of a most important mediation of this tension between hierarchy and grass roots (Levine, cited in Vásquez 1998, 275). For the progressive Church hierarchy, CEBs represent an ecclesiastical essence, demonstrating the arrival of a new era of renovated faith that posits the people as the new social and religious subject (Macedo 1986, 59). In this sense, CEBs, in conjunction with their pastoral support agencies created during the 1970s,[41] facilitate the organization of the religiosity of the masses, tying the popular imagery to the symbolic universe of the Catholic Church.[42]

However, the refusal of Catholic militants to identify with the term CEB is indicative of their refusal of a role dictated by the hierarchy. This refusal symbolized a rejection of ecclesiastical demands to endorse the project of the progressive Church. All of the interviewed militants said that working at the grass roots calls for much more than simply evangelical missionary activity. Even the moderate Brazilian Catholic militants who arrived in the *bairros* during the mid- and late 1980s take their social commitment seriously enough so that they reject the intrusive authority of the ecclesiastical center. For most of these militants, the spiritual quest is closely linked to their involvement with the poor. It is not surprising that the concept of authenticity should tie these militants closely to their *bairro* communities and to the theme of the people. This basic tension is embodied in the role of the Catholic militant or pastoral agent. Constantly challenged to incorporate new local tendencies into their practices, these militants are continually reinventing the identity of the Catholic Church, a process that is to various degrees hindered by the hierarchy.

Within the Catholic communities that emerged during the 1970s, a great variety of transformative methodologies converged. During the early and mid-1970s, the work of Catholic community leaders in the *bairros* was very much influenced by the political, social, and methodological orientations of young radicals, themselves often influenced by the practices of the student movements (Mainwaring 1986b, 110, 164). With the consolidation of the progressive Church in the late 1970s, these diverse practices gave way to a much more unified stance based on the direction outlined by the renovating progressive Church hierarchy.

As a result, the Catholic community leadership of the 1970s, which took a much more vanguardist, politically radical, cultural revolutionary position, gave way to a more moderate and evangelist leadership during the 1980s. Ironically, it was the supposedly progressive stance of the Brazilian Catholic Church during the 1970s that enticed many in the local Catholic community to seek to ally themselves with the hierarchy. However, in the defense of radical dissidents (see also Bruneau 1979, 69), while this alliance worked during the early and mid-1970s, during the 1980s it entangled many local communities and Catholic militants in an uneasy relationship with an increasingly conservative Church (see also Mainwaring 1986b, 110). From the late 1970s onward, the "revolutionary cultural action" (Soares 1988, 339) inspired by Freire gave way to increasingly conservative currents under the dominant tutelage of the hierarchy. This orientation of the 1980s and 1990s muted the previous diverse and radical spirit of transformation and turned itself into an increasingly consolidated, now conservative, voice of the voiceless. In the *bairros*, this ended the most radical phase of the militant Catholic communities.

Catholic *bairro* communities became central to the transformation of the masses into new social and religious subjects. They ensured the successful integration of community members into a consolidated progressive Church, effectively linking the popular classes with the hierarchy. In this sense, these communities occupy an important nodal position, mediating the symbolic exchange between the progressive Church and the people. On the one hand, they constitute a symbolic space in which the beliefs and imagery of the people are constantly being symbolically reinterpreted, incorporating progressive Catholic imagery. On the other hand, the changing local beliefs and practices are constantly integrated into the position of the progressive Church, providing it with a certain dynamism and legitimation. In other words, Catholic communities effect the semantic fusion of innumerable contexts, harmonizing the various voices of the popular sector. Hence, in these communities, popular culture is ridded of the fragmentation and ambiguity encountered by Renato Ortiz in his noted work *A consencia fragmentada* (Fragmented consciousness) (1980).

However, this mediation is always fraught with tensions that arise in the very attempt to synthesize local beliefs and discourses into a unified voice.

Many issues of daily life have not been accommodated by the progressive Church, and, as a result, the inclusive communities where new issues and identities are contested are potential sites for fragmentation. In as much as Catholic militant practices have been encouraging a more critical orientation among community members, these new orientations may escape the realm of a Church that is no longer able to contain them. Under these circumstances, these new actors are expelled from the struggle.

GENESIS AND CRISIS OF THE LIBERATIONIST STRUGGLE

1968–1985

In Jd. Recanto, Jd. Vista Alegre, Jd. Princesa, and Jd. Damasceno, the struggle has been shaped by three main forces: local residents, the progressive Catholic Church, and secular student militants. Local residents have been engaged in many forms of struggle since their arrival in the area. Their aim has been to transform their extremely harsh environment, allowing for individual and communal development. At times, these local concerns acquired a broader focus within a broader political context. Local residents received support and direction in their struggle from Catholic radicals. The contact between these radicals and local residents during the late 1960s and early 1970s—institutionalized in the form of grass-roots nuclei (later called Ecclesiastical Base Communities, CEBs)—created a novel political force, inspired by a concept taken on board by liberation theology: the people. In fact, these militant Catholic community groups, assisted by student militants, cast local political events during the 1970s in terms of the struggle of the people. They encouraged legitimation and hope by supplying an important organizational structure and a strategy for change. Most important, they gave rise to a competent and critical local leadership that began to question institutional structures—including those imposed by the local clergy.

GENESIS

The story of the founding of Jd. Damasceno, conveyed by local residents, tells of the journey from an "infernal poverty to a normal life."[1] According to the story, Jd. Damasceno was born in a mountain of smoldering *lixo* (garbage) covered with a thin layer of black dirt. Residents used to climb up the stinking mountain to erect makeshift huts just centimeters above the *lixo*. The earth was hot from the fermentation process that took place under the thin crust. Their huts were warm even during the foggy winter months. Gas would escape through cracks in the crust, and women would transform these crevasses of the nether world into cooking places. In 1978–1979, the garbage caught fire, and the people got together to pressure the *prefeitura* (city council) to take action. Some of the *lixo* was removed and dumped in Perus, a nearby *bairro*, and the remainder was buried under a further layer of dirt. This layer was finally able to lock the hot inferno underground, creating a solid division between the rotting waste of civilization and human life.

Today, only the enormous potholes in the asphalt, bigger than in the other *bairros*, suggest what may be hidden underneath. These gigantic holes make it impossible to navigate certain streets. Complaints of residents that local buses diverge from their predetermined route to avoid these streets are met with the official reply of the transportation authority that the unstable ground makes it impossible to maintain a regular service (*Folha*, 18 July 1997).

Over the past thirty years, the refuse has disintegrated. With it the memory of its existence has dissipated, creating a story whose origin centers on the *bairro's* poverty. This story gives an idea of how long-term local residents construct the history of the *bairro* and their role in it. It is a story of a struggle to transform an infernal stretch of wasteland into a community; and in this story the people are placed at the center of radical change. "The people," Mônica asserts,[2] "that is us." Mônica and Maria-Conceição later admit that they did not form part of any social movements during the 1970s. In spite of this, by using the term the people in a sense that could have denoted their own involvement, they gave an impression that they were at the forefront of the struggle. Monica explained, "Jd. Damasceno was constructed by the people who successfully struggled for housing, asphalt, schools, water, and health services. The movements were so important here that Jd. Damasceno was the first *bairro* to receive water." In fact, the upper part of Jd. Damasceno was, according to Jacobi (1993), among the last to receive water. This, however, underlines the importance of concepts like the people and the struggle to local political self-esteem. It also conveys a glimpse of a *bairro* culture steeped in a liberationist imagery in which the *caminhada* (journey or procession) of the people into a better future has been worked into local history.

The Construction of a Popular Struggle and the Church

The struggle of the people plays a fundamental role in the founding story of Jd. Damasceno and other *bairros* in the region.[3] Mônica and Maria-Conceição remember other "prehistoric" struggles in the region that must have occurred before 1970. None of my informants, however, recalls any factual details of these early struggles. More than being just myth, however, it is likely that parts of the struggle of the people did actually take place. Partial evidence for this can be found in Lajolo's (1991) documentation of illegal land occupations involving Jd. Damasceno. Her account shows at least the contours of a col-lective struggle in the region.

While concrete references to the origin of these early struggles are scarce, several sources point to the fact that they were fought with the help of com-munity organizers linked to the Catholic Church. Julie,[4] an Irish community organizer and member of the *Congregação Missionárias Médicas de Maria* (Medical Missionaries of Mary Congregation), recalls that a substantial level of pastoral organization already existed when she arrived in the late 1960s. She says that this community work, led by agents of the Catholic Church, constituted the rudimentary social services in the *bairros* (Jacobi 1993, 117). According to Julie, the Catholic Church supplied health and education serv-ices throughout the Brasilândia region. In Jd. Damasceno, the local school was established on the premises of the parish. In Jd. Vista Alegre, Maria da Glória and Edilene[5] remember, public potable water was available only at the local parish. Claudia,[6] an Italian Catholic community mobilizer active in Jd. Vista Alegre between 1974 and the early 1980s,[7] sums this up: "Priests func-tioned as general practitioners, psychologists, lawyers, prosecutors, and jour-nalists all in one." She also remembers the presence of a local leadership —Carmelita and Zé—linked to the Catholic Church. This leadership must have emerged—she is not quite certain about this point—during the late 1960s.

They were the predecessors of Edilene, Maria da Glória, and Cleide, who joined local Catholic community groups in 1970. Such Catholic community activism is also evident in the work of Pedro Jacobi, who quotes Brazilian Democratic Movement (MDB) militants who arrived in the region in the early 1970s (Jacobi 1993, 117). Catholic community organizers thus played an important role in the construction of early collective struggles in the *bairros*.

Nevertheless, Pedro Jacobi (1993) claims that in the Brasilândia region these Church groups were not as politically organized as those in the south of São Paulo. There, Jacobi notes, the Workers' Pastoral acted as the single most important incubator of the workers movement. Jacobi observes that the relatively conservative nature of the Church in the eastern districts of São Paulo gave rise to pastoral work that emphasized the traditional role of the Catholic Church (Jacobi 1993, 127). However, in the light of the work of radical Catholic militants in the *bairros*,[8] Jacobi seems to be overstating the conservative aspect of the local Catholic Church. Furthermore, his research focuses on secular militants, suggesting a bias in favor of a secular opposition movement in the *bairros*.

Some of the work of Church-affiliated community organizers, such as the health center in Jd. Carumbé, was, without a doubt, of conservative character. Initially, the health center set up by Julie and her colleague administered curative medicine as part of a charitable mission. The evidence presented below, however, suggests a rapid radicalization of Catholic projects in the area. Furthermore, given the ideological differences that divided the secular Left MDB student vanguardists—which formed Jacobi's main interview base—and the liberation theology–inspired and supposedly nonvanguardist Catholic militants, it is possible that Jacobi reproduced a bias introduced by these secular Left MDB student militants. This may have led him to read the projects of local Catholic militants as conservative, reformist, or *assistentialist*[9] in nature (Jacobi 1993, 118, 123).

Medellin and Radicalization

In fact, between the late 1960s and the early 1970s Catholic communities in the *bairros* experienced rapid radicalization. By the late 1960s, various Catholic communities were displaying progressive leanings, and Church grass-roots groups appeared to be radicalizing rapidly, according to the statements of

Edilene and Maria da Glória (Berryman 1996, 61). Julie remembers that the radicalization process was fueled by the experience of the harsh local reality and, encouraged by the progressive message emanating from the Latin American Bishops Conference (CELAM) held in Medellin in 1968, by an increasingly militant tenor among Catholic priests and laity. Julie remembers that the diseases she treated:

> were mainly related to malnutrition. Mycosis, scabies, infected scabies. Good food, proper nutrition would have done away with these diseases. Children that we treated at the age of four or six returned to the center at the age of ten or twelve with the same diseases. This revealed that we were just maintaining a system. Hence, we entered the struggle for clean water, food, health centers as these were government obligations. From then on we also engaged in consciousness raising.[10]

Clearly, Medellin served as a catalyst in this radicalization process. Julie remembers: "Medellin opened the ears of progressive Catholics to the 'cry of the poor.'[11] With Medellin, the *caminhada* [journey/procession] had already started. After Medellin things were no longer the same. Already in 1971 and 1972 the message of Medellin was noticeable in the *bairros*."[12] In Julie's case, these influences transformed her traditional Irish Catholic outlook into a profoundly liberationist orientation, a transformation that took place between 1968 and 1972.[13]

These and other influences transformed the Catholic communities in the neighborhoods and inspired instances of collective action. By 1974, according to Edilene, Julie, and Claudia, many increasingly militant Catholic communities had undertaken a local struggle against the high cost of living that formed the *movimento da panéla vazia* (the movement of the empty saucepan), a local movement inspired by the better-known cost-of-living movement (*Movimento do Custo da Vida*), which emerged with the support of Catholic militants in 1972.[14]

The Role of the Progressive Church

In the *bairros*, this radicalization process was further inspired by the overall shift in orientation of the Paulistano Church hierarchy during the early 1970s. This shift toward humanist enlightenment discourses was reinforced on a na-

tional level with the ordination of progressive bishops and the election of Dom
Aloisio Lorscheider, known for his liberationist stance, as president of the
Brazilian National Bishops Conference (CNBB) (Löwy 1996, 87). According
to Michael Löwy, the installation of Dom Paulo Evaristo Arns in 1970 initiated a moral and sociopolitical reorientation of the local Church hierarchy,
turning it into one of the single most organized and committed forces op-
posing the violent abuses of the authoritarian regime (Löwy 1996, 87). While
Löwy's focus may rest too exclusively on the role of the hierarchy in the development of liberationist currents, this change in the São Paulo Church hierarchy's stance toward Christian humanism during a time of fear and persecution
certainly encouraged many progressive Catholics. Claudia, for instance, recounts that Dom Paulo Evaristo Arns's 1972 *Operação periferia* (Operation
Periphery) was very influential in the sense that it legitimized an already existing local struggle.[15] *Operação periferia* aimed to remedy the disproportionate
allocation of ecclesiastical resources in the city by paying more attention to
the fast-growing working-class neighborhoods at the periphery. Religious orders were encouraged to support this initiative by sending personnel to live
in these poor neighborhoods (Berryman 1996, 12). In 1975, based on an extensive consultation process, the archdiocese articulated the priorities of the first
pastoral plan. They were CEBs, the periphery, the world of labor, and human
rights. This agenda was widely endorsed by the Paulistano clergy (Berryman
1996, 13). By pledging the support of the Church behind the neighborhood
struggles, Dom Paulo helped to validate local claims directed at the authoritarian state, offered limited symbolic protection, and shaped the agenda of the
struggle.

The new official orientation issuing from the episcopal center informed
the work of Catholic militants and inspired them to take a more explicitly political position. This thrust of radicalism reverberated throughout Vila Alta
Brasilândia and had a strong influence on local militancy. According to Julie,
during the first half of the 1970s—the most violent and repressive years in the
history of the military regime—many of the community organizations "opted
for a more political posture. CEBs started to form and the creation of a political front was in the air." This change in the official discourse helped to carry
the projects of community-based Catholic radicals to new heights. Julie, for
instance, remembers that: "Within this increasingly politicized environment
we decided to enter into politics too. [We] started the first 'faith in politics'

group supported by the Archdiocese, which did similar work but did not endorse the [political] party analysis work that was presented as theater by our 'faith in politics' groups."[16]

The humanist currents that issued from Dom Paulo's posture were of great importance. "The early and mid-1970s gave rise to a period during which brotherhood was more than a word," Julie recalls, without explicitly mentioning the state-sponsored terror that overshadowed collective action during those years. "This created a strong alliance between people." During the early and mid-1970s, then, a progressive discourse directed against the authoritarian abuses of the state enticed many Catholic militants in the region to seek the proximity of this new Church.[17]

Popular Movements

During the second half of the 1970s, inspired by the impetus of Dom Paulo and profiting from the organizational capacity of Church activists and MDB student militants,[18] the struggle of individual local communities began to transcend *bairro* boundaries (Jacobi 1993). Consequently, the struggle for electricity, water, asphalt, sewers, transport, and the legalization of land titles that occurred during this period gave rise to an inter-*bairro* alliance, referred to by some as popular movements. According to Edilene, the first well-organized struggle was the movement for asphalt in 1978, which united thirteen *bairros* within the region.[19] Similarly, the struggle for water between 1976 and 1982 united a great number of *bairros* from the Brasilândia region (Jacobi 1993). During these years the *bairros* emerged as a new political force within Brazilian politics.

It is difficult to imagine the political mobilization during these years without the work of Catholic militants and the religious imagery whose promise of social and moral justice managed to inspire people. Without doubt, secular militants added an important organizational dimension that encouraged the formation of an inter-*bairro* movement. However, their work was very much defined by the institutional network of the progressive Catholic Church and would have been unthinkable without the political basis, as well as the political and spiritual consciousness, constructed by Catholic militants. For many *bairro* residents the presence of Catholic militants was most encouraging and propelled them into the forefront of the struggle.

RADICAL CATHOLICISM AND
FOREIGN INFLUENCES

Early liberationist attempts at mobilization in the *bairros* displayed a radical diversity. During the 1970s, the neighborhoods were home to various lineages of an ideology commonly referred to as *basismo*.[20] Actuated by Pope John XXIII's appeal to churches in Europe and the United States to place personnel and resources at the disposal of initiatives in Latin America, large numbers of Church affiliates of various nationalities congregated in poor neighborhoods all over Latin America (Beozzo 1996, 28–32). This impetus of foreign priests and lay persons, as Michael Löwy argues in *The War of Gods*, amplified the magnitude of progressive Catholic practice in Latin America (1996, 43).[21] To this should be added the radicalizing influence of women within the Catholic Church, evident in the work of Carol Drogus (1997), for instance. The fact that women are barred access to the hierarchical structures tends to endow them with a freedom paradoxically bound up with this peripheral status. This freedom, issuing from marginalization, may encourage radical action. Julie, for instance, when asked if she supported the ordination of women, replied that she did on a theoretical level only. "In practice," she replied, "such an ordination would bind Catholic women too closely to an archaic institution," a proximity that would stifle progressive action at the grass roots.

As suggested above, the impetus of foreigners within the *bairros* was substantial, and the contribution of foreign women certainly deserves attention.[22] However, their importance remains unacknowledged in Unger's (1987) work on pragmatic liberationist change, and it is absent in most of the literature on Brazilian social movements. Nevertheless, within the *bairros*, the most important Catholic radicals, during the 1970s and 1980s, were foreign Catholic women.[23] For instance, in Jd. Vista Alegre the Italians Claudia, Maria de Lourdes, and Teresa were highly influential in the organization of the local struggle. The statement of Maria da Glória, former coordinator of the local youth center, epitomizes this:

> Everybody here (in Vista Alegre) owes everything to some Italian Catholic nuns who visited when the CJ (youth center) was established. They prepared the ground for the CJ, gave me the documentation, and said, "Now you do it." I said, "Do what?" I had no idea what to do. They showed us how to

struggle, to become politically active, and set our heads straight in terms of independence. We owe everything to them.[24]

Similarly, Julie's influence on the struggle in Jd. Damasceno through the consciousness-raising groups she formed has been substantial, giving rise to what she regards as some of the most committed and critical local leadership. During the mid-1970s, many parishes in the area were occupied by foreign Catholic priests with astonishingly radical leanings. At the forefront of radicalism were the Italians—Padre Ivo, in charge of the parish in Jd. Damasceno, and Padre Alberto of Jd. Vista Alegre. Padre Ivo still evokes amusement among local activist veterans who remember him as "the mad communist." He is especially engraved in local memory as he is supposed to have addressed his flock as "comrades."

Diversity

The approaches of these foreign Catholic militants have been diverse, and their orientations range from explicitly revolutionary vanguardist politics to a conservative Christian social democratic position, politicizing basic needs. Their multifaceted frame of reference differed substantially from that introduced by Brazilian student militants influenced by a very particular trajectory of Brazilian student activism during the 1960s. Shaped by an array of influences at their places of origin, the foreign Catholic militants brought with them a vast and varied repertoire of political mobilization. This emerges clearly from their divergent attempts to construct a local political force. Padre Ivo's work, for instance, may be represented as having a vanguardist Catholic radical edge, while Julie, Maria de Lourdes, Teresa, and Claudia claimed that they were trying to effect change by anchoring their messages more firmly in the culture of the *bairros*. Julie asserts that her orientation was primarily influenced by liberation theology, anti-institutionalism, and a deep commitment to Christian humanist ideals. When taken at face value, this self-confessed liberationist commitment to work at the grass roots, present in the posture of many of these foreign Catholic activists, does resonate with Lehmann's characterization of *basismo* (Lehmann 1996, 33). However, closer scrutiny of these dispositions reveals that they do not culminate in a prostration in the face of an idealized image of popular culture (Lehmann 1996, 18). Rather than arising from an authenticity within popular culture, the commitment of these militants to the grass roots appears to flow from an applied humanism as well as an elitist developmentalism.

Claudia, for instance, appears to have adopted a stance that is quite critical of local residents and of local culture. Her position appears relatively little influenced by liberationist *basista* notions. As a consequence, in her statements she makes no attempts to endow popular culture with a spiritual authenticity. She reported, for instance: "Tuberculosis infections were mostly the consequence of insufficient hygiene, and garbage facilities. It was the work of years trying to educate people not to throw waste simply in front of their doorstep. This campaign did not lead anywhere. Also the campaign against malnutrition achieved no changes because nobody wants to show that they are hungry."

Furthermore, she claims, "Many of the other social conditions (comparing the 1970s with the 1990s) appear unchanged." "There were always groups that were *da pesada*" ("heavy," a local idiom describing those who kill and/or engage in organized crime). Robberies and drugs were common features, and many young people became entangled in them. "The families of Jd. Vista Alegre don't take care of their children," and their upbringing is largely left to the street, she says. At the health center, she treated many bullet wounds, and many children were shot during that era. Even then, the police profited from the local drug trade. While the overall volume of crime may have increased, its nature is still much the same.

Claudia's absence of faith in an authentic popular culture contrasts the symbolic framework of foreigners with that of Brazilian militants working in the area. This may have led foreign militants to be more prepared to accept and—in Julie's case—to respect local orientations. Claudia—not sharing the belief of many Brazilian militants in the authenticity of the people—felt, "The political consciousness of the people was reasonable and that of the leaders somewhat better." This distinguishes her approach most definitely from that of secular Brazilian militants such as Sandra[25] and the MDB student militants mentioned by Jacobi (1993), whose elitist notion of authenticity would lead them to experience a profound disappointment when faced by the reality of *bairro* culture. Ironically, their faith in an idealized popular culture did not necessarily promote respect for local values.

Sandra reveals the strong elitist tendency that underpinned her activism. For her, "The women resembled rough stones (*pedra bruta*). When we arrived [in Jd. Vista Alegre] the conditions were very rustic. No asphalt, no sewers, only a wooden barrack as a school, no electricity. Edilene was unlettered at the time; Maria da Glória and Cleide[26] had absolutely no political consciousness. They had no idea of poverty, class, misery, distribution of income, and so on." In this rather polemical statement, Sandra reveals some of her student militant background, anchored in the legacy of the student activism of the 1960s. In as much as Sandra's involvement in popular politics is indeed sub-stantially shaped by key symbols and concepts elaborated during that era, it resonates better with Lehmann's portrait of a slightly eccentric *basismo* (Lehmann 1996).

Urban Services and Infrastructure

Foreign radicals displayed great diversity in their approach to community work during the mid-1970s. Yet this diversity was reined in—according to Julie—by a common focus on the posture and initiatives taken by the progressive Catholic Church. In order to implement their interpretation of liberationist objectives, strongly colored by the leadership of the archdiocese, they at-tempted to roll back the Church; that is, to disengage the Church from services that were regarded as outside its scope. Julie, Claudia, and Maria de Lourdes —who also spoke for Pe. Ivo and Teresa—agreed that social services are the responsibility of the state. As a consequence, they tried to direct the local need and demand for these services toward the state, creating a more dynamic and, in Pe. Ivo's case, revolutionary atmosphere.[27]

The strategies were simple. Charitable services provided by the parishes were stopped, and efforts were made to turn them over to the state. For in-stance, Mônica and Maria-Conceição remember that Padre Ivo shut the local school built on church premises. Locals would stand in front of the closed school only to be told that the state was responsible for education services and a struggle was needed to force the state to extend this service to the local community.[28] This lack of diplomacy was not met with much local under-standing. Only with hindsight could Cristiane—a local activist of the 1970s—appreciate the struggle for the school of Jd. Damasceno that Padre Ivo fought almost single-handedly. Mônica and Maria-Conceição recollect that his efforts drew largely on the support of Pe. Alberto, on other priests, and on lay people in the region. Moreover, Mônica recalls that rather than provoking a mass uprising, Ivo's maneuver, which aimed at forcing the people to take action, caused a lot of local discontent. Consequently Pe. Ivo saw himself as very much alone at the helm of a popular movement that tried to pressure the state into establishing a school in Jd. Damasceno. In one account of this event, discussed in Jacobi (1993, 127), a resident revealed that the locals understood only after the fruits of Ivo's struggle had materialized and the elementary schools in Jd. Damasceno, Jd. Vista Alegre, and Jd. Carumbé had been built that their political conscience should prevent them from going to the Church school. According to Mônica, however, this experience inspired the struggle for water and other urban services in the *bairros*.

Claudia, Maria de Lourdes, and Teresa in Jd. Vista Alegre followed a similar path, implementing the local struggle for water. Due to their proximity to local residents, however, their approach was more sympathetic with the local ability to digest change. Claudia recalls that when the pump that supplied the only potable water broke down, and the locals waited for the priest to fix it, they were told that there were no funds available. This initiated a local discussion that gave rise to the initiative to enter the struggle.[29] This brief account of early foreign Catholic workers who radicalized *bairro* politics over the course of a couple of years manages to communicate the simplicity as well as the ideological scope of their approaches. This diversity gave way to a rather uniform canon of liberationist practices during the 1980s and 1990s.

Radicality and Transgression

W. E. Hewitt claims that during the mid- and late 1970s, the progressive politicization of the *bairros* carried Catholic militants increasingly beyond the boundaries acceptable to the Paulistano Church hierarchy (Hewitt 1991, 49). The political climate apparently encouraged local Catholic militants to assume a particular political position that was too specific for a hierarchy that attempted to maintain the universality of faith.[30] Michael Löwy elaborates this position by stating, "Not being a political movement, liberation theology does not have a program, nor does it formulate precise economic or political aims" (Löwy 1996, 37). Toward the end of the 1970s and, in particular, with the increasing pressure that followed the accession of Pope John Paul II (Beozzo 1996), the politicization of faith observed by Hewitt was increasingly criticized by the hierarchy. While in São Paulo, *Operação periferia* and the first pastoral plan expressed the hierarchy's official support for a struggle for urban infra-structure, such as health, transport, and education, local Catholic militants stepped well beyond these priorities by openly casting their lot with the discourse of political entities such as the Workers Party (PT) (Hewitt 1991, 49). Julie remembers that virtually all Catholic communities in the *bairros* supported the PT. This change in political and moral/ethical currents swept many local activists toward a more radical practice, bringing them close to what Unger claims was a radical opening of their epistemological horizon and allowing them to recognize that radical change was indeed possible (Unger 1987).

Well aware of the transgressions they were committing against Church directives, my Catholic militant informants asserted that their work was essentially political. Their practices were certainly much more radical than the consolidating progressive hierarchy would have been willing to condone. Ivo, for instance, took an explicitly Catholic-Communist stance that led him into a tense relationship with the local hierarchy.[31] Often against explicit episcopal directions, Julie's "faith in politics" sessions favored particular party orientations over others. Maria de Lourdes, and to a lesser degree Claudia, disseminated the principles of a feminist orientation within the *bairros* that did not place women inside their families but treated them as individual beings. It appears that during the late 1970s these radical militants often abandoned the confines of the Catholic doctrine, searching for new and more suitable practices beyond it.

Such transgressions entice Hewitt to raise the question of the Church's sanctioning practices. In fact, Hewitt's account contains an interesting ambiguity that emerges in relation to the sanctioning of radical CEBs by the progressive Church. In an early passage of his work, Hewitt claims that such a sanctioning was not forthcoming (Hewitt 1991, 44). According to Catholic militants of the 1970s, direct sanctions were indeed rare. However, it appears that over the course of the 1980s the militants became increasingly conscious of the degree of official attention they attracted as a result of their action. Clearly, the Vatican's instruction to subdivide the progressive archdiocese of São Paulo in 1989 added to this vigilance. During the mid-1990s, virtually all Catholic militants took precautions to avoid conflicts with the hierarchy by relegating radical activities to a sphere outside the dominion of the Church.

To act consciously against the dictum of the Church—with or without the direct sanctioning of the progressive Church—is generally regarded as a serious matter. This emerges clearly in the reluctance of local clergy to discuss controversial topics and the frequent requests to me for anonymity.[32] This may explain why Hewitt changes his point of view in a later chapter: "CEBs are creatures of the Church and, to a considerable extent, are subject to its dictates" (Hewitt 1991, 53). In other words, Hewitt witnessed what I call "the consolidation process" of the progressive Church. This consolidation process was driven by a local clergy whose status and power were challenged (Lehmann 1996, 76). Increasingly the clergy managed to remove the more problematic local leadership from the struggle, ending an era of Church renovation from grass roots. This consolidation process constituted an attempt by the progressive Church to regain control over militant *bairro* communities (Vásquez 1998, 108).

THE CENTRALITY OF THE PEOPLE

Local women joined the struggle for reasons that did not necessarily coincide with the political mobilization attempts of Catholic militants. In fact, the issues that led local women to join militant Catholic communities were not raised in the political agenda of popular Catholic communities during the 1970s and 1980s. Only during the 1990s did Catholic militants rediscover these issues and transform them into an essential part of a new liberationist-feminist synthesis. Initially, the confusion often surrounding land ownership in popular neighborhoods in São Paulo serves as the focal point for neighborhood movements. Rallying around the moral order underpinning liberation theology, neighborhood activists are able to resolve seemingly insurmountable legal hurdles.

Mônica left Jd. Carumbé in November 1970 and moved to the comparatively cheap plot of land she had recently bought. During 1971 and 1972 the rest of the hill belonging to a *sitio* (a holiday home situated in the countryside) was illegally subdivided and sold. This resulted in a municipal intervention and a second semilegal subdivision in 1976, during which a land planning agency, PLAVEN,[33] came to supervise the conduct of the owner, Dr. Sérgio Benicio & Soc., who was in charge of this subdivision until the time of my research in the *bairros*. In 1977 the Taxation Department learned that Dr. Sérgio had charged local residents with land taxes that were assessed on his land. As a consequence, the Caixa Economica intervened and ordered Dr. Sérgio to repay the funds and to stop issuing illegal land titles. According to Mônica, who is uncertain about this point, local residents were never able to retrieve these payments. However, as none of the local residents was interested in following up, the issue remained unresolved. During the same year Dr. Sergio resumed his illegal selling activity: "There was talk that everything was illegal and after some time someone suggested that we prove that the deal was legal by trying to register the land at the registry office. It turned out that Sergio bought the land from someone who inherited it but was not yet eighteen, and, therefore, had no legal authority to sell. As a result, the deal was illegal and the people weren't able to legally buy land."

At this point in the local story, the liberationist symbolic universe is evoked, and the struggle of the people begins. All my informants from Jd. Damasceno emphasize that the people got together and struggled for the legalization of their land titles. They formed a movement and were finally able to pressure the government into conceding to their demands. To be sure, the local residents' accounts all assign the lead roles to themselves and stress the centrality of the people in the struggle. The agents of the progressive Catholic Church are without exception represented as tangential to the achievements of the people. Padre Ivo's involvement in this struggle could be extrapolated only by means of an intense questioning process. These accounts indicate a fundamental tension between local residents and Church representatives. This leads my informants to reiterate the official discourse of the progressive Church that is at the center of this struggle.

Many Catholic and secular militants use accounts like the above to illustrate their view that material issues were the driving force behind local participation in the struggle. Claudia, for instance, claims, "With the satisfaction of all needs, a day-care center, water, housing, health, it is difficult to get another meeting out of them now. Before the struggle the people lived on top of the *corrego* [the river that doubles as sewer], and there was still a need to participate." Mônica claims that the movements in Jd. Damasceno stopped because there was nothing left to struggle for. This focus on material issues is also noted by academic observers such as Hewitt (1991, 88) and Drogus (1999, 36).[34] To state that the struggle focused on material benefits, however, would certainly underemphasize the nonmaterial and spiritual endeavors of local women. An overemphasis on material issues ties these observers too closely to the discourse of the progressive Church, as embodied in *Operação periferia* and the pastoral plan of 1975. Ironically, local preoccupations with material benefits emerged in conjunction with the liberationist struggle for urban infrastructure and services. Because of this, many Catholic militants neglected local nonmaterial concerns.

All long-term residents I interviewed declared that they came to the region as a result of their need for cheap accommodation. They had migrated to São Paulo before arriving in the *bairros* and had settled with family members in other parts of the city. Marriage, according to these residents, necessitated setting up their own households. They invested their scarce savings and borrowed from family and friends in order to buy a cheap, illegally subdivided plot situated at the fringe of São Paulo. Here, due to the illegal character of the transactions, land prices were much lower and still within the reach of blue collar labor. While this move to the periphery boosted their disposable income, families had to endure the total absence of social services and infrastructure and had to live with high levels of violence. By the late 1970s, the absence of rudimentary infrastructure such as water, asphalt, and sanitation had turned Jd. Damasceno, in Pedro Jacobi's account, into "one of the most needy *bairros* of the entire region" (Jacobi 1993, 96). The situation in Jd. Vista Alegre, Jd. Princesa, and Jd. Recanto, as well as the rest of the region, was only marginally better than that of Jd. Damasceno.

Cultural Concerns

While the lack of basic amenities and legal uncertainty was acute for residents as well as observers, it would be wrong to posit this as the exclusive central focus of the local women's struggle during the 1970s. In my interviews, virtually all the women who occupied leadership roles emphasized nonmaterial reasons for their participation in Catholic communities.[35] Of foremost importance were loneliness, isolation, and fear of street violence, as well as domestic violence and oppression.

The majority of the interviewed women suffered a severe shock when first exposed to their new environment. The conditions of violence and isolation found in the *bairros* proved difficult for many women. This fear was exacerbated by the loneliness they experienced in the sparsely settled region.

Edilene, for instance, arrived in Jd. Vista Alegre in 1966. "Then there was only jungle and mud—no houses."[36] The population density was so low that she felt very isolated during the first four years. Edilene was "found" by the Catholic community in 1970, and she began to participate in a mothers club that brought her into contact with the wider struggle of the community. Irina moved to Jd. Vista Alegre during the early 1970s.[37] She had recently married in an attempt to escape her authoritarian father. Her first impressions were dominated by the high levels of violence in the area. "The calls for help during the night, the shots, and groaning of the dying." She recalls the fear she felt, coming back from work and hearing cries coming out of the scrub next to the dirt path leading to her shack. This fear drove her away from Jd. Vista Alegre, and it took three attempts for her to settle there. "The initial process of getting used to the city culture was difficult. The change from the *fazenda* [large farm] to São Paulo was hard. You think that things are the same, but they are not. This leaves you half crazy." These issues led her, during the first year after her arrival, to participate in a local Catholic community, where she encountered many other women sharing a similar plight. For her, the Church represents an ideology-charged safe haven for women away from domestic violence: "The Church is a kind of refuge from the oppression of males. Men are pushing the women to Church because they don't know how to treat women well. There, women are very receptive to ideology. When a woman realizes that she is oppressed she is going to demand her rights."[38] According to Irina, the militant Catholic communities of the 1970s taught her and many others about the oppression of women.[39]

Mônica, Maria-Conceição, and Cristiane claim that in Jd. Damasceno many suffered from the violence and perceived insecurity in their new environment.[40] Arriving in the *bairros*, they encountered members of organized crime, who found an ideal hideaway in the relatively inaccessible forest. Mônica from Jd. Damasceno recalls that the whole upper part of the Damasceno hill was "their" territory. The forest was virtually littered with gutted cars whose "hot" parts satisfied the demands of the local second-hand car-accessory industry.

Zinha,[41] a most active and innovative local community organizer, arrived in Jd. Recanto after her marriage in 1975. She told me of the difficulties involved in forming a political community within an environment controlled by organized crime. "The *bairro* was abandoned, lots of drugs, crime, people attended the meetings with a thirty-eight-millimeter gun in their pockets in order to protect themselves from local criminal elements." Levels of local violence were perceived as a threat inhibiting the development of personal and communal ties. Today, Zinha celebrates the establishment of such ties, in the face of the atmosphere of fear that threatened communal projects, as a clear victory over the criminal elements in the *bairros*. This sentiment was shared by many other women I interviewed during the mid-1990s.

This victory over isolation, and particularly violence, formed an important aspect of the struggle of local women and has rarely received the attention it deserves in academic publications on social movements. This struggle was marked by the desire of local women to conquer the *bairros* in order to establish a livable social environment. While tangible material resources formed a part of that effort, they were certainly not omnipresent in the mobilization of these *bairros*.[42] In fact, this struggle in which fear is conquered represents an early attempt to semantically reiterate the liberationist symbolic universe to serve a purpose more pressing for local women.

The importance of this victory still reverberated throughout the *bairros* in the mid-1990s. The claim of women to have created a space of personal and communal security appeared, at times, to contradict the facts of continuing violence. Nevertheless, this discourse claims that women are no longer afraid; that neither domestic nor street violence can undermine the self-confidence of those who have conquered their fear of violence. According to these women, their joint force, articulated through community groups, was able to expel the criminal elements from the *bairros*. In their accounts, this power assumes almost mythical proportions, an empowering myth that is treasured by the generation of young women in the mid-1990s. The periods of violence that still ravaged the *bairros* in the mid-1990s certainly formed a strong incentive for the celebration of this theme.[43] This contestation is absolutely central to the concerns of local women and became the basis for a new liberationist effort during the early 1990s.

The example of these women demonstrates that the battle against deteriorating human relationships created an important but often neglected incentive to join Catholic communities. These orientations were multifaceted and fluid, however.[44] The prospects of better urban services certainly proved to be important, but other issues played an equally important role for many long-term participants in the struggle. The participation of women in Catholic communities often issued from violent, gender-specific, everyday experiences arising from the location of working-class women in society, the *bairros*, and the family. This was, according to Julie, largely overlooked by the predominantly gender-blind liberationist clergy, who treated what were essentially gender and class issues exclusively as a class analysis (Burdick 1993; Drogus 1997, 156; Lehmann 1996, 61). It took Catholic militants almost two decades to adapt their projects to this aspect of everyday life, because the liberationist listening process did not always contain the pragmatic qualities necessary to hear the voices of local women. The political focus of the local struggle was, to a large extent, preconceived and shaped by the outlook of the progressive Church. As a result, women were never invited to make their issues the spiritual or political focus of local movements and always remained in the shadow of an officially endorsed struggle for urban services and infrastructure.

Day Care, Health, Transportation, and Urban Services

In 1973, a pastoral publication talked about the cultural tendencies that priests would encounter in the working-class neighborhoods. The publication focused on violence, promiscuous sexual behavior, greater liberation of women, search for social welfare and social status, mysticism, solidarity, and the necessity for security, concerns that were supposedly characteristic of "lower-class" culture (Soares 1988, 280). While these issues were largely taken up by militant Catholic communities in the *bairros*, Carol Drogus points out that they never entered the official political discourse of the progressive Church (Drogus 1997, 156). For the local clergy, according to Julie, gender issues were assimilated into a moral and ethical sphere. Furthermore, she claims that liberation theology influenced local Catholic militant projects in such an important manner that gender issues fell outside the parameters of their political activity. As a result, the political emphasis of the local struggle came to rest on day care, health, transportation, and urban services.

While topics such as domestic violence, personal hygiene, contraception, sexuality, and women's rights were still being discussed within the communities led by Julie, Maria de Lourdes and, to a lesser extent, Claudia, the struggle for urban services dominated the official political agenda of local militant Catholic community groups. For instance, according to Julie, an increasingly threatened local clergy zealously watched initiatives, such as those attempted by Maria de Lourdes's group, to politicize gender issues. This reluctance to accept that local hardship contained distinct gender-political specificities created a basic tension between Catholic militants, the local clergy, and the hierarchy (Alvarez 1994; Caldeira 1990). Moreover, differences of opinion on the importance of gender issues also divided Catholic and secular militants in the *bairros*.[45]

Claudia and Pe. Alberto, for instance, believed that the only political initiative that enjoyed sufficient centrality in the *bairros* was the politicization of urban resources.[46] For Claudia, the feminist principles that informed much of Sandra's and Maria de Lourdes's work were not particularly important. Claudia embraced the boundaries defined by a local clergy that claimed to represent the progressive Church. Within these boundaries women's issues could be taken up only with the family at the center of the discussion. Stepping beyond these boundaries became increasingly difficult during the late 1970s as the debate on gender issues started to polarize. The official break between feminists and the Catholic Church materialized during the First Paulista Women's Congress in 1979, when the question of female sexuality was politically elevated to a place alongside traditional issues, such as urban services and political participation (Alvarez 1994, 27). During the early 1980s this break was reenacted in Jd. Vista Alegre, causing the fragmentation of the Italian nucleus around Claudia and Pe. Alberto. Even before 1979, however, the development of a focus on gender themes in the *bairros* was predominantly the concern of militants whose limited Church association left them more space to move into the field of gender politics.[47]

Consequently, only in a very limited sense did the preoccupation with urban services arise from the grass roots. To accept claims such as Claudia's, that day care, health care, public transportation, water, and electricity were the only issues that could provide a mobilization platform, and that these issues were detected by liberationist militants' listening (Mainwaring 1986b, 208, 209), would be a misinterpretation of local events. In fact, the focus on these services was to a large degree predetermined by radical Catholic militants, who initiated the struggle for water, health, asphalt, day care, and urban transportation between 1976 and 1982. The fact that Claudia, together with Pe. Alberto, initiated the struggle for water in Jd. Vista Alegre, or that Pe. Ivo initiated the struggle for education in Jd. Damasceno by barring access to locally available resources, demonstrates this clearly. Hence, *bairro* politics during this era was substantially shaped by Catholic vanguardist and paternalist practices in tune with an agenda propagated by the progressive archdiocese.

Claims of Catholic militants that their initiatives have been informed by nondirective practices should thus be treated cautiously (Lehmann 1996, 95).[48] The symbolic influence of the progressive Church distracted substantially from the concerns that brought women into contact with militant Catholic communities. By entering the realm of militant Catholic communities, the specific concerns of local women within the cultural realm of the *bairros* were translated into material issues whose politicization was largely predetermined.

CRITICAL SECULAR AND FEMINIST VOICES

During the second half of the 1970s, the mobilization practices of Catholic radicals, increasingly curtailed by the locally consolidating progressive Church, attracted critical responses from two different camps. Secular student activists who had joined the MDB criticized the emerging *bairro* movements for their closely focused and localist outlook, which eschewed a wider political perspective (Jacobi 1993). More important for collective mobilization within the *bairros*, this dissatisfaction with a focus on urban services was shared by some feminist militants who expanded on the feminine element taken up by Catholic militants and placed women's issues at the center of their projects. These projects would alter the lives of the participating women significantly and would create the basis for modest cultural change in the *bairros*.

The Secular Left

Secular MDB student militants, who aimed at unifying and transforming *bairro* groups into social or popular movements, appeared in the region in 1974. The consequent rise of popular movements in the Brasilândia region, encouraged by MDB coordination, was marked by a tension that, not unlike the student politics of the 1960s, divided the secular vanguardists from a Freire-inspired Catholic Left. In the eyes of the MDB student militants, it was important to transcend the "inferior" politicization of everyday life based on immediate local issues and to achieve a deeper-rooted change on a national level (Jacobi

1993, 116). Jacobi's observations make this clear: "The reformism of the movement corresponds in their view to the incapacity of the population to amplify the struggle which remains very connected with issue-based demands (asphalt, water, creche, etc.)" (Jacobi 1993, 118; parenthesis in the original). To overcome issue politics, the militants of the MDB attempted to give political direction to local activities. Their approach alienated not only Catholic community mobilizers, but also local politically active residents. Following an ideology that built strongly on a tradition of elitist student movements, MDB militants reacted strongly against the Catholic radicals who emphasized a transformation process based on culture.

According to Jacobi, for MDB student activists in the *bairros*, the overall aim of the struggle was the end of dictatorial oppression and, more generally, the end of capitalism (Jacobi 1993).[49] With this in mind, these MDB student militants tried to broaden the struggle of local *bairro* groups, creating regional movements that were supposed to struggle for macropolitical aims, thus leaving the realm of issue-based *bairro* politics. Their proposed methodology was education by elites with a correct understanding of the political economic conjuncture[50] (Jacobi 1993). This position clashed with that of Catholic militants, such as Claudia, for whom the struggle of the people was essentially geared toward creating a society based on Christian norms. Claudia discarded the MDB position as utterly romantic. She was particularly incensed by the MDB's assertion that "the children of the poor need nothing less than university degrees," which she regarded as "absolutely utopian."

Nevertheless, the influence of MDB student militants on local militant Catholic communities was tangible. Claudia claims that they prevented her participation in grass-roots workshops attempting to foster a new culture and identity.[51] Sandra remembered that the MDB militants perceived working on basic needs as terribly backward. Their view was that the people should have reached a stage at which they could understand the fundamentals of political doctrines. Work on needs was seen "like falling back into the dark ages," she said. Sandra also remembers that this very vocal MDB student militant critique influenced the focus of her project.

Jacobi believes that a certain frustration also defined the relationship between MDB militants and local residents. For MDB militants, this frustration was amplified when the numbers of local movement participants declined during the second half of the 1970s (Jacobi 1993, 128). For local residents, the practices of these militants had a lot to do with their loss of interest in the movements. According to Jacobi, a tension between local residents and the MDB militants gave rise to a sense of general distrust among the local population (Jacobi 1993). The MDB student activists assumed a rather paternalist, as well as elitist, posture that overestimated its politicizing impact on the masses. While the population was able to assimilate the discourse of the MDB, Jacobi's account makes it clear that translating this discourse into action proved to be far more difficult for most locals (Jacobi 1993, 120).

This tension explains the odd absence of MDB militants from local memory. By the mid-1990s, none of the interviewed local residents remembered any MDB activities, though long-term residents did remember most other political activity during that era. For instance, Benedito Cintra, the local *vereador* during the early 1980s, is depicted by Jacobi as one of the great mobilizers in the struggle for water in Jd. Damasceno and Jd. Carumbé, but his name has disappeared totally from the local history (Jacobi 1993, 97). This may have been because these militants and opposition politicians were mainly organizing the already-organized elite of the *bairros*. Only community activists such as Julie, Claudia, or Eneida are aware of the role of the MDB militants. It is certain, however, that MDB militants were never able to penetrate the culture of the *bairros* in a lasting way.[52] The example of MDB student militants demonstrates that *bairro* politics were inextricably linked to Catholic militants and the liberationist symbolic universe during the 1970s. In this sense, the presence of MDB militants during the late 1970s and their unsuccessful contestation of the liberationist symbolic space within the *bairros* highlight a failure in the argument of many academics who sought to construct a secular political opposition in the space of the liberationist struggle. However, the experience of MDB militants reveals the strength of the liberationist symbolic universe during that period.

The Feminist Left

A current that left a definite imprint on local culture was the emergence of a feminist force in the *bairros*. In 1976, the specificity of women's experiences in the *bairros* received renewed attention with the arrival of Sandra, a young Brazilian graduate of the Catholic University of São Paulo (PUC/SP). Her feminist background introduced to the *bairros* a focus on identity politics that gave rise to a women's movement. Commissioned by Socio-Educative Youth Orientation (OSEM), a secular organization that worked with local Catholic communities, Sandra started to work as a consciousness-raiser in the region. As a result of their common interest in feminist issues, Sandra and Maria de Lourdes began to organize workshops dealing with topics like abortion, household health, and violence, and they set up literacy programs geared toward politicizing everyday life and forming strong consciousness-raising organizational leadership. In these workshops they encountered Edilene, Maria da Glória, and Cleide, the local women who became the driving force of the daycare and youth center struggle; and by the late 1970s, Sandra and Maria de Lourdes had begun to focus more explicitly on gender issues.

According to Sandra, they started to work with around fifty women who had been participating in militant Catholic communities and who received food subsidies for their participation. After listening[53] to local concerns, they learned that "mothers needed a place to leave their children during their working hours." As this was the only issue the group could agree on, they decided to struggle for a day-care center.[54] Soon, however, the group began to focus on women's issues in more general terms. Issues like "abortion, sexuality, domestic violence, violence in general, health, menopause, and women's rights" became increasingly important, according to Sandra.

This movement grew with astonishing speed. Sandra speaks of an excitement that gripped the women in the *bairros*, which in turn led to the movement's rapid growth in the region. For instance, in 1979, Sandra mobilized many local women to participate in the first women's congress in São Paulo. The meeting drew eighty women from the *bairros*, with Edilene and Maria da Glória among them. The *Congresso Movimento Mulheres* (Women's Movement Congress), organized in 1980, was attended by more than three thousand women. While this expansion was swiftly arrested by the emergence of political parties and their concerns for the women's vote, these feminist workshops facilitated changes in gender dynamics that would produce a basis for a modest transformation of the *bairros'* cultural sphere.

The feminist group that formed around Sandra and Maria de Lourdes during the late 1970s prepared the ground for the liberationism/feminism that emerged in the 1990s. This feminist endeavor contested the symbolic sphere of the *bairros* and disseminated a feminist outlook among local women, in turn facilitating the emergence of the liberationist/feminist synthesis of the 1990s.

Cultural Transformation

According to Alvarez, a sense of achievement that affects all aspects of local cultural life is constructed through women's involvement in the struggle (Alvarez 1994, 16). This certainly occurred in the *bairros*. For many residents, and especially for women, cultural patterns shifted substantially as a result of their involvement in the feminist struggle. Foremost, this novel focus on gender issues boosted their self-confidence and enriched their lives in a variety of ways. Both the local *bairro* leadership of the 1970s and the women leading the land occupation at Jd. Perí Alto in 1996 emphasized that they had gained a new outlook: they had learned that they were able to leave their mark in the local political arena; they experienced resisting and changing the local institutional environment; and they discovered they were capable of executing tasks they had never dreamed of before (Drogus 1997).

Having experienced the way they could effect change in wider society, many participating women began to reconstruct the nature of their space within the *bairros*. Maria da Glória, Mônica, and Irina were among the first of the women involved in the struggle to demand more independence and space to pursue their own lives, and their partners felt the results. On quite a few occasions, according to Maria da Glória, these new demands ended with the violent imposition of male authority. However, she goes on to claim optimistically that those involved in the struggle "who have not liberated themselves and are still oppressed by their husbands are in the minority." For those who were able to stand up to their partners, their relationship with other family members as well as with the *bairro* changed substantially. The participation in the struggle in many ways served as an incubator for their own personal development. Maria da Glória, for instance, speaking in the name of a group of friends who had been at the forefront of political activities in the 1970s, claims:

> Today women are working, participating in social movements, participating in politics. Today I come home at one, two, or three and my husband doesn't dare to ask where I was. If he did he would get an answer like "None of your business." Imagine, women have to secure an income, do the housework, look after the children, have to be women to their husbands, and still have to be submissive?? No way! Men today are like children of their spouses, totally dependent on their women. Women here boss their husbands around.[55]

Throughout my stay in the *bairros*, I found many of Maria da Glória's statements confirmed by the women I interviewed.[56] This attitude was also captured by the survey. When asked if women had more rights in the 1990s than in previous decades, 89 percent of surveyed Damasceno residents confirmed this. When questioned why this was so, 96 percent of this sample asserted a greater liberty in general, 41 percent claimed a greater liberty to work, 19 percent mentioned a greater freedom to enter (*bairro*) politics, and 23 percent responded in terms of legal rights. Maria da Glória states that much of her independence as a woman was learned during the political fight for the youth center and in contact with Maria de Lourdes and Sandra: "They set our heads straight in terms of independence," she recounts. "Today, women are much more independent," and in order to underline this she claims: "They engage in relationships with other women. Today, there are a lot of lesbians in the *bairro*." In this way she is stressing the fact that women have gained the self-confidence to express orientations that collide with the male-oriented culture of the *bairros*.[57]

While the liberation of women may be partial or incomplete in character and applies only to those who have developed their personal ambitions and initiative through political activism, the feminist struggle may have contributed to a modest redefinition of gender roles.[58] On a cultural level, the struggle has done more than just stimulated an intra-*bairro* discussion focusing on gender roles; in many cases, it has actually changed them.[59] Most important for this book, these feminist tendencies, which were never allowed to occupy a central position in militant communities during the 1970s and 1980s, created the basis of the liberationist/feminist synthesis that surfaced during the 1990s.

THE FRAGMENTATION OF THE STRUGGLE

For the majority of local residents who participated in militant Catholic communities, the struggle was over by 1980–1981. Whereas the institutionalists contend that the demise of the popular Church was largely due to the ebbing of institutional support during the 1980s (Hewitt 1998), events in the *bairros* suggest that the deterioration of popular participation preceded institutional changes. In fact, popular support had been dwindling ever since the late 1970s

(Jacobi 1993), when the movements of the Brasilândia region achieved their goals or gathered academic fame. Much of this fragmentation occurred as a result of the fulfillment of local demands or exhaustion (Vásquez 1998, 149). However, for those participants in the movement who saw in the struggle more than a means to the satisfaction of material demands, another struggle involving the contestation of the liberationist symbolic universe began. In 1980 this struggle was strongly shaped by political events. Newly formed political parties, and in particular the PT, increasingly claimed the prophetic voice of the Church. This initiated a transition period into a decade in which the local clergy asserted its power much more directly, and the dominion of the progressive Catholic Church came to cast a much more defined influence over politics and morals in the *bairros*.

The collapse of the struggle in the early 1980s owes much to the fact that many demands had been met (Telles 1986). Much of Jd. Damasceno was urbanized after the violent clashes with forces deployed by Paulo Maluf, governor of the state of São Paulo, in 1980. This violent response resulted in a prompt and determined condemnation by most sectors of civil society. Consequently, Jd. Damasceno was chosen to implement a model urbanization scheme (Jacobi 1993, 99). Mônica remembers that with this sudden extension of urban services, many movement participants could no longer find a reason for their struggle.[60] Confrontations erupted as a result of the sudden availability of resources and accelerated the fragmentation of groups. According to Claudia and Sandra, internal fights broke out over the distribution of opportunities, such as jobs and resources. This divided groups and left traces of bitterness that have survived until today. Once the focus of these groups was reduced to the *bairro* level, local politics pushed regional political events off the agenda. Community leaders, such as Maria da Glória, Edilene, and Cleide, tried to secure their positions of power and closed themselves off from other groups.

Signs of exhaustion appeared among local movement participants. Julie, for instance, remembers, "People were simply tired. They had to take days off from work and had to face the consequent danger of being fired. For years they spent every spare minute in meetings or other community activities." The severe recession of 1982 and 1983 made participation in struggles harder for many local residents. According to Claudia, the *bairros* experienced a dramatic change and many informal businesses sprang up during these years. The mass unemployment that ensued made it difficult to find the material resources to struggle. For those who could not be persuaded to struggle for abstract ideals, or those who could no longer afford the relative luxury of spending their time in political activism, the struggle was over.[61] However, for those locals who became professional militants between the late 1970s and the early 1980s, the struggle took a decidedly different direction. Increasingly they began to contest the liberationist symbolic universe and the role of the progressive Church within it. This introduced a new dynamic into the struggle, a dynamic that was frequently overlooked in the discourse on social movements and on CEBs.

Extermination of Popular Criticism

During these years, in the community frequented by Julie, a small group of local leaders emerged. They decided to act on their newly gained consciousness. For this elite of local militants, Julie asserts, the struggle had taken on other contours. They had invested most of their time in the struggle and their own consciousness raising. They had grown very attached to the Catholic radicals in the *bairros* and maintained close ties with them and their activities. Julie claims that in these individuals the work of critical consciousness raising came to fruition. They had gained a keen interest in wider political issues and displayed a determination to alter existing political as well as economic structures. This successful consciousness raising led a number of local militants to question proceedings within the religious and political institutions that claimed to represent them: "They started to ask their own questions," Julie recalled. Further, this consciousness raising led, in quite a few local militants, to an automatic transformation process in which the acquired critical thought was applied to the local political context, leading to a contestation of the local institutional framework (Vásquez 1998, 124–25).

The formation of political parties certainly spelled changes for political life in the *bairros*. With the opening of a formal political arena, the emerging parties absorbed much of the political activity that was previously tied to militant Catholic groups (Berryman 1996, 67). Political parties altered the local political environment by recruiting the movement participants who had previously been struggling together with the Catholic radicals (Sader 1988). All the Catholic and secular militants who worked in the region during that time agreed that the formation of the parties led to the fragmentation of political alliances. Sandra, for instance, remembered that the women's movement fell apart largely due to the political fights that erupted during this era:[62] "Parties tried to capture votes as they were concerned about who the women would vote for. Political parties have divided everything," she objected.[63] The early 1980s initiated a move away from grass-roots concerns, giving rise to an increasing preoccupation with party politics.[64] Among local residents, this shift created an atmosphere of general disillusionment within the formal political arena (see also Vásquez 1998, 206). However, the birth of political parties was just one factor that contributed to the fragmentation that took place during the early 1980s. Threatened by this *bairro* leadership's demands for democratic participation within Church and parties, officials of these institutions began to edge them out of *bairro* politics.

As a result of the emergence of various political positions and interest groups, local militants became increasingly aware that none of these entities represented their interests. Julie, for instance, notes that at the beginning of the struggle, "It was easy to pretend that the aims of the Church, the Left, and the people were actually the same. Then it emerged that they were not" (Hewitt 1991, 95). This insight was confirmed by the shift of the progressive Church hierarchy away from political matters. After the mid-1970s, the Brazilian Catholic Church embarked on an increasingly liberationist-conservative consolidation (Mainwaring 1986b, 164, 166). According to Julie, the most capable local leadership in charge of catechist groups became increasingly dissatisfied with the closure of the political sphere within the ecclesiastical space. Having been exposed to Catholic radical thought for almost a decade, local leaders had gained a distinctly radical edge. According to Julie, these local activists were strongly inspired by the notion of grass-roots democracy as well as the belief in the struggle as the only expression of democratic political activity. They had internalized a Christian radical political stance that focused on the people as the transformative motor of society. As a result, Julie remembers, they demanded more participatory democratic procedures within that nucleus as well as within the local Church.

Faced and threatened by these demands, the local clergy adopted a more conservative and paternalist stance, asserting their moral authority over the struggle.[65] "It became obvious," Julie remembers, "that the local priests were the bosses."[66] "They were scared to lose their identity" when faced by demands for a more democratic Church. Consequently, within her community the most critical local leaders were increasingly overlooked or, in Julie's words, "'expelled' from the local parish."[67] With the closure of the sociopolitical realm of the Church, many local militants demanded an alternative space within the newly forming political parties. In their search for a radical Christian democracy, they turned to the PT, which during much of the 1980s carried on some of the legacy of the political/moral struggle of the progressive Catholic Church. This point is also made by Phillip Berryman (1996, 67) and by Robin Nagle (1997, 155).

According to Julie, similar incidences occurred within the realm of the PT. In like manner, PT representatives refused to heed popular calls for participatory inclusion. In this light, the promises of the freshly formed PT, carrying on the banner of the popular struggle, rang hollow for local militants. They recognized that their claims were "represented" by social workers, teachers, union administrators, and other elite professionals, while their own demands for direct participation were muted: "They got too close to the power center and got burned. Then, the people started to notice that none of the institutionalized religious or political entities were actually representing their interests and turned off. Then, the whole thing collapsed." In this sense, with the consolidation of the local progressive Catholic Church and of political parties,[68] many of the most capable leaders were lost and the struggle was emptied of much of its progressive potential for transformation.[69]

Toward the mid-1980s, with some exceptions, these critical voices fragmented. As Julie recalls, people withdrew into family life. Bruno, for instance, who had been doing a lot of political work, told me that he became "totally apathetic to violence and politics during those days. In the past I worked a lot for the parties and for movements. Then I didn't want to get involved in this . . . any longer. I only cared about my family." The frustration was that, in effect, nothing had changed; that while the movements had brought some urban services into the area, the political power rested elsewhere. Once again local political participation occurred through a well-remunerated elite intermediation that failed to represent local issues adequately. This ended the struggle for the more politically motivated among the local leadership.

At this stage, both the spiritual and the political protagonists of the liberationist struggle had closed their ranks to the direct participation of those they were claiming to represent. With this, the elitist institutional elements within the liberationist symbolic universe had finally undermined the liberationist message. Faced by these unveiled institutional interests, local militants no longer contested the local symbolic space, but simply distanced themselves from the struggle.

WEAKENING OF THE LIBERATIONIST SYMBOLIC UNIVERSE

The destruction of faith in the authenticity of the working classes spelled the end of the liberationist struggle for student militants like Sandra. The weakening of key liberationist symbols ushered in the decline of the liberationist struggle during the mid-1980s. This tends to be underemphasized in many accounts dealing with *bairro* politics. No doubt attempts at institutional consolidation also played an important role. Sandra conveys the disillusionment that Catholic and secular militants felt increasingly from the mid-1980s on: "The world of the 1970s had definitely gone and the world of the 1990s is endlessly colder and myth freer than the 1970s."

Events in the *bairros*, undermining the motivation of key militants, caused many to withdraw from the struggle in the region. Various factors contributed to their disaffection, giving rise to distinct responses from Catholic and secular militants. Sandra was primarily affected by events that seemed to indicate the inauthenticity of the people,[70] whereas Catholic militants focused on the institutional influences that militated against the struggle. Much of Sandra's dismay issued from the fact that most of the movements initiated by these outsiders had collapsed, lost their radicalism, or been coopted (Gohn 1991; Telles 1986).

Many of the local militants began to develop in a direction not anticipated or desired by community organizers, and consciousness-raising attempts seemed to have failed with all but a handful of militants. These conditions began to undermine one of the core mobilization concepts of the struggle: the belief in the authenticity of the people. Catholic militants like Julie watched as their locals who had gained a critical orientation were forced out of the struggle. They began to doubt that those institutions, which claimed to be the bearer of liberationist principles, were the actual protagonists of such a liberationist promise. Increasingly frustrated by this indirect sanctioning process of the struggle, key Catholic militants stepped back from their political involvement. As faith in the people and in the institutions waned, Catholic and secular militants started to withdraw from the liberationist struggle.

The Myth of Authentic Popular Culture

Sandra, it appears, lost her faith in the people through her work at the periphery. Sandra claims that this loss was brought about largely by Edilene, Maria da Glória, and Cleide, members of the Vista Alegre group that had struggled for day-care centers. Sandra began to question the struggle when those three militants elected themselves as coordinators of the newly gained facilities and began to draw substantial financial benefits and power from their political engagement.

> To see that leaders, our leaders, got bought left, right, and center, that they had learned the political game rapidly and became part of it hurt a lot and destroyed our faith. We believed that the people were somehow good, that they only needed a chance and they would create great things. Women such as Maria da Glória, Edilene, and Cleide turned into professionals—what now? Then, people without any money had access for the first time to some income and that was when the fights over the loot started. At first none of the women had any bossy ambitions. Then we noticed that Maria da Glória started to boss us around and that it [the youth center] turned into her business. Edilene was next in line. Back then Cleide didn't have ambitions. Maria da Glória, Edilene, and Cleide grew and turned into professionals and started to live their lives apart from the movement. When Maria da Glória started to construct her house [two-story white-washed with two cars behind an iron gate] we couldn't believe it and started to ask ourselves, "What are we actually still doing here?" In the early 1980s, everybody still wanted to work for half a minimum salary as monitor, then it turned into one, and today, everybody is complaining about having only one [minimum salary].

Central to Sandra's self-declared loss of faith in the people was the realization that the consciousness-raising process did not necessarily lead to an authentic revolutionary popular culture, as envisaged by student movements during the 1960s. Instead, the consciousness-raising process seemed to give rise to individual attempts to improve living conditions by taking advantage of the struggle. With this loss of faith in the ability of the poor to create an egalitarian Christian culture, Sandra lost her belief in the struggle. Consequently, she embarked on an individualistic path, which led her into career politics. Finding, however, that those *bairro* women with whom she had worked for almost a decade did not support her attempt to capture the political seat of a federal deputy, she was once again fundamentally disappointed. In this sense, the consciousness-raising process of the 1970s proved too successful to accommodate Sandra's reorientation from liberationist struggle to career politics.

During the second half of the 1980s the feminist movement that Sandra had tried to build faced an almost complete fragmentation (Alvarez 1994, 44–53). When this happened, Sandra appears to have lost her belief in the struggle. She claims that the closure of the political system toward the gender question (Alvarez 1994, 44–53) made her see many of the previous achievements in a questionable light.

> Then [in 1987] everything fell apart. Today, "hot" projects no longer exist. The people who changed changed, then the struggle stopped—today we know that there is no continuity. For me it all ended around 1987. Then a lot of us got disillusioned and started to feel that this wasn't going to go right. People [activists with an elite education] started to drop out. Sure, we had all joined the PT by that stage—but by then we felt that the PT had changed too. There was something like a social depression that caught the activists of the middle class then. In 1987 a lot of people suddenly started to talk about therapy, to live in the country. This was the great disassociation of middle class ideals. Money became incredibly important and ideology was lost.

Many elements conspired to produce Sandra's disillusioned image of the struggle. First of all, she seems to have relived those experiences that altered Paulo Freire's views on the authenticity of the people. With the recognition that working-class dreams of a better world also contain individualistic elements and the desire for luxury and upward mobility, the myth of an authentic popular culture collapsed. During Sandra's subsequent move into feminist party politics, both her popular constituency and her own party deserted her. At this stage, the struggle had lost its meaning for Sandra.[71]

Questioning Institutional Promises

The issues that led to the dissociation of Catholic radicals from the struggle in the region were varied. For someone like Claudia, who never experienced profound religious ties with the liberationist struggle, consciousness raising had a more emancipatory objective. While also demonstrating a certain dissatisfaction with *bairro* residents, representing them as irresponsible with regard to child care, Claudia was prepared to accept local events. Once she felt that a certain degree of emancipation had been reached, she moved on to another community with greater need to be mobilized.[72] However, for those Catholics who identified more with the struggle, the changes within *bairro* politics during the early 1980s were crucial.

Julie's disappointment seems to issue from a lack of institutional support and openness toward the working classes. Through her engagement in the struggle, she actively participated in the construction of a radical political and moral culture within the *bairros*. Being true to the liberationist essence as she claims, her involvement displayed a noticeably pragmatist streak that led her to disregard claims that located authenticity in the working classes. This pragmatism enabled her to embark on a radical redefinition of liberationism (see chapter 6). For Julie, "change is natural" and "liberationist practices have to adjust to the changing circumstances of the people." It appears that Julie has never lost her faith in *bairro* residents and preserves her sense of the potential that she finds in each individual. As a result she was able to further the critical consciousness of women residents while adjusting to the changing orientation that emerged in her groups. Maybe not surprisingly, some of the most critical and, according to Julie, capable leadership emerged in her groups during the late 1970s and early 1980s.

Having witnessed the fate of this carefully nurtured leadership, forced out of the struggle by Church and political party actors, Julie's remorse stems more from an institutional closure toward liberationist ideals. For her, the exclusionary political interests of these institutions have militated against the development of a transformation process in which the grass roots could have been actively involved. While certainly aware of other factors, such as life-cycle issues, changing cultural and economic patterns, lack of educational resources, and intra-*bairro* competition for resources, the loss of belief in the struggle and in the possibility for a transformed, just society is central to Julie's analysis. From her point of view, institutional interests have militated against the political force emanating from the *bairros*, truncating the transformative process that was altering Brazilian society. Institutional interests had muted the meaning of Catholic liberation. In other words, institutional interests led the progressive Church to redefine the liberationist symbolic universe in a way that smothered the very idea of liberation.

From Julie's perspective CEBs never existed: "CEBs in an ideal sense"—in a liberationist sense, she claims—"could never emerge because they were never independent of the parish. An ideal CEB would alter the power dynamics within the Church and endanger the [patriarchal] identity of priests. CEBs were never given a chance," she asserts. The term CEB, hence, is by no means neutral. This emerges clearly from the ambivalence other Catholic militants in the *bairros* found in the term. Irmã Maria and Irmã Alba, for instance, made it very clear that their community was not a CEB, though the hierarchy and the local clergy called it a CEB. While the term was frequently used by the clergy of Jd. Vista Alegre and Jd. Carombé, those Catholic militants who had established communities during the 1960s, 1970s, and mid-1980s refrained from using it. For these Catholic militants, the term CEB, having strong liberationist overtones, does not adequately express the practices of the consolidated progressive Church. After it became clear that the Church's option for the poor was indeed only preferential, the term was increasingly felt to represent an imposition by a hierarchy claiming a base it was no longer representing.

In this way the term CEB became—from the early and mid-1980s onward —a signifier for a conflict within the Church. It reveals the rift between liberationist Catholic militants at the base, the local clergy, and a consolidating progressive Church. This rift has been inadvertently obscured by authors such as Hewitt and others who write about CEBs. They tell a story from the point of view of the progressive Church. Here, again, Dom Paulo's statement is useful in emphasizing this point. In stating that "CEBs 'are the Church' and as such must stand 'always united with their priests and bishops'" (Hewitt 1991, 54), he makes them visible. The consolidation process of the progressive Catholic Church, with its pruning of diverse and potentially challenging transformative practices at the grass roots, is brought to the fore. It becomes clear that CEB is a term that aims at constructing a synthesis that disguises important tensions and conflicts occurring within the symbolic universe. It is this consolidation attempt of the progressive Catholic Church that Julie has come to reject.

In other words, by the mid-1980s, many Catholic as well as secular militants had lost their belief in the struggle. While for secular militants like Sandra this loss emanated from a disintegration of the belief in an authentic popular culture, for Catholic militants it was the fact that not only the progressive Catholic Church, but also the Left, had begun to subjugate the empowerment of the working classes to institutional concerns. In the face of these institutionalization attempts, the struggle acquired another meaning for Julie, a meaning that was no longer founded in the liberationist spirit that underpinned her commitment. With the realization that the Church had captured the struggle and changed its context to serve institutional interests, the Catholic militants began to withdraw.[73] Hence Catholic militants became disenchanted with liberationism when the progressive clergy attempted to regain control over neighborhood militants to strengthen their own position, which was being undermined by conservative sectors within the Church (Vásquez 1998, 108). This dispute between the conservative hierarchy and progressive forces culminated in the division of the archdiocese of São Paulo in 1989 and significantly reduced the influence of the progressive hierarchy within the city.[74] Still, Brasilândia remained attached to the progressive archdiocese and, in the same year, was placed in the hands of a progressive bishop, Dom Angélico Sândalo Bernardino, whose commitment to the popular Church led to an astonishing growth of CEBs in the region. Whereas in 1989 only twenty CEBs operated within the region, this number had grown to 106 by the end of the 1990s (Levy 2000, 174).

INSTITUTIONALIZATION AND DEATH OF THE LIBERATIONIST STRUGGLE

Mid-1980s to Mid-1990s

In the Brasilândia region, the 1980s and 1990s ushered in an era of liberationist reinvention. This reinvention was strongly molded by a liberationist archdiocese that, increasingly under pressure from conservative forces within the universal Church, was centralizing its control over its liberationist clergy. The mobilization platform of this liberationist reinvigoration was based on housing (*moradia*), a theme reflected in the archdiocese's pastoral plans during the 1990s. Notwithstanding several successful mobilizations inspired by liberationist militants in the region, institutionally recast liberationist symbols clearly had lost their power to persuade local residents.

LEGITIMATION CRISIS

By the mid-1980s, many *bairro* residents who had participated in the struggle of the late 1970s and early 1980s had lost faith in the promise of general liberation from oppression, injustice, and economic hardship (Vásquez 1998, 125). The recessional economy and growing unemployment, in conjunction with a changing political environment, contributed profoundly to this delegitimation of the liberationist promise, substantially undermining the spiritual content of key symbols like the struggle.

For many residents of the four *bairros*, the twenty years leading up to the mid-1990s had allowed them to construct a relatively comfortable standard of living, escaping absolute poverty. Photos and personal accounts tell of a radical change in the area since the late 1960s. Previously, much of the area, constituting the *sitios* (country retreats) of some wealthy Paulistano families, had been covered with forests, fields, and orchards. During the 1970s, Mônica recalls, in Jd. Damasceno water had to be carried up steep and slippery dirt paths lined with piles of uncollected garbage and the smell of the open sewer (Jacobi 1993). Isolated wooden shacks along a dirt path have turned into two- or even three-story suburban houses that line a paved street; tall iron gates or walls fence off individual properties, giving an impression of a well-established if somewhat unsafe neighborhood harboring modest wealth. By the mid-1990s, the majority of Damasceno residents enjoyed most of the urban services common to the Brasilândia region.

With the success of the struggle, some opportunity was created in the *bairros* of the 1970s. Access to urban services subsidized salaries substantially. Health services, transportation facilities, popular housing, and places in day-care and youth centers lessened the burden on local women.[1] A number of these urban services brought jobs into the region. Day-care and health centers needed administrative and professional staff. Most of the nonprofessional positions were occupied by participants and leaders of the struggling groups of the *bairros* who had proliferated in the struggle. This significantly lifted the living standards of some selected households within the *bairros*. Maria da Glória, Edilene, and Cleide are examples of those who took full advantage of material, educational, and other benefits conveyed by their political activism.[2]

According to local residents, the official recognition of land titles, in conjunction with the extension of urban services, created the basis for a property boom that changed the region substantially.[3] Houses could now legally be sold for a significantly higher price, and the availability of urban services increased the demand for land in the *bairros* even further.[4] Between the mid-1970s and late 1980s, the dramatic increase in population density further encouraged the upward trend in property price levels,[5] leading to a modest increase in local wealth during the mid-1990s.[6] However, while basic amenities could be found in virtually every household, jobs and job security for blue-collar labor were increasingly evaporating.[7]

Between 1977 and 1987, average family real wages in São Paulo fell below their 1967 levels.[8] Among the working classes, unemployment and underemployment climbed to dramatic heights, giving rise to the Campaign against Unemployment led by the progressive Church in 1981. According to the Industry and Economy Foundation of São Paulo, around 20 percent of the industrial workforce was unemployed or underemployed in mid-1983 (Maricato 1985, 277; Brandão, Lopez, and Gottschalk 1990, 102). During the same period, price levels, especially housing costs, increased dramatically. According to the Brazilian Enterprise for Property Studies, rents in São Paulo rose by 500 percent against disposable incomes between 1981 and 1986.[9] These massive price hikes produced the housing crisis of the 1980s (Maricato 1988, 182) and contributed to the famous mass protests, food riots, *quebra quebras* (the collective destruction of public goods), and other manifestations of public strain during that decade.[10]

Within this environment of deteriorating labor markets and job security, previous achievements turned into obstacles for those who had failed to secure their own houses. While the increase of property values in traditionally poor *bairros* represented a boon for those who had moved into the area in the late 1960s and 1970s, it was a curse for the next generation, who formed families in the late 1980s and needed to find their own residential space.[11] Living out of the pocket of their parents or other family members, this largely underemployed generation found it next to impossible to rent or buy any property in the region. Most of the urban wasteland had been occupied, and the chance to buy a piece of cheap, illegally subdivided land had diminished dramatically.[12] The limits to the liberationist promise were clearly drawn for this generation of local residents.

This drop in disposable income was also perceived by my Catholic and secular militant informants active in the *bairros* in the 1970s and 1980s. They claim that the most important difference between the 1970s and the 1980s was that during the 1980s workers' wages were no longer sufficient to purchase a suburban dwelling.[13] According to these militants, deteriorating social conditions, and especially the lack of affordable housing, enticed many low-income families into organized land occupations. In the Brasilândia region as in wider São Paulo many of the attempts to resurrect liberationism were based on this lack of affordable accommodation, and housing became one of three priorities identified by the archdiocese's pastoral plan between 1991 and 1994.

THE INSTITUTIONALIZATION
OF THE STRUGGLE

The second liberationist mobilization that surfaced in the Brasilândia region during the mid-1980s was staged against this backdrop of decaying blue-collar living conditions. Initially successful, these mobilization attempts by the local progressive Church[14] under the episcopal leadership of Dom Angélico Sândalo Bernardino—who generated much fame through his support of popular movements—gave rise to other rapidly growing popular initiatives.[15] Toward the late 1980s, these popular movements turned into one of the strongest and most expressive examples of popular politics in São Paulo (Gohn 1995, 137). In particular, the *União dos Movimentos da Zona Leste de São Paulo* (Union of Eastern District Movements of São Paulo), an umbrella organization closely linked to the progressive Church under Dom Angélico, came to play a pivotal role in the Workers Party (PT) municipal administration between 1989 and 1992 (Gohn 1995, 137).[16] These movements in the Brasilândia region contributed to a larger popular political mobilization. They were increasingly distinguishable from an initial base in the Catholic Church and were more and more influenced by organizations such as the PT and the *Central Unica dos Trabalhadores*, one of the most important confederations of trade unions, founded in 1983. However, this particular example of vibrant, liberation-inspired, popular politics was followed by a spectacular crisis. The crisis prompted various observers to predict the end of liberation theology.

The Housing Movement of the Brasilândia Region

During the second half of the 1980s, the most important liberationist struggle in the region focused on the lack of affordable low-income housing.[17] In Jd. Recanto, a neighborhood association began to take action in 1983. According to Zinha,[18] this association emerged out of the *Sociedade Amigos de Bairro* (Friends of the Neighborhood Association), which, during the late 1970s and early 1980s, focused on the improvement of general living conditions in the *bairro*. During the mid-1980s, together with many other groups in the region, the association embarked on a five-year struggle for working-class housing.[19] Adriana, who settled in Jd. Vista Alegre in 1986, joined this struggle and emerged, together with Roberto, as one of the most important local land occupation activists. Over the space of a decade, Adriana participated in and organized eleven land occupations, all of which were successful, she claimed. In Jd. Damasceno, numerous land invasions took place during the second half of the 1980s.[20] The most important ones occupied the riverbank and an old waste disposal area.[21]

According to Julie, after the mid-1980s these struggles were brought together by pastoral and secular political agents. Given the relatively limited educational background of local militants, pastoral agents and secular militants came to play an important role as consultants. These support structures became increasingly secular (Lehmann 1996, 92; Assies 1999, 218) after 1989 in regions administered by conservative bishops, but in Brasilândia support for the movement's infrastructure remained, by and large, tied to agencies of the progressive Church and to political institutions. According to Adriana, all of her mobilization attempts received substantial strategic and organizational support from the Housing Pastoral (*Pastoral da Moradia*), as well as from the episcopal center. Also important were the involvement of Catholic PT representatives and the consultancy of Church, linked trade unionists, and Catholic University of São Paulo (PUC/SP) affiliates. On various occasions these representatives lent support to struggling groups or represented the regional struggle in a formal political forum.

A brief comparison with the relatively autonomous struggle of Catholic militants during the 1970s reveals that the struggle of the 1980s introduced a much more dependent form of liberationist militancy.[22] The revitalized struggle in the region was, to a great extent, conducted by leaders who were local but whose leadership was much more closely tied to political or Church institutions.[23] Contributing to the change in character of *bairro* politics was the influx of a clergy and laity that saw their role in the struggle in increasingly less vanguardist terms (Berryman 1996, 61–62). Julie recalls that by the mid-1980s, the revolutionaries of the 1970s either assumed a more conservative position or were replaced by a new generation of priests and lay persons whose disposition toward the liberationist struggle was far from radical.[24] This is underlined by the unwillingness of this new generation of priests to lead the struggle in the *bairros*. As a consequence, *bairro* politics was increasingly in the hands of a local lay leadership dependent on the Church. Furthermore, it appears that the role occupied by Catholic and secular militants during the 1970s was split, separating the function of the local leader and mobilizer from the pastoral researcher and strategist (Assies 1999). Hence, the role of Catholic and secular militants who had previously linked the Church to the *bairro* communities was increasingly occupied by local militants whose limited access to education and information tied them inextricably to resources available through the progressive Church.

Ties and Dependencies

Virtually all of the local militants involved in the institutionalized struggle of the 1980s cultivated close ties with the local progressive Church. In some cases this relationship led them to embark on political careers not unlike those depicted by Daniel Levine (1992). Zinha received her initial impulse from a liberationist priest who worked in Jd. Recanto for some years. During the late 1980s, she developed strong links with Sister Maria, who moved into the region in 1986.[25] Adriana participated in some Catholic community catechism groups where she learned about liberationist fundamentals and came into contact with the struggle of popular movements. Shortly after her arrival in Jd. Vista Alegre, she had the opportunity to enroll in a leadership course within the Children's Pastoral (*Pastoral da Criança*).[26] Soon thereafter, she joined the housing struggle in the area. Her relationship to local progressive Catholic institutions was such that she gained access to scarce educational resources and, in 1988, was sponsored by the Housing Pastoral (*Pastoral da Moradia*) to represent São Paulo's popular housing struggle at an international meeting of social movements in El Salvador.[27] Before embarking on a career as a local activist, Roberto, a militant resident of Jd. Vista Alegre, also came into contact with the popular struggles through his involvement with Catholic communities. Irina, an activist veteran of Jd. Vista Alegre, learned about liberationist principles in the local mothers club and in Catholic community catechism groups. During the 1980s she was at the forefront of a group that successfully averted seven eviction attempts.

Local clergy and pastoral agents used an informal selection process that eased out the most critical and autonomous local leadership during the mid-1980s (see chapter 3). During the early and mid-1980s, according to Julie, many of the local priests were seriously concerned about their loss of authority within the *bairros,* and they expended much energy in capturing nodal points within the neighborhoods to consolidate their control and political influence.[28] Institutional support was increasingly available only to the local leaders who followed the directives of local clergy. This filtered out the radical leadership that challenged hierarchical authority, allowing for the consolidation of liberationist practices.[29] The result was the emergence of a docile leadership that was partially entrusted with control over the local liberationist project.[30]

Henceforth, the local leaders who remained in charge of the liberationist struggle were to a large extent prepared to fully embrace the institutionalized liberationist orientation of the local progressive Church.[31] A clear illustration is Adriana's confession that she "was very much influenced by liberationist theology and took it very seriously when they [the Bishops] said that during times of hardship, goods become common." She specified her attachment to the liberationist symbolic universe further during one of the first meetings leading to the occupation of a stretch of land in Jd. Péri Alto (31 March 1996). At this meeting, Adriana explained that this proposed land invasion was actually an occupation, because the area belonged to a public entity or, in other words, to the people. "Public land is God's land," Adriana proclaimed. "The land has no title, the government just claims it belongs to it." Furthermore, Adriana announced, there was still a lot of empty space for God's children. By occupying this land, the people of God would accept God's gift. Adriana saw the struggle as definitely more than a political elaboration; it was the struggle for a new person and a new society, a Catholic liberationist struggle that "if it had succeeded," she claims, "would have created a wonderful society."

The intense link between the religious world and the social struggle manifested itself in many instances of Adriana's daily life. Besides deploying many liberationist symbols in her language, gestures, and prayers, in many ways life itself was a liberationist project for her. Liberationist Christian values informed many of her decisions. On many occasions she emphasized that, if she wanted to, she could make a substantial amount of money by using her significant skills elsewhere. But her life, she affirmed, was the struggle. Rather than dying at home in bed, she preferred to encounter death during the struggle. In her words, being a good person included striving for "a new society in which the people are closer to God."

Hence, for Adriana, but also for Roberto and other local militants, the liberationist message was of enormous importance.[32] For these militants, liberation theology, as they understood it, filled much of their lives and carried aspects of a universal truth, evoked whenever a more pragmatic decision might have taken them in a different direction. This also gave their approach a certain rigidity, which militated against a dynamic reformulation of strategies in the light of a changing environment. Inasmuch as militants accepted liberationist thought as a dogmatic expression of faith, they categorically denied the possibility of pragmatically adjusting to changes. While Adriana's orientation represented in many ways an extreme case, other militants such as Roberto and Irina, as well as a host of lay persons, shared similar convictions that tied their lives inextricably to the dictum of the progressive Catholic Church.

This dependency on local clergy and hierarchy was strengthened as access to financial, education, and information resources came to rest in the hands of Church agents. During the late 1980s, Adriana's initiatives depended heavily on the donations of individual priests and congregations. According to Adriana, her own home, constructed in conjunction with a struggle for public housing, was erected on ground donated by a congregation. Furthermore, the local clergy played a most important role with regard to her economic and political activities. Because these priests occupied strategic key positions, Adriana remembers, they often controlled resources valuable for her group. This financial dependency frequently gave rise to severe conflicts between local priests and Adriana.[33] She repeatedly accused local priests of having diverted funds destined for the struggle for popular housing to finance their own projects. Her quarrel with Padre Oscar in mid-1996 illustrates this. According to Adriana, Oscar—who functioned as a middleman between a Canadian aid organization and Adriana's cooperative—had failed to pass on a donation that was supposed to benefit her cooperative. This financial dependency on local clergy fueled her endeavor to achieve greater financial independence (see chapter 5).

In summary, by the mid-1980s, the Catholic and secular militants who had inspired much of the liberationist mobilization during the 1970s had given way to a local leadership increasingly integrated into Church and political institutions. These leaders emerged principally from the consciousness-raising campaigns of Catholic communities during the early and mid-1980s.[34] Many of them came into contact with militant Catholicism in the catechist groups of these communities. Subsequently, they followed a career path quite common for *bairro* activists that led them through various ecclesiastical agencies, as was the case with Adriana. Here, they acquired the consciousness-raising and political-religious orientation that propelled them to the forefront of the struggle during the second half of the 1980s. However, this close relationship with the progressive Catholic Church and its representatives in the *bairros* signified a dependency in which clergy and hierarchy wielded substantial power over local projects. The leadership careers of local militants were virtually tied to the support of Church agents and subject to their dictum. Even the independent Adriana felt this subjection. This relationship of dependency between local activists and the consolidated progressive Church is underemphasized by Levine (1992).

The local leadership was far less able than the Catholic and secular militants of the 1970s to fathom and integrate new tendencies into their project.[35] Symbols such as authenticity, the people and the struggle had lost much of their meaning by the mid-1990s, but nevertheless this new wave of militants insisted on a dogmatic reading of those symbols. This undermined a much-needed reinterpretation. During the late 1980s, even the most committed liberationist political activists began to discard the notion of a revolutionary popular culture. With this loss of faith, the idea of a radical grass-roots democracy, central to liberationism, disappeared from the formal political arena. Coinciding with this loss of faith in liberationist symbols, local residents learned from experience that even a city administration that promised to continue the liberationist struggle in the political arena could not produce the promised just society.

ERUNDINA AND STATE CORPORATISM

As early as the mid-1980s, it was becoming obvious to local residents that the upward mobility deriving from the struggle was limited and tightly linked to the political regime's willingness to meet local demands with state services. Rising unemployment showed residents that their material well-being was to a large degree based on government handouts rather than their own ability to achieve change through engagement in the labor market. Furthermore, it was ever clearer that state handouts, which trickled down to the *bairros* through political networks, tended to benefit certain key individuals, such as Maria da

Glória, Edilene, and Cleide, who controlled pivotal points in this network. Luiza Erundina, of the liberation theology–influenced PT, was elected mayor of São Paulo in 1988. Her election demonstrated with great clarity that despite radical secular liberationist promises, the liberationist symbolic universe was too distant from the practical problems of policy and administration to allow for anything but a continuation of state assistentialist practices.

For the liberationist forces within the *bairros*, Luiza Erundina represented and still represents a dream candidate. Her popular background—poor and from North East Brazil—as well as her articulate commitment to at least the secular aspects of the liberationist project, aligned her strongly with militants in the *bairros*. Campaigning along the lines of the liberationist struggle, demanding better urban services and the democratization of political power in the city, she promised to construct the liberationist dream: a radical grass-roots democracy. In this sense, she pledged to *"colocar nas mãos do povo o governo de nossa cidade"* (to place the government of our city in the hands of the people) (Kowarick and Singer 1993, 203). One day after her electoral victory, Erundina declared that she—very much in line with liberationist ethics—intended to place human rights, or the right to survive, above the legal contract (*Folha,* 16 November 1988, in Kowarick and Singer 1993, 201).

Once in office, however, the PT was increasingly forced to abandon its promise of radical grass-roots democracy and to participate in parliamentary politics. Contributing to this development was the fact that the PT had won the executive, but not the city legislature, which controlled the budget. After eighteen months in power, Erundina moved away from a radical liberationist *basista* discourse and began to negotiate with other interest groups, such as the private sector. With this shift, the most radical tones of the administration's official discourse were muffled. In just eighteen months, the party that promised to place the government of the city "in the hands of the people" became an administration asserting the slogan: *"Um governo para todos"* (An administration for everybody) (Kowarick and Singer 1993, 205). The PT administration had turned into a capable social democratic government, concentrating strongly on the redistribution of municipal funds benefiting the social sector and establishing new democratic structures. However, the greatest achievement of the Erundina administration (echoing the struggle of the 1970s)—the investment of 48.1 percent of the budget in urban service and infrastructure projects benefiting the people—rang somewhat hollow in the early 1990s.[36] For the overwhelming majority of *bairro* residents, this reallocation of resources did not promise or produce great changes.

One significant change experienced by *bairro* residents I interviewed involved the administration's attempt to foster and organize cooperation between the state and civil society. To facilitate this cooperation, organized groups from working-class Brazil were tied to the administration by *convênios* —a kind of joint venture. As the redistributive channels that attended these groups were, by and large, equivalent to the political channels that tied the PT to its popular base, charges of Left clientelism started to emerge. At stake was the function of the local *vereadores* (city councilors), who at times acted as intermediaries or, more strongly, as a kind of *despachante*—an agent or facilitator—in this exchange of popular political support and state resources (Kowarick and Singer 1993, 213). Local movement leaders with close ties to the administrative processes began to develop a privileged relationship with the administrative center and started to override participatory local structures in order to attract individual benefits (Kowarick and Singer 1993, 213).[37] Given the scarcity of resources within the *bairros*, many local residents I interviewed were clearly aware of these special relationships between PT administration and local liberationist leaders. Within the climate of industrial restructuring, shrinking job markets for blue-collar labor, and neoliberal policymaking of the 1990s, it became obvious to local residents such as Bruno, Claudio, Eduardo, Mônica, and Valdirez that redistributive policies benefited only a few local residents (Macedo 1986, 289). The single most crucial resource the popular sector needed, which neither the liberationist struggle nor the PT administration was able to provide, was employment.

In the early 1990s the limits to popular politics were exposed. The redistributive project of the liberationist Left and especially the liberationist PT came into conflict with the dramatically shrinking base of opportunities in the *bairros*. With this rapidly eroding economic base, also pondered by Manuel Vásquez (1998, 216), the civil rights discourse of the liberationist Left took on the shape of state welfare and redistributive handouts. However, many *bairro* residents saw this mode of existence as undignified.[38] In particular, men I interviewed declared that accepting government handouts was a sign that they were "not man enough" to support their own families. Instead of encouraging local initiative, redistributive measures frequently produced a welfare mentality that aimed principally at attracting more welfare handouts (see chapter 5). Increasingly, it appeared that neither the liberationist struggle nor the PT administration had encouraged the fundamental changes that could have produced a just society.

Instead, the PT administration made it clear to many observers, militants, and movement participants that it considered many of the key liberationist symbols to be based on utopian romanticism. In dealing with the political reality of São Paulo in the early 1990s, the administration discarded the core values contained in symbols like the struggle and the people. Henceforth, the struggle was no longer carried to an ultimate conclusion, but was assimilated into elite politics. As a consequence, the promised just society turned into a promise of social welfare handouts. In this manner, the whole liberationist symbolic universe lost its representative power. This loss of purchase of the liberationist promise was absorbed into a much larger disillusionment with regard to democracy that underpinned popular sentiment toward corrupt formal politics (Vásquez 1998, 206; Nagle 1997, 116).[39] In this sense, mobilization attempts during the late 1980s, and especially during the 1990s, took place within a context profoundly different from the mobilization of the previous decade, when the struggle for democracy still symbolized a "heroic stance" against the abuses of a monolithic military regime and the promise of radical change for the better.[40]

In fact, by the 1990s, the liberationist struggle lacked some of the inspiration, hope, creativity, and pragmatism that allowed militants during the previous decades to construct a synthesis between popular politics and progressive Catholicism. In the mid-1990s, even the more radical liberationist clergy and laity in the *bairros* no longer attached great symbolic meaning to concepts such as the authenticity of popular culture. Increasingly disillusioned with the lack of popular response to the liberationist project, these Catholic militants found it more and more difficult to believe in symbols such as the people, which lay at the heart of the liberationist symbolic universe.

THE FRAGMENTATION OF LIBERATIONIST SYMBOLS

In one of his frequently witty, cynical, and polemic statements uttered in mid-1996, Padre Pedro, one of the self-defined liberationist Catholic priests who worked in Jd. Vista Alergre and Jd. Carombé, aired his frustration with respect to the liberationist cause:

The masses (*povão*) here will not rise at the best of times. Their basic state of being is so insecure that they don't trust anybody and follow absurd paths in the pursuit of economic improvement. If you show them an official document about some event, they will look at it and will ask, yes, but what is it *really* like? They are so disoriented, a condition that is worsened by the fact that they can't read, that they don't know whom to trust. They have received so many blows in their lives that they are unable to identify real chances from imaginary ones, or real obstacles. The decisive factor becomes the stature of a person, the discourse, the looks, the status, etc. They are easily led to a wrong conclusion.[41]

While it is possible to understand Pe. Pedro's despair in the face of what appeared to be apathetic *bairro* residents, the statement also carries a peculiar connotation. By representing his community as apathetic masses (*povão*), Pe. Pedro refuses to believe in the transformative potential of the people (*povo*). This casts the theological foundation of his position in doubt. By referring to local residents as "masses" rather than "the people of God," Pe. Pedro destroys the very historical basis on which liberation theology came to rest. This burden to awaken the alienated masses, also noted by Vásquez (1998, 267), noticeably distinguishes Pe. Pedro from the mainly pragmatist community mobilizers who worked in the *bairros* until the mid-1980s.

By the mid-1990s, Pe. Pedro seemed to view liberation as resulting from a more efficient way of communication—in his case, a community radio.[42] By creating community radio stations, Pedro argues, popular culture, and with it liberationism, can be revived. I only began to fathom the importance of his work for other projects during a subsequent visit in August 2000. Pedro sees the key to this revitalization in a democratized access to mass communication. An official statement of Radio Cantareira FM 102.1 exemplifies this:

Community radio is closer to the people, remembers the names of individuals, congratulates their birthdays, turns the people into a news item, hears the people, informs and raises the consciousness of the people, supports the popular struggle, and searches for a better life as well as social change, etc. . . . By focusing on the local dimension and by emphasizing the struggle of local communities, the community radio contributes to the organization of the people.

While this project statement still carries the seal of the liberationist symbolic universe, its context reveals how the liberationist message has undergone some significant changes. By the mid-1990s, Pe. Pedro's liberationist quest reveals a greater distance between the people and the Church, a distance that is to be breached by the new medium. With a few exceptions, this new medium turned into an anonymous voice of the voiceless, preaching the liberationist cause. However, despite being broadcast by an eager clergy and laity, it was often lacking communicative exchange. Priests who did not feel comfortable with the new medium tended to deliver long monologues. Furthermore, the unidirectionality of these radio transmissions underlined the elite posture assumed by the local liberationist Church in the 1990s. In this respect it was reminiscent of the student movements of the 1960s (see chapter 2). Hence, rather than exploring the reason for this distance between the people and the progressive Church, the Church emphasized finding new and more effective means to amplify its message.

Attempts to Stem the Fragmentation

The practices of this disillusioned clergy and laity contrast starkly with the initiatives of local militants. By the mid-1990s many local leaders were determined to assert the authenticity of the working classes and tried to reignite the power of liberationist politics. On many occasions this was done by taking the traditional liberationist symbolic universe and rearticulating it in the light of new tendencies within the local political sphere. Adriana, for instance, tended to reelaborate all politicized topics in terms of her version of the liberationist struggle. A case in point is her attempt to form a women's movement. The *Associação Mulheres em Luta* (Struggling Women's Association) carried scant feminist messages and was principally another vehicle through which to organize land occupations. Women's issues were important only inasmuch as a strong female identity appealed to local women and facilitated mobilization. The lack of a significant gender dimension was underlined by the fact that *Mulheres em Luta* was headed by Gilberto—a man—whom Adriana had designated to lead the land occupation.

During the mid-1990s, Adriana used *Mulheres em Luta* to revitalize the neighborhood association that she and others had set up during the late 1980s. This association was to facilitate the housing needs of many young *bairro* residents who had established families and needed their own homes. Over seven years a wide range of occupational strategies were tested; they resulted in unsuccessful attempts to purchase cheap urban land collectively. By the mid-

1990s, the association was on the verge of collapse, and its leaders—including Gilberto—had lost their initial inspiration. To infuse new energy into the local struggle for housing, Adriana merged several of the groups that she coordinated, thus managing to reactivate stalled local political commitment. By combining the leadership of various movements with the constituency united by the neighborhood association, Adriana succeeded in organizing the first meetings during early 1996 that would lead to the land occupation at Jd. Peri Alto (see below).

The political, social, and economic context of the 1990s undermined attempts to reignite the liberationist struggle.[43] Key symbols, such as the people and the struggle, had lost their power, largely because their liberationist messages no longer fit the context of the 1990s and so did not make social, political, or spiritual sense. As a result, the majority of land occupation participants were never integrated into the liberationist struggle: meaningless symbols had lost their erstwhile integrative and mobilizing power. Local leadership was unable to rearticulate these symbols in a manner that would incorporate these participants. Some authors focus on particular facets of this decline, such as the conservative reorientation of the Brazilian Church (Hewitt 1991, 103; Della Cava 1986; Doimo 1986), the upsurge of violence within communities (Doimo 1995; Vásquez 1998), or the growth of Pentecostalism (Burdick 1993; Mariz 1994; Lehmann 1996). Their works do, indeed, contribute to an understanding of this fragmentation, but they fail to note that much of it issues from the emptiness of the liberationist symbolic universe. The incidents detailed below—from land occupations that took place during 1996 in Jd. Peri Alto and Jd. Paraná, *bairros* near the neighborhoods studied in this volume—demonstrate this emptiness.

An important challenge contributing to the fragmentation of collective identities arose from participating local Evangelical groups.[44] During the land occupation at Jd. Peri Alto, Evangelical participants constituted an important force that undermined the ability of the liberationist leadership to unite the group under the banner of the people. While the struggle was initially conceived as an ecumenical vehicle open to all religious denominations, by the mid-1990s it was difficult to overlook the fact that the liberationist struggle was an essentially Catholic endeavor, if only because of official consolidation of liberationist projects in the agencies of the progressive Catholic Church. Consequently, the Evangelical participants in the occupation increasingly grouped together and challenged the authority of the liberationist Catholic leadership. Unable to open the liberationist symbolic universe to accommodate this Evangelical constituency, local militants failed to prevent the fragmentation of the struggle.

The Evangelical Challenge

Adriana opened one of the meetings that led to the land occupation in Jd. Peri Alto with a liberationist prayer: [45]

> God bless the path (*caminhada*) we are on,
> God bless the people who really need housing,
> God bless the persons who are helping and supporting us and are entering with us in the struggle,
> God bless the dreams, and I believe that if we poor stop dreaming our lives will come to an end. And what is the greatest dream of the poor? It is to work and to own a house. And I believe that to own a house is a little more important. Once we have our own house, it is possible to work without any disquiet or to look for other work.
> May this dream turn into reality for the entire group here as it did for the small group of the FNT (*Frente National dos Trabalhadores,* National Workers Front) . . .
> And I am certain that if you are very persistent and struggle with determination and have faith in God and in you, we will get our own home.

Through this proclamation, the liberationist flavor of Adriana's approach to the struggle is clearly visible, echoing elements of Konrad Berning's film *Pé na Caminhada* (see chapter 2). Instead of a priest, however, it was Adriana who assumed the spiritual leadership of the struggle. By rejecting any public office, she made it clear that her aim was spiritual and not material. This posture, drawing heavily on Catholic liberationist symbolism, was increasingly questioned by group participants. Some Pentecostal participants immediately questioned the Catholic domination of the supposedly ecumenical character of the struggle.

The first sign of tension surfaced early during this particular meeting. Adriana tried to overcome the fear of the participants present, faced with a possible forcible eviction, by claiming that the occupation would be supported by the Catholic Church and that this institution was a mighty partner indeed. Someone in the audience made a quiet reference to the absence of the Evangelical Church in Adriana's statement. Encouraged by this remark, Adilson, an FNT coordinator, volunteered that various Evangelical communities also lent their support to the occupation. The question of the relative power of these institutions had remained unexplored up to this instant. In Adriana's speeches, the Catholic Church usually held center stage. This represented a point of contention for Evangelical participants. Before the occupation, meetings were largely organized through Catholic Church networks, and the Evangelicals remained barely audible. However, this changed during the first months of the occupation. This period demonstrated only too clearly that symbols such as the people and the struggle failed to serve as the ecumenical glue that could produce a Catholic/Evangelical liberationist synthesis.

Overwhelmingly, support for the occupation came from agencies with strong links to the Catholic Church. For instance, the presence of Bruno—an architect from the Housing Pastoral—who contributed much of his time, knowledge, energy, and resources to getting the project under way, was most important. Furthermore, the group was able to draw on invaluable legal support in the form of consultants from the Human Rights Pastoral and had the support of individual trustworthy liberationist priests.[46] Politically, the group was represented by two PT deputies who belonged to the Catholic militant faction within the party. Those who occupied the land enjoyed the media coverage of "Rede Rua," a Catholic Church–sponsored TV journalism project.[47] In addition to this substantial progressive Catholic support team, the occupation enjoyed—at least initially—the assistance of some FNT lawyers and coordinators.[48] However, most of the support was provided by individuals with strong ties to the progressive Catholic Church.

During the actual occupation, this representational weight of the progressive Church was undermined by the action of Evangelical group participants. In fact, the Evangelical participants gathered such political strength during the occupation that they became one of the dominant factions. Most of these group participants joined in the land occupation when Catholic coordinators lost control over events. This occurred on the second day of the occupation (27 April 1996), when the 100 initial occupants found themselves in the company of 250 uninvited free riders. These free riders moved in at such a breathtaking pace that, by the end of the next week, more than six hundred families had been registered by the occupation administration. Very quickly it surfaced that a substantial number of *crentes* (believers or Evangelicals) had moved onto the area. This constituency was concentrated in several of the six areas into which the occupation had been subdivided. Night after night, the main topic of conversation around the open fire in these subdivisions was the Evangelical faith. This religious-political propagandizing was rewarded with some success and, within the first three weeks, two of the six elected area representatives declared an Evangelical orientation. From this initial position, the Evangelicals revealed an extraordinary ability to catapult internal politics to the top of the movement's agenda, increasingly undermining the authority of the liberationists.

This eroded group solidarity. While half of the leadership tried to construct a liberationist struggle focusing on the broader effects of their action, many Evangelicals were consumed in a quest to proselytize and wrangle for power. For leaders like Adriana the struggle was very much a spiritual endeavor that brought its participants closer to God and to a Catholic faith. Evangelical leaders, however, were alienated by the religious, and in particular the Catholic, content of this struggle. In fact, they saw it as their mission to evangelize at least parts of this Catholic venture. However, their partial success was possible only because the key liberationist symbols had lost their rallying power for most of the occupation participants, whatever their religious persuasion.

The Honest Worker

A fundamental lack of group solidarity had already manifested itself during the night of the actual occupation on 26 April 1996. Under the intimidation of a police squad that arrived around 3:15 a.m., Adriana tried to motivate and mobilize the frightened occupants, who were ready to abort the occupation. She did this by recommending counter strategies, placing pregnant women, invalids, and children in the front row. In addition, she appealed to the justice of their cause, by trying to unite those present in the struggle of the *honest worker*, who in time of severe need has no other option but to claim a piece of public land. Under a battle cry that united poor workers in the struggle, Adriana encountered some difficulties with actual participants in the occupation when they arrived at the word *worker*. Many looked confused and found the word a stumbling block. As a consequence, it took several attempts for Adriana's battle cry to get past the term worker without fading into insignificance. A possible reason for this surfaced during the following week, when it turned out that forty-three of the fifty-two participants who attended an occupation administration meeting defined themselves as unemployed, or as doing odd jobs (*fazer bico*) to survive.[49] Furthermore, it emerged that for most men who participated in the meeting, the inability to identify as honest worker represented a loss, sorely felt, a point also noted by Cecília Loreto Mariz (1994, 123). Those interviewed declared that not being a worker left them in an undefined realm where they found themselves in the undesirable company of *the vagabond*.[50] In this sense, the deterioration of the economic environment and the associated shifts in culturally meaningful concepts exacerbated the loss of the symbolic efficacy of terms such as the people.

The potential for the occupants' success was closely related to their political ability to construe their claims as legitimate. This legitimacy was defined within the symbolic framework of liberation theology.[51] Core concepts that are generally accepted as legitimate liberationist claims included the poverty of the honest worker, which obstructs his right to lead a dignified existence. At every possible instance, *bairro* residents would, when faced with Brazil's formal political economy, claim the authority of this absolutely honest poverty. The physical force of the arriving police was to be undermined by the absolute poverty and powerlessness of the occupants. This would reinforce the legitimate character of their occupation. As no pregnant woman could shovel dirt on a cold night to build herself a dwelling, genuine need must exist. The next step was to demonstrate the honesty of the constituents: "We are all honest/modest/poor workers (*trabalhadores humildes*) here," was an exclamation that was regularly made during an encounter with the forces of the other, elite, Brazil. A third step entailed the declaration that those present accepted the law. No one was out to usurp private property, only to find a solution to intolerable hardship and was willing to pay for that. This moral strategy—a general feature of the liberationist mobilization of the late 1980s—was significantly undermined by the presence of the *marginals*, defined as such in liberationist discourse and outside its framework of poor.

The Marginals (Os Marginais)

Forced by a deteriorating labor market, a number of movement participants engaged in illegal activities to complement their disposable income. In liberationist terminology, these movement participants were described as marginals,[52] outside the struggle. This conceptualization of the people within the

liberationist symbolic universe obstructed the symbolic integration of a segment of occupation participants in Jd. Peri Alto.

The importance of the marginals (*os marginais*) could already be sensed
during meetings to prepare for the land occupation. Based on the experience
of previous land occupations, Adriana gave graphic instructions on how to
avoid rape and violent clashes. Throughout the meetings it was generally
emphasized that the occupants would share their lives with unknown people
whose intentions might be dubious. In addition to particular directions—such
as not to send a fourteen-year-old daughter in a miniskirt or hot-pants to the
occupation and to remain aware of the possibility of foul play—there was
much expression of fear that such events could sabotage the chances for success of the occupation. However, though the impact of marginal elements
was anticipated, the leaders of the occupation underestimated the impact on
their project of organized crime, drug trafficking and consumption, and domestic violence.

Some of those who joined the land occupation during the first weeks were
involved in the local drug trade or affiliated with the trade of stolen car parts.
They soon began to form groups and started to dominate one particular area
and its representation. A number of guns and drugs were available in the occupied areas, and their use presented a major problem. Adriana and Gilberto
(who was elected general representative of the occupation) received death
threats; violent fights over women, drugs, and property erupted; and there
was at least one drug overdose.

This undermined much of the liberationist legitimacy conjured up through
the image of the honest worker who, according to the movement leadership,
occupied this area because of absolute need for housing. The presence of occupants who engaged in illegal activities tarnished the legitimacy conveyed
by the image of the law-abiding honest worker. This also provided ample opportunity for the occupants' legal opponent, Electropaulo. With astonishing
efficiency, the legal team of this electricity giant managed to denounce the legitimacy of the occupation. Their evidence detailed the number of occupants,
those engaged in illicit activities, and occurrences that conveyed the illegitimate character of the land occupation. They had a declaration of occupation
participants alleging that the administrators of the occupation were, in reality,
real-estate speculators. Some of the participants asserted that cases of domestic violence correlated with the incidence of drug sales and theft of con-

sumer goods.[53] Without doubt, the actual behavior of the marginals, and the liberationists' framing of them as a separate class of illegitimate poor, significantly obstructed the liberationist moral/political strategy.

More than just undermining the moral/political image of the land occupation movement, however, the presence of this armed group obstructed the internal organization, as well as democratic procedures within the occupation. Threatened area leaders retreated from their positions, leaving the occupation administration without much-needed support and stability. Furthermore, internal conflicts among area representatives tended to escalate in the presence of firearms, making it necessary to have centrally organized debriefings and conflict-resolution sessions.[54] The presence of members of organized crime groups was a strong distraction for the administration, and many hours of administrative work were lost as a result of violent threats. Such incidents undermined the motivation of support staff and leadership to a point where they gradually lost faith in their project.

After some months, marginals developed political ambitions and gravitated toward the center of political power within the occupation. During the latter stages of the negotiations with the state's public housing commission (CDHU) and Electropaulo, the formation of a legally recognized association was required. During the election process that led to the nomination of an administrative body, the marginals garnered around one-quarter of the vote,[55] thus gaining an important political foothold within the occupation administration and emerging successfully from the aggressive wrangling and jostling for power that had begun during the first weeks of the occupation.[56] For the occupation leadership, the unexpectedly strong political presence of marginal elements created grave obstacles. These marginals not only undermined the public image of the occupation and the leadership's control, but were able to form a strong block, contesting representative power within the occupation.

Political Contestation

Formal political interest groups further undermined the liberationist struggle on which the land occupation rested. While the leadership was able to avert political challenges stemming from outside the group,[57] it suffered great difficulties in maintaining control over political factions among occupation participants. The political conflict between supporters of the PT and those of the Brazilian Popular Party (PPB) created a constant ideological tension, but also tended to polarize group members and distract and confuse the leadership. Furthermore, by achieving a partial victory inside the occupation, the PPB faction split the group's political posture. The weakening of key symbols such as the people and the struggle had dissipated the synthesizing power that united the struggle of the 1970s. This allowed for the emergence of political divergences that gave rise to two independent political support teams, each claiming to speak in the name of the same collective.

Within the first days of the occupation, politicians and support teams from a variety of parties appeared in the area. Since it was a municipal election year, many politicians took particular interest in the occupation and went to considerable lengths to mobilize some popular support for themselves. However, while visits from city councilors (*vereadores*) and state deputies (*deputados*) were frequent, only a few were able to gain a following among the occupants. This was largely due to the directives of the leadership not to accept any political assistance except from the PT. Non-PT politicians who did gain ground did so through an election aide who participated personally in the occupation.

Such an election aide, the representative of Area Two in particular, maintained strong ties with a local PPB *vereador* (Garib). His attempts to steer the entire occupation leadership into his particular political camp caused significant administrative tribulations. Offering his help as a powerful patron during the initial weeks of the occupation, he tried to muster support within the administrative committee. Adriana, who tended toward the PT, rejected such a sponsorship outright. The subsequent successful mobilization attempts of this area representative were achieved in a clandestine manner. An incredible amount of misinformation and slander, generated to unseat the liberationist administration, turned the occupants against their representatives. Only an equally aggressive counterpropaganda campaign proved capable of disarming this slander. However, the liberationist-PT camp had to expend much energy and scarce resources in countering this challenge. Exhausted by the many tasks and emergencies they confronted, the leadership was unnerved and demoralized by this challenge from within the occupation.

By the time the association was formed, this political opponent had built such a solid support base that he was able to capture the presidency. By that stage it was clear that Adriana had lost her moral and political hold over the occupation. While the defeated leadership, with Gilberto at the top, tried to work within the new political constellation, Adriana withdrew from the occupation.[58] According to her, the fragmentation, fights, and jostling for power were unprecedented, and she felt that the minimum of group solidarity was no longer sufficient to conduct the struggle. From that moment onward, the vestiges of liberationist moral and political connotations left within the struggle were lost.[59]

As a consequence, the original liberationist participants of the occupation began to withdraw from the area. Largely out of dissatisfaction with the individualist orientation that the group had adopted—which manifested itself in the wrestling for political and religious power—but also out of fear of the marginals, the vast majority preferred to abandon the occupation movement. As a result, of the one hundred families that had planned and initiated the occupation of the area, only a dozen remained seven months into the occupation.[60] Those who remained attached themselves to other more powerful factions such as the Evangelical constituency or the PPB. In other words, the people had disengaged themselves from what they perceived as no longer their struggle. With the realization that they had nothing in common with the fight of the other increasingly dominant factions within the occupation, they declared the end of the struggle.

These events were by no means exceptional. Another land occupation in Jd. Paraná, near Jd. Vista Alegre and initiated in October 1995, displayed similar features. The occupation began with the illegal sales of land titles carved out of a protected environment area. As the residents of this illegally occupied area faced eviction in April 1996, Alexandra, a member of the local liberationist laity, tried to organize and channel local efforts by constructing a liberationist movement. However, her efforts were frustrated by events similar to those experienced by Adriana and Gilberto, forcing her to suspend her project in mid-1996. The events that occurred during the occupation of Jd. Paraná illustrated vividly that the liberationist symbolic universe could no longer synthesize individual interests nor inspire movement participants to adopt an outlook based on popular solidarity in a struggle for liberation.

During the very first meetings that Alexandra organized, she surmised that it would be extremely difficult to transform this occupation into a liberationist struggle. During these meetings it was clear that strongly defined individual interests running along political, economic, and religious lines were undermining her attempts to unify the fragmented occupants. Furthermore, the presence of a strong constituency of marginals[61] excluded around one-third of the occupants from the proposed struggle of the honest worker. While liberationist symbols certainly informed the local discussions, they were not able to provide the occupants with a central outlook that could have united these various factions. As a consequence, the local movement fragmented into numerous groups and individuals who began to undermine each other, giving rise to a mobilization chaos.[62] According to agents of the Housing Pastoral such as Bruno and local leaders like Adriana and Irina, the profound fragmentation of the struggle during the mid-1990s is unprecedented.

In the example of the land occupations at Jd. Péri Alto and Jd. Paraná, the fragmentation of key liberationist symbols such as the people—a term that in the liberationist symbolic universe is based on the identity of the honest worker and diametrically opposed to the marginal—portrays a profound change that has altered the face of *bairro* politics over the decade leading to the mid-1990s (Lehmann 1996, 61). In addition, it displays the inability of the local liberationist leadership to adjust its strategies and practices to this altered reality.

Various factors conspired to produce the general weakening of the symbolic force that had cemented the political and moral dominion of the progressive Catholic Church during the late 1970s and early 1980s. Progressively, many residents of the low-income periphery were no longer captured by the symbolism expressed in the struggle of the people; and those who still cherished this universe composed too small a group to lend weight to liberationist mobilization efforts. Consequently, core concepts that were of enormous importance for the struggle of the 1970s—such as the struggle aiming at the creation of a society that granted a humble but dignified existence for all honest workers or, rather, the people[63]—were no longer able to encompass the reality of low-income residents. The story of Saint Francis that underpinned these key symbols could no longer capture the imagination of local residents. The severe tension between various factions over the course of the occupations demonstrated that the liberationist symbolic universe was no longer able to muster the authority or popularity necessary to unify the struggle.

CONCLUSION

During the 1980s and 1990s key symbols of the liberationist struggle increasingly lost their meaning for movement participants, Catholic militants, and *bairro* residents in general. As a consequence, the notion of an authentic popular culture was increasingly discarded by key liberationist politicians and Catholic militants. However, with the local hierarchy's attempt to resurrect the liberationist struggle during the mid-1980s, these concepts informed the actions of a local leadership that was left in charge of liberationist popular politics. This catechist group and pastoral-educated leadership were far more prepared to let the directives of the progressive Catholic Church remain un-questioned. Furthermore, given limited access to finance, education, and in-formation, local leaders became heavily dependent on the input of pastoral agents, the clergy and the progressive hierarchy. This institutionalization cre-ated a palpable inflexibility and lack of autonomy, obstructing pragmatic re-definition of key symbols.

Furthermore, the mass unemployment that occurred during the lost decade of the 1980s undermined the credibility of the promise of liberation. Increasingly, *bairro* residents realized that the struggle had not liberated them but, rather, had made them dependent on neoclientelist networks comprising the state, political parties, and the Church. Disillusioned about the politi-cal and moral aims of the consolidated liberationist struggle, those who participated in bairro politics during the late 1980s were much more aware of the individual interests involved. The coming together of these tendencies with the resurrected liberationist struggle demonstrated that the liberationist project had lost much of its symbolic power. In particular, symbols such as the people and the struggle had been emptied of the meaning they carried during the 1970s. As a consequence, by the mid-1990s, only extremely com-mitted local leaders such as Adriana maintained their faith in the liberationist project.

5

DOGMATIC LIBERATIONISM AND PRAGMATIST RESPONSES TO EVERYDAY NEEDS

Key liberationist symbols lost their authority during the late 1980s and 1990s, leading movement participants and organizers to discard the symbolic meaning of authenticity, the people, and the struggle. As a consequence, by the mid-1990s, only the most committed local militants such as Adriana maintained their belief in the struggle. However, within the growing crisis faced by liberationist militants during the early and mid-1990s, these local activists tried to pragmatically adjust their projects to the significantly altered environment of the 1990s. In Adriana's case, this meant integrating her liberationist project into the market economy. The case study presented in this chapter details that such an endeavor was stifled by the ethics contained within dogmatically read liberationist symbols and the radical *basismo* that they inspired. Adriana's endeavor was substantially undermined by the resistance issuing from influential factions of the Catholic Left. The evidence calls into question the assertions made by Levine (1992, 18) and Unger (1987) that the people inspired by liberationist thought are able to pragmatically adjust this body of thought to new contexts. Instead, the evidence tends to resonate with the somber *basismo* outlined by Mainwaring (1986b) and, more recently, by Lehmann (1996).

COOPERATIVISMO

During the late 1980s, rising unemployment levels, especially among young people, prompted local activists to embark on employment-generating projects. Inspired by the liberationist struggle, they established popular cooperatives—cooperatives that, unlike the elite cooperatives frequently formed within the Brazilian economy, were supposed to create communities in which the Brazilian poor could live, work, and earn together, without replicating the exploitative relationships commonly found within unmediated market economies.[1] In this endeavor, local activists have received strong support from the progressive Catholic Church and Catholic militants, as well as Catholic factions within the secular Left. While emerging out of a concern for local unemployment, popular cooperatives very much constituted a moral and political project deeply rooted in Catholic theological tradition. They represent an attempt to create a new basis for a more dignified survival of Brazil's popular classes. More than that, however, popular cooperatives, as brought into being by liberationist Catholic assistance, were envisaged as a means to produce a just Christian society based on values inspired in many ways by liberation theology.

However, such popular cooperatives in São Paulo were exposed to major changes. During the 1990s, their environment was transformed almost completely. Politically, neoliberal ideology and practice undermined the legitimacy of social assistance policies by making it unlikely that popular cooperatives would receive financial assistance from state bodies. Furthermore, those segments of the nongovernment sector sponsoring popular cooperatives were plunged into a financial crisis and thus unable to assist these projects sufficiently. With the drying up of traditional funding sources, popular cooperatives were increasingly forced to reflect on their dependence on external, and especially Church, agents. In various cooperatives, this gave birth to a desire to disengage from often constraining assistance networks and to gain greater financial, administrative, and even political independence. For the *Cooperativa Convivência,* a popular cooperative on the northern fringe of São Paulo, this meant surviving solely by engaging with an increasingly globalizing market. This attempt, however, unleashed some formidable clashes, which turned the cooperative into a stage on which factions of the Catholic Left, liberationist spirituality, and decisionmaking based on a market economy collided with full force.

During my fieldwork in Brazil in 1996, I had plenty of opportunity to witness and to become involved in these clashes. This chapter is a brief account of the tribulations of the *Cooperativa Convivência* in which I participated. The dream of Adriana, the administrator of this cooperative, was to construct a flourishing popular cooperative that would realize the values of liberationist anticapitalist humanism in one of the most savage capitalist markets in Latin America. The attempt to realize this dream formed the basis of battles described in this chapter, battles that lured her into venturing beyond the boundaries of consolidated liberationist thought. Adriana's endeavor turned out to be extremely challenging and, to an outsider, confusing.

The symbolic and institutional universe of the liberationist Left, in conjunction with a *bairro* culture extremely antagonistic toward elitist Brazil, limited this project substantially. As a consequence, unable to symbolically recreate the liberationist influences that had shaped her project, Adriana locked the cooperative tightly into Left assistentialist policies. It became my view that the circumstances undermined Adriana's twin goals of enhancing the life chances of the residents, especially unemployed adolescents, while building a local militant Catholic community in her *bairro* of Jd. Vista Alegre. Indeed, within the space of Adriana's cooperative, the contradictory forces contained by a liberationist symbolic universe and political network have unraveled, threatening to extinguish the local project that strove for a pragmatic adaptation to a new context.

Tensions arose from attempts to accommodate the political climate of the 1990s and the limitations of an institutionalized liberationist symbolic universe. A dilemma resulted from Adriana's dogmatic insistence that Christian humanist principles derived from liberationist symbolism had to underline the cooperative's involvement in the capitalist market. Furthermore, the liberationist values embodied in Adriana's decisions, in many ways premodern and anticapitalist,[2] coexisted uneasily with the acceptance of the capitalist market by the Catholic faction of the social-democratic Workers Party (PT), which, nonetheless, maintained a revolutionary liberationist discourse. This friction was aggravated by practices of the liberation theology–inspired revolutionary movement of the landless (*Movimento Sem Terra*—MST), which resorted to exploitative capitalist principles to purchase propaganda material. Forced to find new forms of survival in the mid-1990s, local residents tried to venture in new directions, leaving the projects of the Catholic and secular Left behind. This not only produced discord in the residents' relationship with liberationist Left factions traditionally active in the *bairro,* but also clashed with the residents' own antagonism against elite Brazil. These tensions emerged in the context of my activities in a local cooperative. While the realm of discourse contained these tensions only implicitly, the actions and events that almost devastated Adriana's small popular cooperative were able to expose them rather clearly.

The story that unfolds here is very much bound up with my intervention in that cooperative. It was largely through this intervention that many of the facets of conflict emerged with clarity. My account is subjective and interpretative; I am at once a central actor, reporter, and interpreter. In this, however, rests its strength. The conflict-ridden premise of Adriana's project would have been difficult to uncover by methods other than my invited intrusion into that realm. Discourse analysis, for instance, would not have been able to pick up these conflicts, as Adriana's discourse focused very much on what should be rather than on events and evidence about costs and production methods. In discourse, Adriana generally defused potential tensions and depicted the cooperative as a success story. A more empirical, document-oriented methodology would have had little to work with, as hardly any written evidence was available. Pure nonpartisan observation would have been impossible, too, within the political climate of the *bairro.* That much is made clear by a local priest's comment about another researcher: "Researchers who arrive in the *bairros* with mainly three aims, to finish a Ph.D. by writing about the Brazilian misery, to party on, and to taste *mulatas,* are no longer welcome."

My account of the emergence of these cooperatives is based on the statements of administrators or members of local cooperatives themselves, local agents of the Catholic Church, and the local representative of CARITAS (*Caritas Internationalis,* the international agency of social assistance affiliated with the Catholic Church). These local accounts tend to underemphasize the positive role played by CARITAS in the region.

ORIGINS OF A COOPERATIVE

The lack of basic services and urban infrastructure has remained the basis for mobilization by the major political parties of the Left, such as the PT and the PDT, as well as the local progressive Catholic Church, forming the basis of the state assistentialist projects of these organizations. Many of the ideas of this liberationist Left revolved around radical redistributive demands in conjunction with the creation of a new counterhegemonic culture that embraced a liberationist anticapitalist humanism. This symbolic backdrop would inform employment-generating projects and especially the formation of cooperatives, empowered to create the economic basis of a new communitarian anticapitalist system. In the *bairros*, Catholic leftism had been molded to fit the local culture. It was, by and large, deeply suspicious of outsiders, extremely local in outlook, exclusive in nature, and dogmatic in its approach (Mainwaring 1986b; Lehmann 1996). These radical *basista* features are still commonly found in pastoral agents and in influential personalities in the welfare bureaucracy.[3]

Since the late 1970s, the disposable income of the popular classes has dropped by more than half.[4] The transition to democracy in 1985 made little difference in the downward spiraling of real wages. In this respect, the democratic years display features similar to those known popularly as the belt tightening years under authoritarian rule. In the early 1980s, this decline in real wages had been accompanied by "the worst recession of the century," followed by another "worst recession of the century," in the late 1980s. In Jd. Vista Alegre the 1980s are remembered as the years when workers were no longer able to choose their jobs and, henceforth, were chosen.[5]

During the 1990s, the deterioration of the job market for blue-collar labor continued unabated, annihilating the purchasing power of the poorer people that resulted from the currency stabilization plan (the Real Plan) introduced in July 1994. Informal labor relations replaced job safety and security, leaving a large segment of the workforce without union protection. The national opening toward global markets in connection with industrial restructuring produced deep changes in the Brazilian job market. The scope and speed of these changes were profound. In the twelve-month period of July 1995–July 1996, São Paulo's industry shed 292,668, or 12.5 percent, of its formal jobs. This decline is representative of trends throughout the 1990s, with the exception of 1993.[6] The result was a rapid informalization of labor relations and ensuing unemployment or underemployment. Bearing the brunt of these developments were young, poorly educated males. In the *bairros*, according to all the community organizers I interviewed, youth unemployment had already assumed dramatic proportions during the 1980s.

According to community organizers, by the mid-1980s, youth unemployment and the growing involvement of young people in the world of organized crime dominated local meetings. By this stage, women frequently had to sustain the whole family on a substantially lower wage than male breadwinners in better times, and many had to cope with the alcohol, violence, and gambling habits of their unemployed husbands. As women had hardly any free time, the instruction of the growing generation was left to the streets. Here, media-stimulated desires for the goods of the global youth-consumer culture and the lure of a more glamorous, as well as macho, lifestyle created the incentive for many adolescents to work as *aviões* (drug couriers) or to get involved in other illicit activities (Zaluar 1996; 1994; 1990). Under threat of losing their sons, or having actually lost them in the war for drug territory, local women expressed the need to create employment and education projects in order to draw adolescents away from the streets. According to local community organizers, the first cooperative was erected within an atmosphere of violence and fear that isolated *bairro* residents and threatened to undo most of the sense of community.[7]

The arrival of Sister Maria and several other members of a Canadian Catholic order in 1986 gave local community organizers and militants new incentive. Taking the local grievances seriously, and armed with some international and national financial backing, these nuns established workshops that would eventually turn into cooperatives. One workshop was aimed at extending vocational training to adolescents. The other was focused on the employment needs of women. Toward the end of the 1980s, the workshops became an incubator for cooperatives. Local women and militants learned the basis of cooperativism on these premises and expanded their technical expertise. When *cooperativismo* reemerged on the agenda of state and Church agencies in the early 1990s, this project had already disseminated its principles locally.

State agencies had, up to that point, given astonishingly little attention to generating employment. This changed only partially with the election of Luiza Erundina and the PT in 1988 (see chapter 4).[8] Professionalization and employment projects administered by the *Secretaria do Bem-Estar Social* (Social Welfare Department) displayed a strong charitable character. Many of these projects revolved around the reproductive needs of the popular classes and were interlinked with other redistributive policies.[9] Under the tutelage of this department, discussions were held among organized groups of the population to create awareness of productive local opportunities. Within the context of these groups, people discussed production techniques, administrative practices, and the marketing of certain products. These group discussions created the foundation for community bakeries, brick fabrication projects, broom workshops, and community kitchens, which sprang up in the neighborhoods. Here, it was argued by the authors of *São Paulo para todos*, a publication that reflected on the achievements of the Erundina administration, "Workers have an opportunity to become active in all productive or commercial cycles, improving the living conditions of the entire community, those who produce as well as those who acquire the produce" (*São Paulo para todos* 1992, 38). In most of these projects the *Secretaria do Bem-Estar Social* would function as a starter—it provided the necessary equipment—"of an activity that is generated for the actual community" (*São Paulo para todos* 1992, 38).

Dominating the elaboration of employment-generation proposals within the *Secretaria* was a vision of local nuclei producing locally for the local market. Community production nuclei were thought to constitute a *bairro* market, in many ways separate from the capitalist market, benefiting producer as well as consumer. However limited in scope and design, these attempts exemplified the faith in the market shared by some Catholic liberationist factions within the PT. Employment creation—beyond very limited vocational training and the incorporation of pressure groups into the municipal administration— was left to the private sector or to agents of the progressive Catholic Church.

By the late 1980s, youth unemployment and violence had gained much academic and media attention in São Paulo (Pinheiro 1992; Adorno 1992; Zaluar 1990). Various international organizations, state agencies, and, principally, the progressive Catholic Church became sensitized to the problems. In the Brasilândia region, various initiatives by United Nations (UN) organizations, CARITAS, the Housing Pastoral, and other Church agencies gave assistance to cooperativism.[10] Courses were organized to create the ideological foundation, and joint ventures were signed with FABES, the social welfare branch of the state.[11] By 1991, CARITAS had sponsored some nineteen popular cooperatives in the region.

While the administrative training was extensive, in the sense that it inculcated the virtues of *cooperativismo* and gave comprehensive introductory instruction in these priests' own counterhegemonic communitarian values, the design and implementation of these projects was haphazard. According to Francilene, the local CARITAS representative, hardly any previous feasibility or impact studies were undertaken. As barely any resources were invested in professional support staff, the supervision and training of cooperative members in administrative matters as well as the follow-up service was mainly left in the hands of Catholic priests.[12] Adriana remembers that technical support was limited to emphasizing the role of suffering and sacrifice in the cooperative enterprise and to pointing out the need to curtail individual material aspirations if the cooperatives were to survive. In short, many priests saw the cooperative as a vehicle to foster a new antimaterialist, noncapitalist culture. According to Adriana's accounts, *cooperativismo* was turned into a spiritual quest, the fruits of which were to be harvested in a far distant future—so distant, in fact, that it might not benefit the current generation of cooperative members. Sister Maria remembers that fewer than half of the nineteen cooperatives survived the second year.[13]

In late 1995, at the time of my arrival in the area, only four of the initial nineteen cooperatives had survived. Three were still functioning, and one existed in name only. None of those still functioning was able to sustain itself without the steady inflow of financial assistance.

THE CASE STUDY

The *Cooperativa Convivência*—the name refers to some of the underlying liberationist ideals of the cooperative's founding members—administered by Adriana, was one of these survivors.[14] Adriana's close affiliation with the progressive Catholic Church, the PT, the *Movimento dos Sem Terra*, and the *Frente Nacional de Trabalho* (FNT) certainly boosted the resilience of her cooperative. Over the years she has activated a political network that reaches from Mario Covas (former governor of the state of São Paulo) to Luiza Erundina (the former mayor of São Paulo) and from the managing director of the state bank, BANESPA,[15] to Herberto Betinho da Souza, the famous sociologist.

In spite of her impressive political connections and substantial expertise, her cooperative had been on the edge of financial bankruptcy ever since its inception. Though set up to function as a training center for adolescents, teaching the crafts of shoemaking and dressmaking, the cooperative had a dramatic turnover of members. By the time I met Adriana, the majority of the more than twenty adolescents had deserted her,[16] and cooperative was a fancy term for what was in fact a family work/sweat shop. There were no orders, hardly any inputs, no cash, and the infrastructure that somehow carried a price tag of more than R$53,000 was in ruins. Hardly any of the machines worked, and wages—if one can call R$50 per month a wage—had not been paid for more than four months.[17]

In January 1996, looking back on five years of hard work and financial failure, Adriana asked me to devise a project for the cooperative and to teach its members the market. She wanted to demonstrate to everybody, and especially to fellow residents she frequently labeled stupid and lazy, that "The people are able to administer." She often claimed, "The poor have very narrow minds. If they would spend as much time forming positive movements as they do sabotaging their own operations, they would smash the Brazilian system." This formation of positive movements in conjunction with an increasingly troublesome dependence on local clergy and hierarchy led Adriana to question her own welfare and Church dependency and introduced the notion of self-sufficiency to her political aims. As a result, she decided to hire me on a voluntary basis, making it explicit that she wanted me to introduce market principles to the workings of the cooperative. Restructuring the cooperative along these lines would, she thought, turn it into a success story.

Over the next twelve months, two colleagues and I tried to establish a project that would eventually introduce the concept of self-sufficiency as well as basic accounting, administration, marketing, and production supervision skills to the cooperative. Toward the middle of 1996, despite the semiliteracy and lack of mathematical skills of my "students," I succeeded in communicating the basic concepts of pricing, cost/benefit analysis, niche markets, style, and quality control. At the same time, I realized how Adriana's attachment to a legacy of institutionalized liberationism and *basista* tendencies clashed with the practices of Catholic Left factions. Furthermore, I learned what it was like to try to persuade a dogmatic liberationist Catholic of the logic of the market. The ensuing tensions between Adriana and myself resulted in a metamorphosis that, over months, transformed my persona from a white knight carrying the sword of reason into, at best, an empathetic coworker and, many times, a frustrated as well as helpless bystander, increasingly aware of the constraints that militated against the proposed rational solutions.

The nature of the project that emerged over these months owed much to the fact that it could not be tied to a larger project of the Catholic Left for furthering viable cooperativism. Other considerations entered into my attempts to shape the project. As Adriana had already pragmatically entered markets that were distinguished by desperately low profit margins, it seemed important to me to communicate the basis on which these markets operated. The aim was to facilitate a more informed decisionmaking process. In this case, leftist niche marketing seemed the only viable means to make the cooperative profitable. So my colleagues and I assembled a group of PT-friendly shop owners, who were lenient about quality and delivery and willing to change their international suppliers for local popular cooperatives. The additional profits that accrued to shop owners from this substitution were to be split evenly between them and the cooperative. Our first aim was, thus, to modify the production methods of the cooperative in order to satisfy the demands of clients.

Adriana founded the cooperative in 1990–1991. Inspired by the idea of co-operativism since the early 1980s, Adriana's impetus for action was found in Sister Maria's workshops and various other catechist groups. Successfully, she attracted the funding that a group of cooperative members would invest in a self-constructed workshop and the necessary machinery. Having participated in various workshops, run by agents of the progressive Church, that aimed at constructing values that would sustain the cooperative, the members of the new cooperative soon started to produce garments and footwear for the local market. Almost immediately, they experienced a number of seemingly insurmountable problems, most of them related to administrative practices and technological expertise. This prompted Adriana to search for a sponsor of an education program who would communicate administrative and technological fundamentals. Such a course was finally sponsored by the National Workers Front (FNT). A teacher was contracted who was supposed to instruct cooperative members for one month and offer a support service for a further three months, terms that were not fulfilled. Consequently, the cooperative had to rely on the expertise available within the group.

As a result, the cooperative created survival strategies that were reminiscent of the practices that surfaced with the political struggle in the *bairros* during the second half of the 1980s. Business to Adriana was closely related to fundraising and political networking—the things she had learned through the struggle. On a wall inside the coop she advertised her gratitude and indebtedness to a dozen political and social institutions that had, in one way or another, assisted the success of the coop. This list included the *Pastoral de Moradia* (Housing Pastoral), *Pastoral da Criança* (Pastoral for Children), *Fé e Alegria* (Faith and Happiness), CARITAS, PT, FNT, *Sindicato dos Bancários BANESPA* (Bank Employees Union of BANESPA), *Ação da Cidadania* (Citizenship Action), *Forum das Cooperativas Alternativas* (Forum of Alternative Cooperatives), SESC (*Serviço Social do Comércio São Paulo*—Social Service of São Paulo Commerce), *Cúria da região Brasilândia* (Curia of the Brasilândia region), *Ludic Afric* (an Afro-Brazilian organization), a Canadian University aid organization, *Solidária Idade* (a NGO), and eventually OCCA (Coordinating Organization of Alternative Cooperatives—the association that my colleagues and I formed to assist cooperatives), to mention just a few.

While this extensive support network facilitated the initial functioning of the cooperative and assisted it during financial crises, it represented the very point of departure for Adriana's desire for independence. Without direct access to credit and without business administration skills, Adriana's cooperative became heavily dependent on this support network for financial and administrative resources. Agencies and individuals of the progressive Catholic Church directly controlled the events within the cooperative. For instance, the association that administered the cooperative was dominated by priests, nuns, and other Catholics with predominantly liberationist leanings. This group influenced the overall direction in which the cooperative moved and obstructed Adriana's attempts to adjust the procedures within the cooperative to the exigencies of the market. Furthermore, pastoral agents provided technical and administrative support to the cooperative, and priests were often left directly in charge of marketing, fundraising, and other administrative proceedings. As a consequence, the cooperative's development was strongly shaped, even controlled, by Catholic agents.[18] Most important, as most of the finance issued from sources administered by agencies inspired by liberation theology, fundamental business decisions needed to coincide with the symbolic orientation of these lending agencies.[19] As the overall emphasis of these agencies rested on the construction of communitarianism and family values, the core of the project needed to reiterate this position.[20] Within the context of an increasing funding shortage of donor agencies and a changing political environment in which assistentialist policies were increasingly difficult to justify, the constraints imposed by this network tended to override its usefulness. This initiated Adriana's struggle for greater independence.

This desire for greater self-sufficiency, however, coexisted in a contradictory manner with Adriana's administrative practices, much informed by the principle of political leverage. In fact, most of the internal workings of the cooperative were based on a mix of pressure group politics and welfare clientelism based on liberationist values. Cost/benefit analysis, pricing, and other instruments that normally facilitate the decisionmaking within firms played only a marginal role. It took me some months to realize that Adriana's methods did not, as I had previously assumed, result from a lack of expertise, but issued from a distinct choice she had made. In fact, while Adriana sought to cut her dependencies by entering the market successfully, the liberationist symbolic premises on which her project rested, and the context within which it operated, tied the cooperative inextricably to forms of state corporatist assistance.

Structural Resistance

The fact that the principle of state corporatism dominated much of the debate of cooperativism within Catholic Left circles was brought home to me during a meeting of the *Forum das Cooperativas Alternativas* (Forum of Alternative Cooperatives) at the end of July 1996. The forum, I was informed, was an organization with strong links to the progressive Church that had been established to make popular cooperatives more viable.[21] During this meeting, which lasted for four and a half hours (with content that should have occupied one and a half), I grew more and more confused. Contrary to what had been claimed previously, the Forum had less to do with making the cooperatives more viable than with linking their claims to specific political agents. Discussions focused on how cooperatives could try to occupy more space in a landscape of political assistentialism, and the most important item on the agenda was the elaboration of a pamphlet that would search for support in political assemblies. Another factor that revealed the forum as a political pressure group was the absence of any committee or consultancy dealing with production and administration techniques. While the forum covered the sociopolitical spectrum of cooperatives well, it did not take account of the market requirements. Meetings orbited endlessly around political issues such as housing, employment, and the right to receive state subsidies. The intent of the pamphlet was to tie the forum and affiliated cooperatives permanently into an association with the state. Dilemmas to do with production, marketing, and administration were thus overshadowed by an almost exclusive preoccupation with political representation.

The "development strategy" of the progressive Catholic Church rests almost exclusively on Catholic morals and values. For this Church, social problems are read in terms of spiritual and political questions. Within the liberationist symbolic universe, politics opens society for the proposed spiritual renewal of its moral fabric, producing the basis for a just society. The forum should be regarded as the direct heir of this legacy. Built on a liberationist foundation, shaped for more than two decades by a struggle that gradually lost its spiritual symbolism, the forum gradually focused almost exclusively on the political dimension of the cooperatives' dilemma, which was to be resolved through state assistance. However, in the case of the forum, state assistance had become an end in itself. In this sense, the forum stands for a corrupted struggle, which, by the mid-1990s, had lost much of the symbolic link with the liberationist framework that stood for the construction of a just society.

Within this context, Adriana's striving for self-sufficiency represented not only a break with assistentialism in general, but also a major break with a Left that clung to the fragments of a liberationist tradition. In this sense, Adriana's subsequent attempts to redirect the overall orientation of the forum in order to facilitate a greater emphasis on microeconomic issues entailed a political redirection, a redirection strongly resisted by most of the Catholic Left agencies involved.[22] Adriana's new direction, and my involvement with the cooperative associated with it, was observed with growing concern by these agencies. As a consequence, it became harder for Adriana to secure credits and assistance. Pastoral agents started to criticize Adriana for her new approach and withdrew their support. Increasingly my persona became the target of critical voices.[23] Hence, for a local militant who entertained strong links with the Catholic Left to pragmatically venture toward the capitalist market and adopt some of its tools was by no means an act looked on with neutrality, and the obstacles to such a politically sensitive venture were substantial. These constraints tend to be underemphasized by authors such as Levine (1992) and Unger (1987).

Priests, pastoral agents, bureaucrats, and political statists who occupied influential positions—"influential" meaning capable of influencing decisions about project funding—began politically and financially to undermine Adriana's attempts to adapt her project to the changing *bairro* environment. Furthermore, these individuals had decided that I was not on their side, the side of the Catholic Left, and that my activities were endangering their project—working at the local level for a Brazil in which human relations would triumph over market relations. For the Catholic Left, Adriana's cooperative had in many ways become a showcase denoting the success of this project. Not unlike the student militants of the 1960s, these bureaucrats harbored very set ideas about what their authentic popular culture was to contain. Despite the fact that their promotion of an authentic popular economy impoverished local liberationists like Adriana and her coworkers—changes to their project from the grass roots were certainly not welcome. Ironically this very insistence on the popular economy enticed Adriana to demonstrate that the people's economy could indeed be successful. In this instance, local radical *basismo* mirrored the elitism of Catholic Left bureaucrats.

Basismo *and the Political Promotion of the Popular*

Another political facet of Catholic Leftism inhibited the development of a more adequate response. Adriana's proposal for a credit cooperative,[24] tabled during the meeting of the forum described above, demonstrates this clearly. This proposal not only further exemplified Adriana's attempt to leave the realm of assistentialism—she envisaged no external financial support from formal organizations or the state—but also delineated the boundaries that arrest members of the subaltern classes in their attempts to increase their choices. In this instance, the clash between the popular and the formal was made explicit. When the proposal was out in the open, Hélen, the lawyer, intervened, alerting everybody to the complex legal requirements such a financial lending institution needed to fulfill. The great majority of the coop representatives declared that they wanted to construct a popular entity and not a formally registered one. Alberto, another coop representative, entered the discussion and told of an incident in which the administrator of such a popular entity emptied the cash register without incurring any repercussions. Legally, the members of that popular venture were powerless to respond. The coop representatives were silenced by these disclosures. Largely unaware of the difficulties that would accompany the formation of such a venture, and without the expertise that would enable them to run such an institution, their discourse was mainly dreaming, unrooted in reality. Favoring informal popular ways appeared to exclude considerations of legal proof and documentation. In other words, the popular met unhappily with the requirements of the modern state. In this instance, the idea of a popular economy, which is often featured in discourses of the Brazilian Catholic Left, strongly influenced by a liberationist symbolism that locates authenticity in popular culture, widened the rift between the popular and the elitist Brazil and radicalized the notion of local *basismo*.

Basismo occupies an important space in the mobilization platform of the Catholic Left. Through this concept, local antagonistic sentiments rejecting elite society are tied to the party political promise of a democracy issuing from the grass roots. The decisive link between the two is facilitated by a vision of early Freirean thought that left the decisionmaking process, by and large, in the hands of the popular classes. For Freire, the ways of the humble (*o povo humilde*), which were—in a liberationist sense of authenticity—closer to the will of God, were integrated into a social-democratic setting. Still, during the Paulistano municipal election campaign in 1996, a rather populist appeal to the wisdom of the people formed an important element of the strategy.[25] Over and over, it was emphasized that elitist Brazil had created room for the practices and wisdom of popular Brazil. For Adriana, this presented a welcome opportunity to justify her preference for popular solutions over elitist ones. For Adriana, "elitist decisionmaking"—the kind that required knowledge not available in the *bairro*—was beyond her experience and led her into epistemological territory in which she did not feel in control. Furthermore, this mode of thinking permeated the Brazil that had rejected her and that she had rejected. Her world was popular Brazil, the Brazil of the simple, honest, and modest people (*povo humilde*). She stereotyped the signals of social and racial discrimination she encountered and provoked in the other Brazil, thus widening the gap between the two countries.

Her relationship with what she defined as the bourgeois Brazil was marked by a profound antagonism. During an earlier period, when she had worked as youth coordinator in the region, this had led her to encourage the local youth to engage in *arrastão*[26] as a means of acquiring global consumption goods. Her antagonism was also a source of her sympathy toward land occupations. Adriana enthusiastically confronted the Brazil that oppressed her gender, color, and class and that found her ideology and culture aesthetically displeasing. The *basismo* discourse of the Brazilian Catholic Left, demanding that the elitist, Europeanized, bourgeois Brazil adapt to the popular Brazil, corresponded nicely with Adriana's world view. Consequently, she rejected the complicated methodology and culture of the market, demanding that the market adapt to the people. A whole tradition of *basismo* permeated her rejection of market requirements. This attitude exalted the unbending and exclusive localism that the loose federation of popular communities favored over all other forms of association linking locals to the outside.

Hence, one can easily imagine the dilemma Adriana faced when trying to do business with the Brazil she detested. In spite of my persistent efforts, she would never venture into the downtown middle-class shopping areas where the profit margins were potentially greater. Her rejection of elite Brazil forbade her to initiate any contact with that segment of society she detested. This form of unbending *basismo*, hindering the development of local subjectivity, was noted by Mainwaring (1986b). Encouraged by pastoral agents and priests who reject outsiders, and especially impulses that emanate from Brazil's educated elite (Mainwaring 1986b, 215–19), local people are limited in their choices because the gap between the social worlds is widened and contact points are limited. In this manner, radical *basismo*, which springs from a belief in the authenticity of popular culture, insulates, hinders, or even stops the local development process (Lehmann 1996; Vásquez 1998, 275).

Boundaries Set by the Symbolic Universe

An often dogmatic reading of the liberationist message significantly restricted the available options. The *Cooperativa Convivência* carried strong religious premises that shaped the practices of the cooperative. It is easy to underemphasize this important facet, which forms part of liberationist subjectivity. During the year of my activities in the cooperative, this underlying religious principle grew in importance. The more cooperative members and, in particular, Adriana, grasped the instrumental logic of the market, the more they rejected this logic. Only in the face of intense external and internal pressures, which threatened the survival of the cooperative, was Adriana forced to adopt tools such as cost/benefit analysis. In this instance, liberationist theology may actually limit the ability of local residents to adjust their practices to changing contexts. At this point David Levine (1992) and Unger (1987) miss an important aspect of the symbolic dimension of liberation theology, when they underline the pragmatic potential of liberationist subjectivity (see chapter 1). Instead, as this case study demonstrates, the subjectivity that would be necessary for such a recasting can be stifled by the arresting grip of universal truth, contained by the symbolic sphere of liberationist Catholicism.

The power of this grip emerged most strongly during instances when the cooperative was doing well. Whenever the cooperative was able to close a major contract that promised some financial gains, Adriana, strongly inspired by Christian humanist ideals, wanted to share these gains with other unemployed members of the community. She was often aware that her liberationist Catholic background presented obstacles to her projects, and she often blamed her convent upbringing for her inability to overstep certain boundaries. Her religious premises manifested themselves in various ways.[27] During the time of the land occupation at Jd. Piri Alto, in May 1996, she came into contact with many capable but unemployed people. Believing strongly in the principles of charity, sharing, and cooperativism, she soon—to my despair—invited these unemployed occupants to work at the cooperative. This initiated a debate during which I tried to persuade her that this substantial increase in labor power could turn previously profitable deals into potential disasters. After days of ongoing bickering, the atmosphere became increasingly tense. Adriana told me that if this was the principle of the market, she did not want to have anything to do with it, as it was an un-Christian principle. For her, the bottom line of the cooperative was to employ as many people as possible. Cost factors were, from this perspective, next to inconsequential. Three months later, the cooperative had no contracts and no work. Adriana, however, insisted on paying wages until all the cooperative's resources had been drained.[28] Insisting on a management style based on Christian principles, Adriana frequently undermined the ability of the cooperative to develop a more stable production.

The liberationist premise on which the cooperative was built informed all production and administrative practices. For instance, the strong emphasis on human relations and communal procedures led those cooperative members who secured the production commitments of the cooperative to accept the frequent absence of other members who benefited from the efforts of the for-

mer. Another major obstacle, issuing from the focus on communitarian structures, necessitated endless meetings, which seemed to consume at least twenty
hours of Adriana's week. Meetings formed an integral part of Adriana's life,
and she did not think of them as a chore (Nagle 1997, 153). During meetings,
identities were formed, dreams of a new future formulated, and one's sense
of importance stimulated. Meetings were held to chant, to pray, to reinforce
one's disposition to struggle, and to break the everyday monotony. The one
thing generally missing in meetings was a chairperson to keep the discussion
on course. Productivity was not necessarily an issue for members, however,
because they had plenty of time and did not necessarily appreciate the increase
in productivity. Furthermore, for coop members, the division between production and reproduction was of no interest. The *Cooperativa Convivência* was
a place to live together, not to be hyperproductive.

It is difficult to delineate the way in which Adriana's Christian liberationist
premises affected the events within and around the cooperative. While they
tended to inform every decision and action, they manifested themselves only
rarely in a clearly articulated manner. The examples above, however, manage
to convey some of the instances in which the spiritual content of the liberationist symbolic sphere leave a noticeable imprint on local practices. This imprint decidedly militates against a successful integration in the market and
creates dependencies on support networks, which, through their political/
moral exigencies, reinforce this particular orientation. In the case of the cooperative, many of the attempts to alter modes of activity were captured by this
support network, embodying substantial elements of liberationist thought.
Of equal importance, the proposed pragmatic changes led to significant conflicts within the cooperative, laying bare the incompatibility of Catholic liberationist humanitarianism and the instrumental basis of decisionmaking
imposed by the market. Adriana's attachment to the values contained within
the symbolic liberationist universe enticed her to divest the cooperative of all
available funds in order to quell local hardship. As a result, the cooperative
never prospered or expanded, continuing on the edge of bankruptcy. In the
light of the experiences of the *Cooperativa Convivência* and of other experiments of cooperativism (Scurrah 1984a; 1984b), it seems rather likely that a
successful synthesis that would allow popular cooperatives such as Adriana's
to participate in the market, while remaining faithful to the exigencies of their

symbolic universe, would require the support of joint Catholic Left forces. Unfortunately for cooperatives such as Adriana's, such a project is far from being elaborated, as the following illustrations will reveal.

Contradictory Responses of the Catholic Left

When dealing with Catholic Left forces beyond the immediate sphere of contact of the cooperative, cooperative members were exposed to highly contradictory signals that at times represented a serious threat to the survival of the workshop. It is certainly true that Catholic liberationist principles do not always inform the practices of the Catholic Left. In fact, one of the fundamental contradictions within the Catholic Left—the conflict between a Catholic Left that is still trying to construct a new liberationist, anticapitalist, humanist culture, and the Catholic social-democratic Left that has accepted the primacy of the market—came to be embodied in some of the crises that the cooperative confronted. Different readings of the liberationist symbolic universe not only undermined the livelihood of *bairro* militants, but also weakened the residue of an empowered collectivity.

Interestingly, the business involvement most detrimental to the survival of the cooperative was that with the Catholic Left. The following example bears witness to the rather contradictory encounter of market-mediated Left forces. Looking for work in order to occupy her army of idle cooperative members,[29] Adriana closed a contract with the PT. The deal entailed the production of several thousand T-shirts for the municipal election campaign of Luiza Erundina, one of Adriana's political allies and idols. The price the PT was willing to pay posed a dilemma. It was so low that formal commercial producers had shown little interest in the deal. In classic capitalist fashion, the contract was handed over to a cooperative sweat shop of the informal sector, in this case Adriana's cooperative. For Adriana, supporting the campaign effort of the PT while gathering work for the coop members were the most important impulses that prompted her to accept the terms. Her popular approach to cost/benefit analysis had convinced her that she would at least break even.[30]

Some weeks later, the majority of the cooperative members had looted the coop cashbox and left, revolting against the administration's inability to pay wages. The PT deal had turned into a major financial debacle for the cooperative. It is ironic that a contract with a faction loosely affiliated with the Catholic Left had substantially endangered the project of *bairro* residents, who were trying to live on noncapitalist principles. Here, solidarity and community, forming the focus of the cooperative, remained unrequited and experienced a response that differed in no manner from the normal capitalist practices. In this instance, the lack of a consolidated approach that could have featured popular cooperatives as a valuable element was most obvious.

This development was subverted in the course of a further major crisis that emerged as a result of another deal Adriana had struck, placing Catholic liberationist values at the core of the decisionmaking process. This event proved to be even more enigmatic because the business partner, the *Movimento dos Sem Terra* (Movement of the Landless, MST)—another of Adriana's political allies—not only entertained close links to the liberationist Church, but also encouraged popular cooperativism within its own ranks. The deal, the production of 3,000 caps for the MST, became an even greater disaster. Working through the costing during the next workshop, we calculated that the coop had to produce at least one cap every eight minutes in order to pay each coop member a salary of R$120 a month. The reality was that it took close to forty-five minutes to finish a cap. Hence, salaries shrunk below the level of a living wage for coop members. Up to that point, Adriana had failed to tell me that the deal included the printing of the caps, an additional cost that would affect overall losses. Then, the coop delivered the first seven hundred items. They were returned the same day: the MST rejected the shipment due to the poor quality of the goods.[31] Again, it is ironic that the MST not only paid a price well below market rates, but also demanded a level of quality that went well beyond the popular. This lack of cooperation within the space of what can be loosely termed the Catholic Left was highly suggestive of the rift between elite organizers and popular participants. While the directives given to the popular constituents strongly emphasized the adherence to liberationist political and moral principles, the relationship between these organizations and the popular militants of other Catholic Left factions proved to be, at least in this instance, exploitative.

For the cooperative members, this meant that they had to pay to replace the seven hundred rejected caps and find a much more expensive screen-printer able to satisfy the demands of the MST. The depth of the misfortune did not surface until a detailed analysis of the process was attempted in the customary forum. During this workshop, it emerged that the cooperative had already lost several thousand Reais and, thus, everybody's salary for the next couple of months. Furthermore, Adriana was identified as the key person responsible for these losses. In the ensuing conflict the cooperative threatened to disintegrate.

At this point, the inconsistencies contained within the Catholic Left almost extinguished Adriana's attempt to integrate her project into the market economy. While experiments such as Adriana's business relationship with the MST could have given rise to a larger and more fruitful cooperation between forces of the Catholic Left, the lack of communication between individual projects was compensated by the mediating capacity of the market. This not only undermined the credibility of the Catholic Left, but also sent highly contradictory signals to other protagonists of the liberationist project. However, in spite of the extremely adverse experiences that Adriana had had with these factions of the Catholic Left, she continued to idolize this Left with a fervor reminiscent of spiritual dogmatism.

Spiritual Dogmatism

The dogmatic character of Adriana's liberationist orientation hit me with full force. Liberationism often gave rise to a dogmatism—underemphasized by most authors who deal with subjectivities inspired by liberationist thought, such as Unger (1987) and Levine (1992)—that annihilated any pragmatic redirectioning of projects. Adriana tended to read in absolute terms much of the political content of the liberationist message, rendering any secular critique of the Catholic Left impotent. Forced into a corner by a secular analysis of the above events, she shifted the issue onto an ethical and political plane, thus allowing her to assert her authority. She defused the conflict by branding the market principles she had learned as capitalist and, thus, not compatible with Christian values. My position in the cooperative was undermined by the fact that I was associated with the wrong narrative—the narrative of the elitist bourgeois Brazil, of the oppressor, of the market, the morally corrupt, the other, and, definitely, the outsider. With this moral critique, Adriana punctured my discourse and with it the sense of responsibility and accountability that the crisis had stirred. This was a strategy she frequently used. Whenever the logic of the bourgeois Brazil threatened to undermine her liberationist

Catholic position, she declared its message either unknowable or immoral. Hence, throughout these events the actions of the various Left factions involved were never questioned.

This was very much in line with Adriana's overall relationship with the Catholic Left. In many ways, the mixing of Christianity with Left ideas had lifted the Left beyond the realm of criticism. While Adriana threatened at times not to vote for the PT during the municipal elections of 1996, these threats were never serious. Despite the many times she tried to persuade PT candidates of the importance of a concerted campaign against unemployment in the *bairros,* and the many times these candidates rebuffed her with the answer that, yes, such an item existed in their catalogue of commitments, Adriana never turned her frustration into a radical critique. She still believed that she was a part of the struggle of the Catholic Left. And, to a certain extent, she drew satisfaction from the fact that her cooperative was featured as an example of the success of assistentialist policies in a TV campaign promoting Luiza Erundina, the PT mayoral candidate, while being only too well aware that this success existed on the TV screen only.

It was evident to Adriana that her friends from the Left looked somewhat out of place when they came to the *bairro* for an election rally in their fashionable suits and with their battalion of helpers with mobile phones that never seemed to stop ringing. Awkwardly clinging to a makeshift chair in Adriana's dusty garage, surrounded by unemployed bricklayers, construction workers, seamstresses, and metal workers, these friends, distracted by the ringing of the phones bearing most important messages concerning parliamentary procedures, were unable to provide any answers to the local drama. With great political dexterity, the friends were able to guide discussions into the realm of the possible, what could be done in the *Cámera dos Vereadores* (city council), where they had a real impact. Others, like Aldaíza Sposati—PT *vereadora* and candidate in the municipal election campaign in 1996—launched very eloquent critical discourses that featured all the wrongs of the Brazilian state. These discourses, nevertheless, left the small local audience without answers.

Luiza Erundina herself told how things really were. "She's the best of all," someone said. "She tells how things are." She proved her worth as a politician, displaying her knowledge of percentages and facts and arguing for policies— replacement of the health policy implemented by the outgoing mayor, Paulo

Maluf; continuation and expansion of his housing projects; investment in education; increases in security at the periphery; and many more. However, the only political enthusiasm generated by the rallies at Jd. Elisa Maria—a *bairro* in the region—was that of the cheering squad that accompanied her. The audience appeared largely skeptical. By the mid-1990s, the liberationist rhetoric that still dominated the discourse of these PT candidates was perceived as just another political discourse that could hardly bridge the gap between the popular and the elitist Brazil. Any references to the liberationist struggle that had inspired millions of Brazilians during the 1970s to believe in real social change had been extinguished.

Adriana, too, noticed that the issue of income generation was in danger of slipping from the PT's political agenda. She vowed: "I vote for those who have an answer to income generation." "The times are over when I just vote for anybody from the Left!" "They do something for us, we do something for them." Adriana, however, still hoped that the PT would be able to design a real solution to the problems at the periphery, and she wanted to be part of this. Her dismay was obvious when the issues that she perceived as most pressing hardly received a mention in the campaign. Although the PT might have been uninspiring, fragmented, and aloof from its base here in the *bairros*, for Adriana it was still the best party. One of the few times I heard Adriana launch a critical remark about the PT was during the era of political bickering between Luiza Erundina and the candidate for vice mayor, Aloísio Mercadante, when it appeared that Mercadante was quite unhappy about the fact that he had to run as an appendage to Erundina. Returning from a PT congress, Adriana was angry that the focus of the PT seemed to have shifted from the plight of the low-income periphery to career politics.[32] However, even this instance of criticism gave me a sense of how much the Left was bound up with Adriana's worldview. Criticism of the Left would have been tantamount to a critique of her way of life as well as her Catholic beliefs.

While for most Catholic militants and local residents the liberationist authenticity-induced link between spirituality and politics had become problematic or meaningless, Adriana insisted on a reading that located universal truth within the realm of the Catholic Left. This spiritual dogmatism, encouraged by an institutionalized liberationism (see chapter 4), undermined most initiatives that could have meaningfully adapted the liberationist symbolic universe to the context of the 1990s. In this sense, Adriana's dogmatic interpretation of the liberationist message limited the available alternatives significantly.

CONCLUSION

I realized that Adriana's political principles and Christian norms tied her project inextricably to a form of assistentialism. Her mixing of politics and business was not, as I had previously assumed, a confusion, but the very result of a guiding liberationist symbolic framework and cultural practices. The themes of rebellion, antagonism, and rejection in the face of elite Brazil created a significant tension when combined with the need and desire to do business with that same segment of society. Years of Left activism in the *bairros* had turned them into sites of oppressed identities defined against the backdrop of elite society. The sense of being a poor, black, unemployed worker and mother, amplified by the consciousness that she was living in a marginalized peripheral suburb, produced a reaction against elite Brazil. Bound up with this antagonistic local culture was an absence of technical expertise and administrative competence, of which the locals were well aware. This accumulation of negatively charged identities was resurrected and invested with positive meaning by the PT through its celebration of the popular. Doing things the popular way was elevated from a forced reaction in the face of social exclusion to a supposedly viable socioeconomic alternative. Through this celebration of the popular, the intolerant side of *basismo,* such as anti-elitism, was awakened and its radical exclusionary localism stimulated. Culturally, this theme was developed by a Catholic Left set on instilling noncapitalist principles into popular culture. Blending with Adriana's dream to live in a more holistic and organic manner, the radical Catholic Church promoted a new anticapitalist culture, in which concerns about human reproduction rather than material production were paramount. In individuals like Adriana, the growing together of local antagonism, liberationist Catholicism, and secular Left Catholicism produced a stubborn local political and cultural outlook. In the absence of a project that could endow this local outlook with a positive evaluation of productive requirements and tie its local endeavors into a larger economy, Adriana's quest for a solution to unemployment achieved independent of party and state was condemned to failure. Ideological tensions between Left factions and between these and her local culture not only turned the cooperative into an extremely expensive experiment, but also undermined her own political influence as one of the key militants in the area. Exacerbating all this was Adriana's obsession with turning the cooperative into a success story for *basismo*.

In many ways, the utopia of the progressive Church, in conjunction with the assistentialist position of the Left in general and the PT in particular, devoid of a perspective that could tie projects like Adriana's into a wider strategy, had locked local agents into a position of dependency. After almost two decades of state corporatism and charity handouts, local residents like Adriana were fairly certain about the limits to redistributive policies. However, their attempts to turn their initiative and creativity into projects exploring new avenues of development were hampered, not only by their position of relative exclusion and *bairro* localism, but also by an attitude of the Catholic Left that regarded these ventures in production for the capitalist market as intrinsically aberrant.

The case of the *Cooperativa Convivência* questions Unger's (1987) and Levine's (1992) faith in the ability of local residents to adapt the liberationist message to different contexts as it conveys the difficulties faced by local liberationist actors when they tried to implement pragmatic changes. Adriana's endeavor was undermined by politicians and bureaucrats holding key positions within the support network of the Catholic Left. As a result, cooperative members were locked into a relationship of state assistentialism and welfare dependency. This tendency toward state assistentialism was solidified by a radical *basismo*, which, together with a dogmatic reading of the liberationist message, arrested local development initiatives. The case of the *Cooperativa Convivência* illustrated that Adriana's spiritual dogmatism significantly hampered the reinterpretation and recasting of liberationist symbols, hindering an accommodation of changing sociopolitical and economic contexts.

RESURRECTING THE
LIBERATIONIST SPIRIT

"What is then the discourse of the '90s? Maybe we don't need a discourse of the '90s?" In this statement, Julie suggests a new project in the making. Her two questions convey a glimpse of the political direction of this project and contain a hidden critique aimed at the activities of the liberationist clergy and laity, eager to reignite the liberationist struggle in the Brasilândia region. Julie believed that the issues important for *bairro* residents had shifted, and attempts to revive popular politics along traditional liberationist lines were not taking this into account. "For the people," she claims, "the struggle is over." Rather than insisting on a mobilization discourse that would have characterized earlier initiatives, Julie argues, the potential organizer needs to listen. By entering the realm of the *bairro*, she claims, it is easy to distinguish a new project in the making.

Despite Julie's sentiment, the 1990s do indeed have an overarching discourse; Julie herself has promoted it. In fact, despite Julie's claims that the struggle is over, the discourse of the 1990s is based on creating a new context for intra-*bairro* tensions, combining liberationist and feminist currents.[1] By explaining the social realm in terms of religious authenticity, this rereading of *bairro* conditions has constructed a new link between radical Catholicism and local politics that is reminiscent of the liberationist movement of the late

1960s and 1970s (see chapter 3). What emerges clearly is that this reinterpretation demands substantial skill levels, knowledge, sensitivity, and access to local as well as global information sources. Furthermore, as this mobilization attempt is by and large constructed within the symbolic and institutional space of the progressive Catholic Church, such a conceptual renovation is most likely dependent on the initiative of Catholic militants. Most academic studies of popular politics in Brazil after the mid-1980s have a pessimistic outlook (Alvarez 1994; Escobar and Alvarez 1992). In this sense, I construct a counterpoint to the dire revisionism that dominated the work of authors dealing with Latin American popular politics (Burdick 1993; Lehmann 1996; Salman 1996).

CATHOLIC MILITANCY IN THE MID-1990s

During mid-1997, the ongoing episcopal concern for the liberationist struggle in the Brasilândia region gave rise to numerous attempts to readjust the liberationist message to a rapidly changing social and cultural context. Among these, the Archdiocese of São Paulo itself was engaged in an initiative to reform its mobilization capacity along traditional lines. To this end, it redefined the liberationist synthesis of the 1970s and 1980s, based on a struggle against oppression, to accommodate the dominant social-critical currents of the 1990s. Social debt was the principal theme of the Third Brazilian Social Week (*3a Semana Social Brasileira*, 16–19 September 1997) (*dívidas sociais*). The pamphlet inviting participants to this week emphasized the need to create a new mobilization platform incorporating new groups. Meanwhile, initiatives such as the Forum of Citizenship in the Defense of the North Eastern Region (*Fórum da Cidadania em Defesa da Região Noroeste*)[2] and the early project of Radio Cantareira surfaced in the *bairros*. They were complemented by initiatives to rejuvenate the activities of the ailing Housing Pastoral by recruiting and educating a new local leadership.[3] Local responses to such ventures, however, had been rather limited, leading to a profound disillusionment among the liberationist clergy and laity working in the *bairros*.

This lack of local enthusiasm for the traditional liberationist struggle gave rise to a relentless critical analysis of existing religious and political alliances. Severely hit were candidates of the Workers Party (PT), such as Aldaíza Sposati. After a brief period of popularity, they faced expulsion from local

Catholic communities that were most critical of attempts to increase political capital by irresponsibly politicizing local events.[4] Local community leaders, seriously concerned about the diminishing financial support for their projects, no longer found any sympathy for political campaigns that jeopardized these funding sources by publicly appropriating the struggle of local militants. Increasingly, the liberationist faction of the local clergy and laity turned to new and more promising projects. By late 1996, Alexandra, in charge of Radio Cantareira, had become interested in gender issues. At about the same time, Pe. Pedro began to experiment with charismatic practices within the space of his new parish. Aiming at constructing a new synthesis that would incorporate the successful practices of Evangelical Churches (see chapter 4), elements of historical materialism, and a liberationist engagement for the poor, Pe. Pedro began, in September 1997, with sessions reminiscent of religious group therapy that acquired increasingly cathartic qualities. He assembled up to forty of his community members to discuss the psychological hardship and suffering endured by local residents. One of the initiatives most inspiring to local women in the region tried to mobilize *bairro* residents by appealing to their femininity.

THE PROJECT OF THE 1990s

Despite Julie's claims that the liberationist struggle is over, the feminist currents that have been spreading in the *bairros* since the late 1980s have been built on redefined early liberationist practices. These currents are based on assumptions and contain constraints similar to those of the liberationist mobilization of the 1970s. The issues tie grass-roots protagonists to Catholic feminists.

When Julie claims that one needs to listen in order to hear the discourse of the 1990s, she is referring to a group of women in the *bairros* who have been challenging local gender roles. This challenge draws on a chorus of women no longer willing to tolerate gender imbalances in their households. Given the context of increasingly politicized gender tensions in the *bairros,* it is not surprising that a group of women, calling themselves *elas* (the shes) have gathered much local fame. The name *elas* has become synonymous with a weekly community radio program (Radio Cantareira) produced by this group.[5] During the hour-long program, *elas* discusses issues of particular importance to women that are hardly ever addressed. Topics such as domestic violence, rape, drugs, menopause, legal aspects of separation, and adolescent pregnancy are debated in an open manner and are given context by relating them to events that occur in the *bairros*. The program welcomes community participation and publicly debates the themes raised by local women. The women behind *elas* do not pretend to be experts, but answer as friends, giving their program the atmosphere of a coffee-table conversation. The format allows public discussion of issues that usually remain behind closed doors. The wider aim of *elas* is simply to offer support to local women. To this end, *elas* is trying to establish a community support network that could contribute to a balancing of gender relations in the *bairros*. Through the act of listening, then, Julie—who turns out to be the driving force behind *elas*—has fathomed the heart of women's concerns.

When Julie emphasizes the importance of listening, she reveals her strong attachment to liberationist thought and methodology. Listening is at the core of the liberationist prescription in working with the base. As one of the architects of early liberationist practices in the *bairros*, Julie has always kept this work with the base in the forefront of her activities;[6] and methodologies that surfaced with early liberationist thought still informed her orientation in the mid-1990s. However, unlike others using the dominant liberationist practices, Julie respects the reality and outlook of those in the group around her, and she is very careful not to inundate local initiatives with her own discourse and projects. Moreover, her listening should not be taken as a veneration of popular wisdom, such as Mainwaring (1986b, 215) and Lehmann (1996) describe.[7] Instead, the listening that Julie has in mind echoes the liberationist spirit of Medellin and requires mutual respect and dialogue. Through this listening, she perceived that women's issues were only indirectly related to the absence of resources and urban infrastructure. In this sense, Julie's perception is much more refined than that of the liberationists featured in chapter 3, who often presumed what they would hear when they listened. The three decades during which she shared the experiences of local women enabled her to comprehend women's strength and the nature of their struggle as it emanated from the *bairros*. By integrating these experiences into a theological and institutional context, Julie effected a departure from the masculinist liberationist discourse of the 1970s and 1980s described by Drogus (1997) and Lehmann (1996, 61).

While Julie's listening attempts to meet local women on their own territory, it does not in itself achieve the grand Freirean goal of nondirective, education-driven, self-transforming mobilization. Notwithstanding that her discourse contains a strongly egalitarian quality, there remains no doubt that Julie continues a traditional liberationist methodology and politics. This liberationist basis to Julie's activities is revealed by her disguising of her own central role in this group, mirroring the liberationist methodology that places the people at the center of its quest.

Julie's influence within this community of women is certainly crucial. Julie enjoys an enormous popularity in Jd. Damasceno, attributable only in part to her residence in the *bairros* for more than three decades. Local residents told me that she has amply demonstrated her commitment to the local population. The fact that her religiosity does not appear to stand between her and local residents—as is often the case with local priests—enhances her popularity in the eyes of local women.[8] Julie's proximity to *bairro* residents is highly valued, and a number of local women have sought her opinion and spiritual guidance. Her status as a foreigner, her education, and her links to the Catholic Church tend to reinforce her standing as a sort of counselor. This widespread popularity enables Julie to guide discussions without resistance to areas and issues that most of her local women friends would rather avoid. While generally remaining in the background during discussions and radio programs, she is able to guide debates about these issues by posing occasional leading questions. According to Julie, politics is one such topic that must always be carefully introduced, as the majority of the women prefer to leave politics out of discussions. In this sense, Julie encourages these women to explore new topics and to confront new issues.

However, the action of *elas* does not remain solely on a discursive level, and Julie's role as an unintrusive moderator has often made action inevitable. As a consequence, women who participate in her group are known to find practical solutions to problems posed by everyday life in their reflections. For instance, husbands are asked to participate in household chores and are encouraged to share their salaries more equally with their partners. On several occasions, those who proved recalcitrant were forced into line. Group members whose partners entertain extramarital relationships have contemplated and enacted a form of passive resistance.[9] Women who are victims of domestic violence have expelled the perpetrator from the premises. In such cases, Julie assists with job-search and day-care facilities, enabling women to construct an independent existence. Undoubtedly, Julie plays a central role in this feminist movement. This is also evident from the fact that she herself has become a focal point of frequent attacks. For example, discontented males often claim that she is the cause of the increasing disharmony that awaits them in their households.[10] In this way, *elas* not only challenges entrenched gender dynamics on a discursive level, but deals with them on a practical day-to-day basis. Moreover, it is equally apparent that the push for an applied feminism within Jd. Damasceno does not simply arise from the grass roots, but has substantial roots in the ecumenical liberationist-feminist discourse.[11]

Keeping Julie's central role in mind, it is hard to overlook a certain similarity between *elas* and the mothers clubs of the 1970s. During that decade, the motives that enticed women to seek out mothers clubs were very similar to those of Maria-Conceição, Cristiane, Mônica, Cecilia, and Mara, who form —together with Julie—the core of *elas*. Then as today, the escape from monotonous daily activities, domestic oppression, isolation, fear, and violence dominated the accounts of local women. *Elas* deals with topics that also provoked much polemical debate in the mothers clubs of the 1970s and gave rise to a rather radical discourse still popular in the *bairros* in the mid-1990s (see chapter 3).[12] Nevertheless, the group distinguishes itself clearly from Church-inspired mothers clubs of the 1970s and is not just a high-tech version discussing women's issues over the airwaves.

One of the most important distinguishing features is that *elas* focuses predominantly on women and explicitly on femininity, while in the mothers clubs of the 1970s gender imbalances were secondary to issues such as urban services and infrastructure, which were central to the liberationist struggle. Rather than relegating the specifics of women's lives to an intimate and subordinate space within a Catholic community, gender issues form the official and publicly aired central concern of this group. Hence, as Drogus (1997) also noted in commenting on a similar theme, within a Catholic context, the message of *elas* is highly contentious and, in many regards, novel.

The use of a Catholic community radio station to broadcast gender issues that are not part of a traditional Catholic message adds much to this novelty. On the one hand, the radio program effectively disseminates information valuable to local women. Details about medical facilities, safe houses, and tips concerning popular medicine and abortion are aired in the *bairros* at large. On the other hand, the program functions as cultural mediator and promoter of identity politics. By lifting issues such as domestic violence onto a public plat-form and rendering them visible, *elas* disseminates and reinforces the moral principle that any aggression against women is unacceptable. In this admit-tedly limited sense, *elas* is able to define and challenge cultural practice. By clearly denouncing the violent act of a perpetrator and making the voice of the victim public, the program invites the community to take sides. Through this, a system of collective judgment is being activated that often transgresses traditional Catholic values.

In contrast to the secular feminist initiatives of the 1970s and early 1980s, *elas* is action oriented. While the project of Sandra and Maria Teresa was mainly concerned about the dissemination of information and representational pol-itics, *elas* tries to operationalize the conclusions drawn from group discussions and has stimulated concrete attempts to change the lives of individual women. To this end, *elas* has formed a support network that encourages and empowers women to take the necessary steps to reform their lives. As a consequence, *elas* has attracted the attention of a large number of women within the *bairros*.

Moreover, *elas* is not an isolated instance of mobilization in the *bairros,* but is integrated into a wider network that deserves the label movement. Besides *elas*, other feminist projects have been emerging in the *bairros,* and gender and femininity have become the focus of virtually all Catholic communities headed by Catholic militant women. For instance, the cooperative in Jd. Recanto (see chapter 5) has been providing professionalization classes containing a strong gender consciousness-raising dimension.[13] Furthermore, during 1997, Radio Cantareira adopted an increasingly gender-conscious line, largely reflecting the change of orientation of Alexandra, the administrator of the community radio station. Progressively, these projects have espoused reflections, focusing on instances of oppression that have been undermining the physical, mental, and spiritual well-being of women in the *bairros*.[14]

In other words, *elas* forms part of a larger project that is lending practical and moral, as well as emotional, support to women in difficult situations. By making use of the community radio, *elas* is breaking down communication barriers, raising sensitive issues onto a public discussion platform in a manner appreciated and understood by local women. In this sense, *elas* makes public certain private issues and constructs a communal women's support network that encourages and facilitates initiatives that potentially alter the cultural sphere of the *bairros*.[15] Within the space of groups like *elas* a new liberation theology–inspired project has been constructed that differentiates itself significantly from the focus of the liberationist struggle of the 1970s and 1980s.

CATHOLIC LIBERATIONISM-FEMINISM IN THE MAKING

Despite the extensive history of feminist mobilization in the *bairros*, even sensitive Catholic militants such as Julie began to politicize gender only a decade after secular militants had mobilized local women along gender lines. In fact, the interest of Catholic militants in gender issues seems to have risen concurrently with the decline of secular feminist mobilization attempts. This liberationist-feminist synthesis could surface only after the institutionalized liberationist struggle had lost its symbolic power over Catholic militants such as Julie. With this detachment from the traditional liberationist struggle, Catholic militants were able to open themselves to the potential contained within a global ecumenical feminist discourse.

Julie's method, while using an approach that follows Freire at least in spirit, cannot escape the directive element in a liberationist consciousness raising that is now feminist. Even though Julie does not impose direction on her group but, in large part, allows group participation to lead the way, Julie is certainly guiding the political and spiritual initiatives of the women. The construction of a feminine utopia derives at least partially from her search for a better and just society. As Levine rightly claims with regard to the liberationist mobilization of the 1970s, it would be a mistake to assume that this feminine initiative emerged full-blown from the grass roots (Levine 1992, 23). Julie, for instance, began to politicize women's issues only during the late 1980s and early 1990s. While women's concerns formed part of her projects during the 1970s and 1980s, the direct focus on and politicization of "how to be woman" within the *bairro* context emerged only after more than two decades of her work in the *bairros*.

In many ways, such a gendered outlook could emerge only in the late 1980s. Until the mid-1980s, Julie was intensively involved with the traditional liberationist project and shared its focus. Consequently, considerations of gender and femininity took second place to issues that were the focus of the liberationist movement. Only by the mid-1980s, when her disenchantment with the struggle allowed her to consider her experiences in the *bairros* in a different light, did gender issues gain importance in her work and theology. For this new sensibility of *bairro* femininity to arise, Julie needed to acknowledge the end of one particular form of liberationist struggle.

The inability to break with the traditional liberationist struggle of the 1970s and 1980s has undermined many attempts of militants to develop a new form of religious-political synthesis. Correspondingly, the theme underlying comments of interviewed community leaders with regard to the content of the newly inaugurated Radio Cantareira during late 1995 was that the programs were dated and no longer corresponded to the reality of the *bairros*. Only after Alexandra tried to replace the traditional liberationism contained in the radio transmission did these opinions change. However, the case of Radio Cantareira also demonstrates clearly that the local liberationist network of priests constrains such attempts by insisting on following a liberationist tradition. This persistence has contributed to a certain populist dilution of the liberationist project, as some local clergy and politicians such as Luiza Erundina added a carnival touch to their attempts at mobilization, often resulting in form's dominating content. Unable to see beyond a traditional liberationist horizon, many liberationists tried to frame the same message in a more appealing and often simplified manner to elicit new popular interest.[16]

Hence, one of the most important preconditions for the construction of this liberationist-feminist synthesis was the deconstruction of the traditional liberationist struggle promoted by the progressive Church. In this sense a successful reframing process can occur only after the limitations of the old symbolic universe have been perceived. Adriana's liberationist endeavors have been strongly inhibited by her inability to detach herself from the liberationist doctrine. Only after Catholic militants such as Julie were prepared to accept the end of the traditional liberationist struggle could new intellectual and theological currents assume greater importance within the local symbolic universe.

Global Ecumenical Feminist Currents

Most influential for the development of the Catholic feminist project in the region was the emergence of a globally connected, ecumenical feminist discourse whose tenets gained strength during the second half of the 1980s. In the *bairros,* initiatives were strongly shaped by an ecumenical encounter of women reflecting on the question of what it was like to be a woman in their denomination. This encounter inspired further attempts to politicize gender imbalances within Christian communities in the *bairros*. Furthermore, it tied local initiatives to a global point of reference that gained validity during the late 1980s.[17] By stimulating a local discussion that led to the creation of various conferences and forums, the global ecumenical feminist discourse shaped the local Catholic feminist space significantly and produced the conceptual basis for an inter-*bairro* feminist network.

At a local level, these discourses encouraged a group of Catholic women, comprising Sister Alba, Julie, and other Catholic radicals, to experiment with women's concerns. They began to search for a language and theology that could frame local conditions and accommodate the notions of gender and femininity. This endeavor gave rise to what I would call pastoral feminism— a feminism encountered predominantly in local Catholic communities that draws on the notion of femininity rather than the politics of difference. Increasingly, they attracted other women connected with the regional Church and institutionalized some of their aims.

It is difficult to underestimate the importance of the institutional network for the development of this local feminist initiative. This network integrated individual projects into the larger struggle of Catholic women, uniting diverse theological, political, and spiritual orientations. Furthermore, this network provided a source for moral-spiritual and, to a certain extent, financial support,[18] reinforcing the view that the reinterpretation undertaken by the group, which distanced these women from the episcopal directives, was legitimate. Experiences were discussed and evaluated and strategies developed. This network also provided a common base from which the liberationist-feminist synthesis could be generated. Hence, the emergence of this feminine Catholic initiative in the *bairros* is very closely tied to the emergence of an ecumenical feminism. This stimulated a Catholic feminist posture in the *bairros*, a posture that benefited greatly from the local institutional network.

In 1990, influenced by Barbara, a highly vocal, feminist militant Methodist pastor, Sister Alba, co-administrator of the Jd. Recanto cooperative / workshop, laid the basis for the Woman's Pastoral (*Pastoral da Mulher*).[19] In this manner, Catholic feminists in the region had succeeded in anchoring their concerns in the structure of the local hierarchy and thus institutionalizing the feminist project. The Woman's Pastoral seems to enjoy great popularity in the region, and events organized by it have, according to Francilene, a feminist protagonist at the curia of Bralisândia, enjoyed increasing popularity, culminating in the gathering of some four hundred participants to celebrate International Women's Day in 1997.[20] While creating an important feminist forum in the region, this institutionalization of feminist currents introduced a tension between those Catholic militant feminists whose prime focus was *bairro* culture and those who would have liked to give feminist issues greater weight within the formal political, as well as the ecclesiastical, realm.

By the mid-1990s, a group of women, including Julie, Diolinda,[21] Francilene, and most other influential Catholic women in the region, had formed around the Woman's Pastoral. These women began to cement their ties and united local groups in a broader feminist alliance, which coordinated the information flow between various local entities and organized groups, events, and discussions in the region. According to Francilene, many of the feminist initiatives that surfaced during the mid-1990s have been influenced by the efforts of these Catholic feminists.[22]

During the mid-1990s, certain local Catholic militants assumed an increasingly political position within what was progressively portrayed as the Catholic feminist movement. Strongly influenced by the work of Sister Ivone Gebara,[23] the most important Catholic feminist theologian in Latin America, this group of Catholic militants began to develop an institutional and political agenda. As a result, quotations from Ivone Gebara's publications began to appear with great regularity in episcopal pamphlets. Sister Gebara's work was of particular importance to women such as Francilene, who was by and large responsible for these pamphlets. Shaped by her extensive involvement with the liberationist Catholic and secular Left, Francilene found her political and spiritual leanings well accommodated by Gebara's work. As a result, her orientation predominantly politicized the lack of urban resources and gave the project a more traditional liberationist interpretation.

Furthermore, this link with traditional liberationism was reinforced by her strong professional links to the episcopal center. Maintaining close contact with Dom Angélico Sándalo, Francilene's position mirrors some of the features of the liberationist stance delineated in local episcopal directives. In October 1997, Francilene supported the Catholic faction within the PT under the leadership of Luiza Erundina, reiterating an alliance between CEBs and the Catholic PT that had already begun to unravel in the *bairros*.[24] Reading from the public posture of Francilene, taken as an example, the orientation of these liberationist Catholic feminists contains a strong formal political agenda and is heavily influenced by an academic-theological feminist discourse. These institutional links and political orientations are certainly not sustained by all Catholic militant feminists, a fact that exposes some of the divergences within this alliance.

The first intimation of a fundamental tension inherent in the feminist union became apparent in mid-1996. While the central concerns for community groups mediated by Julie were pastoral feminism, friendship, mutual support, and community, the focus was much more on the formal political level for liberationist Catholic feminists such as Francilene. The conflicting interests of these two positions emerged clearly in the Woman's Ministry, which was proposed by the liberationist Catholic feminists.[25] According to Francilene, such a woman's ministry would be able to express concerns that priests are often not able, comfortable, or willing, to touch on. As Julie observed, however, such a ministry "would institutionalize what local women have been doing for decades." By institutionalizing these practices, local women would cede their meager authority to a novel expert institution in the *bairro*. Over the course of a public discussion held on Radio Cantareira, it turned out that Francilene's project—the creation of institutional opportunities for feminist seminarians who would further the Catholic feminist cause in the region— was diametrically opposed to Julie's interests, which aimed to empower local women. Alongside Francilene's social assistentialist position, an institutional logic surfaced that tended to direct local projects into the arms of the progressive Church. By trying to maximize the visibility of projects and institutional legitimacy, a task that requires the satisfaction of certain institutional requirements, Francilene was diverted from the pastoral feminist project Julie espoused.[26]

According to Julie, the politicization of local concerns by a coordinating body tends to render them vulnerable to the political agenda of that same body. While Julie has hesitantly accepted the proposals of the liberationist Catholic feminists,[27] she distrusts their attempts at institutionalization and would like to construct this new feminine liberationist synthesis outside the institutional realm of Church, state, and political parties. The focus of her group, as well as her rejection of overarching discourses, lends weight to her concern that a centralized movement may abduct local femininity and harness it for other political ends. In the light of her experiences with the leadership of the progressive Church and political parties during the 1970s and 1980s, her rejection of overarching discourses is well founded. For her, the most important activity within this new synthesis is to listen in order to maintain an authentic contact with *bairro* women that is free of the manipulation involved in premature political or ecclesiastical institutionalization. For liberationist Catholic feminists such as Francilene, this focus is too narrow and local, and the temptation is too great to impose a political agenda on the practices of local groups in order to give a contemporary political dimension to their eclectic localism and distaste for elusive larger issues.

With this focus on institutionalized politics, liberationist Catholic feminism in the *bairros* appears to harbor an intrinsic contradiction that emerges most clearly in the following statements. When asked about the origin of the cultural feminine subcurrent that I had noticed in the *bairros*, Francilene answered promptly: "That comes from here!" meaning, from a curia-inspired elite discourse. An instant later, however, Francilene rejects any elite feminist academic or theological influence, like, for instance, that of Ivone Gebara, and argues, "This feminism derives from the people." In this way she reiterates a contradiction that permeates the entire line of liberationist mobilization from the student movements to the consolidated liberationist Church, claiming that Catholic feminists, by representing the voice of the voiceless, tie local women unilaterally to their project. As a consequence, by assuming an expert and leadership position, activists like Francilene inadvertently tended to dominate the agenda of local groups, overriding local orientations. The case of the Woman's Ministry demonstrates this clearly. Francilene's passionate pledge to invest the next ten years of her life in the cause of local women partially reveals that she was by no means driven by political ambitions. Instead, her dominion over local groups emerged from a well-meaning Left institutionalism that incorporated a *basista* spirit,[28] a spirit that, due to its posited belief in the popular, carries many of the qualities that Greenblatt (1996) has called "marvelous possession"—a term that makes a metaphor of the dogmatic belief in religious authenticity. Having acquired the liberationist heritage of an elite movement that tries to be one with the grass roots, liberationist Catholic feminists such as Francilene have not yet come to terms with the fact that their approach will preclude such a union.

Central to the historical tension that has underlined much of the liberationist mobilization in the *bairros* is the conflict of interest between the local cultural and the global political, or, more specifically, between community development and the spirit of religious *basista* politics. As soon as a group takes on a religious-political *basista* perspective, local cultural issues are likely to fade into the background. By accepting and cementing their role as elite catalysts and coordinators, liberationist Catholic feminists are carried away from the concerns and interests of local women, as for instance with their proposal of a woman's ministry. This, however, does not prevent activists like Francilene from claiming to represent the voice of local women. As a result, women's voices in the *bairros*, so attentively listened to by Julie, are in danger of being swamped by an impassioned political leadership that is tempted to impose its own agenda on this new struggle.[29] However, during my stay in and visits to the *bairros*, this conflict gave rise to an animated dialogue among Catholic feminist factions that was always informed by a common goal of advancing the cause of local women. During this dialogue, Julie's arguments appeared to have more purchase.

Catholic feminist currents in the *bairros* have been inspired by a global ecumenical feminist discourse and amplified by the work of Ivone Gebara. These influences, combined with a liberationist methodology, have given rise to a new project that has united local women, including women attached to the Church, by embracing and harnessing a feminist femininity. However, diverging positions do exist within this alliance. Despite the political-cultural tensions that inhabit this alliance, it appears as if intellectual and theological differences were never allowed to endanger the alliance. The symbolic framework that underpins this alliance carries sufficient unifying force to subjugate individual positions to a unanimously accepted cause.

GENDER AND FEMININITY WITHIN A CATHOLIC SYMBOLIC SPHERE

This reframing of the symbolic realm takes on a further dimension in the context of the progressive Catholic Church. As also noted by Sonia Alvarez (1994) and Drogus (1997; 1999), feminist initiatives frequently suffered from a deradicalization stemming from the initiatives of a gender-blind progressive Church.[30] In this sense, the symbolic as well as institutional realm of the progressive Catholic Church poses a significant obstacle to Catholic feminist projects.

In this reinterpretation, Julie's ability to enter the cultural realm of the *bairro* and to encounter women on their home ground is highly important. Her ability to do this seems to derive from her liberal interpretation of faith and religiosity. Julie believes that the liberation theology of the 1980s and 1990s, as embodied in the progressive Church, has become so dogmatized that its protagonists subvert pastoral work and fail to engage with the real concerns and priorities of local people. Though she is part of the old guard that has elaborated liberationist practices, she was never prone to seeing liberation theology as an absolute doctrine. Julie regards liberationism as a question of faith and vision, not as one of doctrine and predetermined strategy. Based on this faith, she is able to reframe the context of the 1990s with an open-ended liberationism that refuses to suffocate local voices. By differentiating between faith and dogmatic theology, Julie has been able to construct a spiritually independent space that allows her to experiment with theology, while never abandoning her faith. This enables her to work beyond the boundaries set by the clergy.[31] Listening in to the *bairros* with this disposition, and guided by a Christian feminist discourse, Julie has been able to perceive the severe tensions that most Catholic militants have preferred to ignore.

As a result of a spirituality that exemplifies her anti-institutional stance, Julie's relationship with the local hierarchy is an ambiguous one. However, she has the ability to negotiate these ambiguities within an acceptable institutional framework. Not unlike the liberationist thought that surfaced during the late 1960s, Julie's orientation carries the wish to reform what is, from her point of view, a dogmatic and patriarchal Catholic Church. The gender imbalances within and outside the Church serve, for her, as theological points of departure for a more contemporary reading of key Catholic concepts such as family, authenticity, and the people. Julie believes that the concept of family simply helps to disguise extremely exploitative power dynamics in the *bairros*. Unions customarily referred to as families by the local clergy and hierarchy have, she claims, very little to do with a genuine union. Understanding, dialogue, love, and sexual exchanges satisfying to both parties are too often replaced by violent oppression and exploitation. Furthermore, she also criticizes gender relationships inside the Church and dreams about a women's boycott of Catholic conferences that would protest the lack of women's status within the hierarchy and leave convention halls empty: "If I would make any of this [her feminist activism] public, I would be very quickly zapped," she replies when asked how much of her feminist orientation was known to the hierarchy. As a consequence, she would not broadcast her revolutionary feminist desires within an ecclesiastical forum, and her talk of empty conference halls remained reserved for a small audience of trustworthy individuals. Officially, Julie acknowledges episcopal prescriptions, framing her women's group within acceptable theological parameters.

Justifying her practices in the face of the hierarchy, Julie claims that producing a condition more conducive to the well-being of women in the *bairros* would also create a sound basis for the family. As a consequence, men would also benefit. This focus on a universal union, she asserts, differentiates the local Catholic feminism from the feminism encountered in the United States.[32] As this argument is far from being generally accepted by clergy or hierarchy— the majority of local priests saw in this proposition primarily the desire to deconstruct the family[33]—Catholic feminists like Julie carefully construct an official posture that seems consistent with Catholic dogma. Active, at the time the interviews were conducted, within a liberationist diocese under the authority of Dom Angélico Sándalo, however, Julie was not facing the highly explosive counterrevolutionary warfare against feminism depicted by Jean Franco in the case of the Archdiocese of Buenos Aires (Franco 1996). As a result, she is able to air some of her views without incurring the episcopal accusation leveled at Buenos Aires Catholic feminists, which claims that they promote a cultural revolution that is not in the interests of the Catholic Church (Franco 1996, 1).[34] However, as Drogus (1997) rightly points out, the support of Dom Angélico Sándalo is limited and consists mainly of a tacit agreement to tolerate Catholic feminist ventures within the diocese.

Despite her relative liberty, Julie is extremely protective of the space she has built together with her friends. By stemming the symbolic colonization attempts of the hierarchy,[35] Julie, as well as other Catholic militants in the region, created an autonomous realm in which this new liberationist feminist synthesis could emerge. By limiting institutional access to the community space, they are able to discuss and politicize topics that would transgress the boundaries set by the progressive Church.[36] Outsiders remain generally uninformed about the feminist position that these Catholic militants encourage. For months, the origin of the feminist currents that I had detected in the Jd. Recanto cooperative workshop remained obscure. Avoiding any reference to the gendered catechism that had helped to inspire these currents, Sister Maria followed the liberationist discourse and claimed that they were locally derived. Julie was equally reluctant to volunteer any information about her feminist activism. Only after months of field activity was I invited to catch a glimpse of the pastoral feminist work that took shape under her tutelage. Until that point, I was under the impression that the feminism in her group evolved from the grass roots. Thus, listening to the people appears to be part of a semantic strategy that protects the projects of these Catholic militants, a factor that Lehmann (1996) fails to note in his work on *basismo*. By deploying a liberationist discourse, they obscure their aim to change gender imbalances not only within the *bairros,* but also within the Catholic Church.

However, this is precisely where the project of pastoral feminists such as Julie, that of liberationist Catholic feminism, converges with that of local women. All groups harbor a strong dislike of what they perceive as the chauvinism of gender-insensitive priests, who actively undermine the position of women in the *bairros* and in the Church.[37] *Elas* has been particularly critical of representatives of the Church, leveling charges at individual priests of gender insensitivity. Priests who refer to nuns in the diminutive (*Irmāzinha*) and treat them as they would treat the laity certainly function as a catalyst for Julie's cultural, and Francilene's political, activism.[38] Yet, all parts of this feminist alliance recognize that the paternalism of the clergy is the result of a machismo encoded in the Church hierarchy as well as the wider society. Consequently, the Catholic feminist movement not only embarks on a theological venture that seeks to rediscover a feminine God; it also elevates the feminine principle within the cultural sphere in order to free women from an inferior position assigned to them by a patriarchal society. Even more ambitiously, from their antipodean position, they try to posit the feminine principle as the universal podean utopia of the mid-1990s.[39] This endeavor gives rise to symbolic strategies that often associate femininity with aspects of religious authenticity.

Feminine Authenticity

Mirroring the distinctions between pastoral and liberationist feminism are major differences in how this feminist utopia is being constructed. As with the liberationist discourse of the 1970s and 1980s, the concept of authenticity plays a major role. Both projects endowed femininity proper with latent qualities that are spiritualized or ordained from God's creation. However, the pastoral feminists emphasize an authenticity that arises in the interaction between women, while the authenticity contained by the project of liberationist feminists displays ontological qualities. Liberationist feminists take this a step further and locate authenticity in a feminine reading of poverty. While these interpretations represent a departure from the teaching of the progressive Church, they each shape local projects differently and give rise to a range of interpretations.

For Julie as for other pastoral feminists, the "discourse of the 1990s is about friendship and community." It is not about the veneration of an illusionary authentic popular culture that contains an immaculate sense of community, deriving from the condition of the poorer classes or an idealized vision of poverty (Gebara in Vásquez 1998, 248), but rather the construction of such community and friendship. In Julie's project, authenticity is posited primarily in interaction and only secondarily ontologized in femininity. Julie hopes that interactions that lead to friendship, support, and understanding, can generate a space in which women can discover themselves and lead more liberated lives.[40] At this particular historical moment, she argues, it is especially the task of local women to be working together to build a better *bairro* community. This project, she claims, contains the seeds of a new (liberationist) struggle for a better and more just world.[41] Because such a world cannot be built by applying fixed strategies, Julie is determined not to foster any particular attachments to ideology or dogma. She wants to simply encounter local women as a (Catholic) woman and not as a member of a religious order.[42] From a Catholic conservative point of view, this is a polemical statement; Julie once again departs from the realm of institutionalized faith.

However, when Julie calmly states that if she had to decide between being a nun or a woman, "My choice would fall on the woman," she has not abandoned her faith. In an interview with Elizangela Cordeiro, published in the *Voz da Esperança* (vol. 3, no. 33, September 1997), Julie makes this clear. Answering the question if it was possible to separate her identity as nun from that as woman she states: "Maybe in the beginning, but at the moment I am one. In this month I will complete my sixty-second year. I feel at home with myself. In the beginning, I was preoccupied with what others thought about me, but now I am myself and that's it." In this moment, Julie's theology expresses a new sense of religious authenticity, an authenticity that carries women well beyond the symbolic realm of the progressive Catholic Church. When identifying as woman, it appears, Julie invests femininity with religious qualities. This religious femininity derives, Sister Barbara Bucker claims, from women's "latent qualities," which are not admitted by society[43] (Bucker 1997, 22). Femininity is framed within a new religious utopia, and authenticity acquires, as it did for the liberationists of the 1970s, an ontological quality.

Embarking on this rather radical reworking of liberation theology, Julie leaves liberationist feminists, such as Francilene, behind. Rather than effecting a radical break with liberation theology, Francilene integrates her feminist tendencies and creates a feminine version of the people. For Francilene also, the poverty of these women is in the forefront, a poverty that is politicized by focusing on the absence of resources and by highlighting gender relationships as shaped by the distribution of resources within the *bairros*. This orientation coincides with Francilene's liberationist social assistentialist perspective—one that makes sense in terms of her professional activities and her relationship with the episcopal center: "Dom Angélico tries, but he just doesn't understand," Francilene claims, referring to Dom Angélico's apparent gender blindness. For her, creating the link between pastoral feminism and the liberationist episcopacy, the integration of the Catholic feminist movement would require not much more than to "accept the notion that women are among the most oppressed in the *bairros*."

Julie's notion of authenticity differs substantially from Francilene's. While Julie's authenticity points toward quite radical cultural change, Francilene's interpretation of the feminine utopia leads her toward a traditional liberationist struggle. Nonetheless, these differences do not stand in the way of an effective new synthesis in the making.

In other words, while local women have been working on women's issues for nearly three decades, these issues were only formally acknowledged with the development of a gendered outlook among Catholic militants. In this sense, the new liberationist-feminist synthesis could emerge only after Catholic militants had been exposed to a global ecumenical Christian feminist discourse that inspired the first Catholic feminist initiative in the region. Furthermore, it is difficult to imagine that this project could have emerged without the institutional structures that facilitated the construction of feminist communities in the region. However, such a link also conjures up spiritual and institutional constraints that Catholic militant feminists must address. Hence, the feminist alliance in the *bairros* surfaced as a result of a convergence of local gender tensions, regional institutional structures, and a global ecumenical Christian feminist discourse. In addition, this new project rests on a revised liberationist framework that locates femininity at the center of an eternal search for religious authenticity.

THE RESURRECTION OF THE STRUGGLE AND EMPOWERMENT

Given the degree of fragmentation of popular politics in the Brasilândia region, the feminist movement described in this chapter represents a significant new development. Representing one of the few political forums that have been expanding in recent years, the movement has been able to instill a new dynamism into *bairro* politics. In fact, this new liberationist-feminist project was able to resurrect some of the liberationist spirit and gave rise to a new struggle for social justice. This struggle, however, unlike the previous liberationist endeavors, focuses strongly on local inequalities. Does this allow us to speak of an empowerment of local women?

When Julie's friends, for instance, talk about their project, the sense of importance that they attach to their cause is clear. *"Elas* is friendship and support that you don't find anywhere else in the *bairros,"* Maria-Conceição explains. Mônica adds: "It gives a sense of security and achievement, to be part of something important." All the women who form part of *elas* have noted how their involvement with the group has changed their lives. Supported by the other women, Cristiane has opened a small grocery store that gives her financial independence that shifts the power dynamics within her household. Maria-Conceição completed an education program; now she is teaching basic literacy and basic sociopolitical analysis within the *bairro*. This gives her the resources and self-esteem to demand democratic procedures in household decisionmaking. Mônica summarizes this: "Women are strong, and *elas* shows how strong they really are."

Equally, when Cecília, Ruth, Sônia, Iris, and Teresa, adolescents active in the Jd. Recanto cooperative workshop, position themselves with regard to their femininity, self-confidence and excitement underlie their accounts. The main thrust of their discourse is to lead economically and sexually independent lives. For these women, a good education that would allow them to construct such lives formed their core ambition.[44] Furthermore, they were determined not to let themselves be dominated by their partners and were confident that by deploying their femininity they would be able to manage any male aggression and violent situation they encountered.[45] In this sense, they displayed a certain superiority that they drew from their femininity, enabling them to manage the machismo that they faced within their *bairros*. As it was for the older generation, the ability to evade violence without being harmed is of enormous importance. Drawing on a discourse of feminine power, they are able to construct an almost mythical strength that facilitates independence and brackets fear, to a certain extent, out of their lives.

This sense of achievement is reinforced by comparison of the culture of friendship, mutual support, and courage that has been nurtured within these groups and the toughness that defines their encounter with the *bairro*. The difference between these aspects of *bairro* life is quite profound and offers a glimpse into why local women have been searching for a space in which they can develop their femininity. It is also clear that the space that they have constructed, and in which I interviewed them, adds greatly to their sense of security and protection. Taking these various instances of feminine practices into account, I would argue that Catholic militants, such as Julie, have been able to rediscover the passion that, for instance, Unger (1987) sensed in the wake of the liberationist mobilization of the early 1970s. They were able to resurrect and transform the liberationist spirit that was lost in the early 1980s. Moreover, the initiatives depicted in this chapter sustain my argument that some instances of empowerment did indeed take place.

It does appear that at this stage, the actual impact of this empowerment on the practice of local women is limited. While these women are able to inspire other women to refuse to tolerate abuse, these refusals suffer from a lack of the sustained determination needed to eliminate such exploitative situations. Julie and other group members such as Elite, Maria-Conceição, Cristiane, Mônica, and Cecilia agree on precisely this point. While women can be enticed to take a decisive step, intense family and other pressures often lead to a reversal of this decision, renewing the circle of abuse. Similarly, the young women participating in Irmã Maria's cooperative in Jd. Recanto seem to discard easily their gender consciousness. Francilene, one of the administrators, claims that while young "women may be more intellectual today, their behavior has changed only marginally. As soon as they get involved with a partner, they lose control over their own lives." This is somewhat surprising, given the very articulate and decidedly feminist content of their discourse.

Therefore, it is rather likely that local cultural practices have yielded only marginally to this new feminine discourse. However, Julie's group has ignited an often-heated debate that actually challenges gender roles within households, *elas* enjoys great popularity, and the discourse of many women displays a greater self-confidence that derives from the idea of femininity. These examples should not be ignored. In fact, the very presence of these feminine-feminist currents demonstrates that a cultural contestation is taking place. Furthermore, the events described in this chapter show that this contestation not only occurs on a level of discussion, but also has been translated into action. While the outcome of this contestation may sketch an inconclusive or unsatisfactory picture for the observer, the contestation itself should be read as a sign of social change.

Moreover, this new Catholic feminism has affected the attitudes of the local clergy. While initially facing a fairly reactionary audience, Catholic feminists have, within the past seven years, gathered the support of a substantial number of local priests. After rejecting what local priests identified as a consolidated attack on an already weakening family structure, they have accepted some of the proposals of these women's groups. During mid-1997, Pe. Pedro still found it incredibly difficult to talk about *elas* in a neutral manner—he customarily raised his voice, arms, and eyebrows in a theatrical gesture—but he was certainly able to appreciate the importance of the group, a growth in his attitude of twelve months earlier. At the episcopal level, Catholic feminist militants have encountered a far more difficult obstacle. Here, their concerns are heard and mostly ignored (Drogus 1997).

This new feminist synthesis forms part of an essentially Catholic project, and Julie's initiative faces constraints imposed by the guardians of the symbolic universe of the Catholic Church. These constraints have been reinforced inadvertently by Catholic feminists who would like to link participating groups to the institutional sphere of the progressive Church. Through this proposal, institutional authority reenters the project. By linking local groups to a larger movement in order to gain greater strength at an institutional-political level, Catholic militants abbreviated the local consciousness-raising and self-determination process. As a consequence, their attempts to tie local groups to an elite representation tend to override local concerns. Inasmuch as a Catholic militant woman is bound into and dependent on an institutional Catholic network from which she draws much support and stimulation, her affiliation opens the political and spiritual development of local groups inadvertently to the institutional and religious structures of the Catholic Church.

CONCLUSION

The preceding two chapters have demonstrated that the frequently noted symbolic reelaboration process is contingent on far more than Unger's (1987) collective pragmatic spiritual responses to shared experiences (see chapter 1). Instead, the endeavor is based on an intricate negotiation process that brings together global, regional, and local themes. For Catholic feminism in the Brasilândia region, the themes were identified and drawn together by a multitude of militants linked by institutional networks. These militants had at their disposal significant access to information and education facilitating the mediation among *bairros*, the Church, and global discourses. Furthermore, they shared a symbolic framework that served as a basis for their common interests and beliefs.

The symbolic and institutional universe of the progressive Catholic Church may encourage the mobilization of popular groups under its tutelage. However, it may also undermine those mobilization attempts that carry militants beyond Church authority. For militants who maintain strong symbolic and institutional ties with this Church, institutional support therefore becomes crucial.[46] Symbolic reelaboration attempts must take account of the constraints that issue from this symbolic institutional space and build a strategy that integrates the new liberationist-feminist synthesis into this fabric.

The construction of a new liberationist synthesis is thus likely to emanate from militants who have access to the necessary theological and educational background to accomplish such cohesion. Moreover, they need a disposition toward faith that allows them to manipulate the symbolic universe of the Church. In other words, militants need more than spiritual strength to develop a theological standpoint that may contradict that of the Catholic Church. They also need the political expertise and education to defend this point of view in the face of the significant pressures emanating from an increasingly dogmatically inclined clergy and hierarchy.

In this light, Adriana's failure to construct a new synthesis outside the realm of Catholic-state assistentialism appears preordained. From her local position, constrained by limited access to financial, educational, and information resources, her view of global themes was often extremely fragmented. Insisting on single-handedly embarking on a new project that entailed a radical reelaboration of institutionalized liberationist practices, Adriana was unable to draw on the support of other militants. In fact, due to the highly sensitive political content of her project, issuing from an attempted blending of market economy with liberationist ideas, her initiative potentially alienated most of her former political and religious allies. Hence, Adriana's inability to frame her project in terms more acceptable to her Catholic and secular Left support network undermined her endeavor dramatically. Moreover, her inability to break with a doctrinal reading of a liberationist symbolic universe, reinforced by strong *basista* tendencies, incapacitated the development of a new synthesis and tended to lock her into outmoded strategies and patterns of action.[47]

In order to establish a new liberationist-feminist synthesis, Catholic militants like Julie needed to gain distance from the traditional liberationist struggle. Only after they had achieved a complete break with the institutionalized liberationist symbolic universe could symbols be reelaborated to embrace feminist currents. Furthermore, the symbolic reelaboration process is by no means a simple consequence of a collective pragmatic spiritual response to shared experiences, as posited by Unger (1987). Instead, this reelaboration is based on an intricate and extremely demanding process, encompassing the mediation among institutional, spiritual, and local spheres, which is likely to surpass the abilities of local militants. While spiritual pragmatism has a place in this process, especially concerning the action of Catholic militants like Julie, it appears that the liberationist project of local activists remains inextricably tied to the initiatives of elite militants who are able to construct a new synthesis in such a manner that it appears to comply with the boundaries of progressive Catholic guidelines.

LIBERATIONISM AT THE END
OF THE MILLENNIUM

What would become of the liberationist movement if it were to extinguish the *basismo* at its core? To shed light on this question, I am sketching the contours of major institutional and political trends affecting the *bairros* and beyond. During the second half of the 1990s, much of institutional Catholic politics and secular political culture was shaped by pluralization. Ironically, this pluralization has undermined *basista* militants within Brazilian religious and secular politics. After nearly thirty years of *basista* grass-roots politics, it is difficult to imagine Brazilian politics without *basismo*. However, I will delineate three possible scenarios: a liberationism without *basismo* bound to the Church, an elite *basismo* detached from both the aegis of the Church and the grass roots, and a postmodern *basismo* tied to the politics of the spectacle.

In Latin America and Brazil, the agenda of the Catholic Church is dominated by a project to stem what David Martin (1990) has called the Pentecostal explosion. This, the Church declares, threatens to extinguish "the Catholic Faith at the heart of Latin American culture." Officially launched at the Latin American Bishops Conference in Santo Domingo in 1992, the papal response to the Pentecostal "menace," framed in terms of the "new evangelization," has done much to unite dissenting Catholic factions in holy battle. The liberationist movement in the Brasilândia region is no exception and has been successfully enlisted in an attempt to regain Catholic dominance in a rapidly pluralizing religious market (Berryman 1999, Vásquez 1998, Lehmann 1996).

In the face of stiff Pentecostal competition, Latin American bishops devised a number of strategies to streamline the Catholic Church in Latin America. These include (1) an improvement in the relationship between Church and state. In Brazil, a healing of Church and state relations hinges on the Catholic Church's capacity to bring under control the highly politicized *basista* militants within the popular church. (2) On the level of worship, the strategy involves pluralization of Catholic projects and devotional life away from the focus on liberationism and leftism. This pluralization includes opening up São Paulo's Catholic imaginary to the mystical effervescence of the Charismatics, the Catholic Charismatic Renewal Movement (CCRM). (3) On an institutional level the strategy encompasses a restructuring of administrative practices and procedures (Gill 1998, 2, 27). The thrust of institutional restructuring borrows much from managerial discourses prevalent in NGOs and international organizations aiming at an effective investment of scare resources.

At the *bairro* level the implementation of these imperatives has ended the tacit agreement between recalcitrant grass-roots militants, such as Julia, and the old liberationist guard, personified by Dom Angélico, that allowed for experimentation and innovation but only within the liberationist project itself. Increasingly, a new generation of liberationists has devised new strategies to keep alive the liberationist project in a pluralized Church. Forming alliances with other movements within the Brazilian Catholic Church, such as the Charismatics, the liberationist Church has shifted its emphasis away from direct action at the grass roots and toward greater involvement in institutional politics as it supports the pursuit of liberationist goals through its structures and resources

ON CHURCH AND STATE

On 10 March 2001, Cardinal Cláudio Hummes, Archbishop of São Paulo announced the ordination of two new auxiliary bishops. Contrary to widespread expectations, the ordination went to two progressive priests, thus signaling a reconciliatory approach and a preparedness to bridge the gap that has opened since the division of the Archdiocese of São Paulo in 1989 between liberationist and conservative clergy.[1] This gesture must have put at ease many a liberationist priest in the *bairros* of São Paulo, who hitherto feared that Dom Paulo Evaristo Arns's replacement would further purge the liberationist personnel from positions of influence in the archdiocese. Thus reassured by the local hierarchy, liberationists were invited to take their place in a recentralized Church. Similar signs indicating that liberationists had a place in a pluralized but more centralized Church are also visible in the Brazilian National Bishops Conference (CNBB), where, according to Father Oscar Beozzo, candid observer of the Brazilian Catholic Church,[2] a new generation of dignitaries is able to move easily between entrenched political positions of left and right.[3] This movement between political differences, it seems, is at least partly inspired by a recognition of the need for unity in the face of the threat of Pentecostalism and particularly neo-Pentecostalism.[4] While this reconciliation on the basis of threatened supremacy ensures the survival of some liberationist initiatives, it also dissolves much of the radical spirit and creativity that underpinned liberationist projects during the 1970s and 1980s.

Until the end of 1998, the last year Dom Paulo Evaristo Arns held office, the progressive Church was an enthusiastic supporter of the Movement of the Landless (MST), the CUT (a trade union federation), and the Catholic faction within the Workers Party (PT). More important still, the progressive Church provided a widely endorsed symbolic framework that galvanized opposition forces against the government. During September 1997, *o grito dos excluidos* ("the cry of the excluded"), the pastoral theme promoted by Dom Paulo between 1995 and 1998, became the moral platform that united opposition groups against governmental economic policies (*Folha*, 8 September 1997, sec. 1, p. 5). Yet the impact of this pastoral theme and the liberationist message at its core extended far beyond political groupings directly connected with the Church and dominated the agenda of secular nongovernmental organizations (NGOs) and movements during most of the 1990s (Hochstetler 2000, 173).[5] After 1998, and with the installation of Dom Cláudio Hummes, this highly politicized voice subsided, signaling a new and less politicized Catholicism in São Paulo (see also Serbin 2000b).

By August 2000, the drive to separate explicit political involvement from religious practice had become more noticeable in São Paulo. As the bishops strove to reassert the Catholic identity of the Brazilian nation by reestablishing a Church-state relationship that underscored mutual interests (Gill 1998; Serbin 2000b), politicized liberationism became untenable. From the point of view of a new generation of prelates such as Dom Fernando Antônio

Figueiredo,[6] a leading figure in the CCRM in São Paulo, the politicized Church was a phenomenon of the 1970s. According to Dom Fernando, the politicized Catholic Church was a response to the military dictatorship, when the Church was the only forum for dissent. After the dictatorship, political parties began to form, and many of the militants no longer frequented the Church. This, in his view, spelled the end of the politicized Church and called for a new focus on devotional life and more traditional forms of religious worship. For Dom Fernando, the political activism of today's Catholic militants takes place entirely outside the bounds of the Church. "They mainly entertain lose ties with the Church," he claims. The term *luta*, Dom Fernando explains, no longer applies to the context of the 1990s, as it denotes a situation of confrontation—a clash. Contemporary conditions, according to the bishop, call for a more subtle approach of learning and cooperative exchange. This new approach should appeal to a plurality and take account of the multicultural tendencies within Brazilian society: "In the past *cultura popular* (popular culture) was a very closed concept." Dom Fernando would like to open this concept to incorporate the various regional cultures such as those of *Pernambucanos*, *Mineiros*, and *Bahianos* that were homogenized under the heading of *cultura popular*.

Dom Fernando's views help us discern a project to pluralize the Brazilian Catholic Church in order to make it more palatable to the state and a range of potential worshippers. With the withdrawal of the Church from politics, the popular Church has been fundamentally reconfigured. In the new ecclesiastical framework, the liberationist movement becomes just one increasingly depoliticized faction. Once charged by academic observers with the task of transforming Brazilian society morally and socially and democratizing the Catholic Church from the bottom up, the popular Church has been emptied of its militancy in the institutional politics of both Church and state. This has clarified the relationship between CEBs and social movements, asserting the religious character of the Ecclesiastical Base Communities (CEBs). Thirty years after the rise of Eder Sader's ideal actor (see chapter 1), the separation between Church and secular political forces has been (almost) completed. While many liberationists would reject this sketch of ecclesiastical changes, it is difficult to overlook that there has been a gentle but palpable purge of *basista* ideas. Recast in such a pluralizing ecclesiastical context, unsympathetic to *basista* tendencies, liberationist activism takes on an entirely new role. Liberationism has become something like a project at work in civil society, forming values and inspiring religious visions of social justice rather than engaging directly in political struggle. This new role is significantly shaped by the new evangelization project and its emphasis on enculturation[7] (Vásquez 1998, 248; Gill 1998).

In theory at least, enculturation defuses the tension introduced by the vanguardist *basismo* (see chapter 2), which positioned well-trained elite militants above the alienated, uneducated masses. The hierarchical mode of communication introduced by vanguardist *basismo* has been replaced by a conversational mode based on mutual exchange and understanding of equal parties.[8] With this, the *basista* attempt to turn the masses into social agents has given way to a preoccupation with spiritual guidance. From this viewpoint, politically neutral liberationists are henceforth able to concentrate on community development activities and promoting democratic values at the local level. At least in this sense, Vásquez's prescriptions have become reality: CEBs will no longer be "placed in the role of having to awaken an alienated, resigned, oppressed class, and thus will not have to resort to elitist condemnations of popular culture and religiosity" (1998, 267).

Being nudged out of the Church, Catholic activists intent on pursuing an overt political mobilization of the grass roots are increasingly forced to anchor their projects in the secular realm.[9] Yet, according to Hochstetler, this realm too has changed dramatically since 1985. Before 1985 grass roots–based social movements, deeply suspicious of any dealings with the state, sought to construct autonomous centers of governance. After 1985 activists formed part of state-focused political parties, pressure groups, or NGOs integrated in global communication networks (Hochstetler 2000). If this reading of a new Brazilian democratic politics is correct, the space available for radical liberationist activists with a commitment to grass-roots mobilization has diminished in the secular realm as well as in the Church. While movements such as the MST might still follow a method reminiscent of the struggle of the 1970s, an era of liberationist militancy seems to have drawn to a close. What then is the role of liberationists within this new political and ecclesiastical context?

PLURALIZED FAITH

> There is only one Church. Besides, it is questionable if the label progressive makes much sense today, as the contemporary progressives tend to react quite often against new currents.
>
> Dom Fernando Antônio Figueiredo, 8 April 2000

At the beginning of the new millennium, the symbolic universe that underpins Catholic religious practice in São Paulo, once steeped in images inspired by liberation theology, is taking on a distinctly different shape. In a recent article Manuel Vásquez comments, "In Catholic circles today, one is more likely to hear references to a new evangelization, a new civilization of love, and enculturation than to liberation, the struggle (*a luta*) or the path (*caminhada*) toward the kingdom of God" (Vásquez 1999, 3). Clearly this new symbolic framework has been strongly shaped by the new evangelization campaign, promoting an embrace of the Charismatics and a more effervescent form of worship. Suppressed during the administration of Dom Paulo Evaristo Arns (1970–1998), the Charismatic movement has turned into a major force within the new evangelization. Drawing on the euphoric style and method of neo-Pentecostalist churches, the Charismatics, publicly represented by Pe. Marcelo, have launched a very competitive televised product (Chesnut 1998). Media presence, merchandising, and the entrepreneurial style of individuals such as Pe. Marcelo have turned the Charismatics into a well-established and extremely popular element of the local Catholic Church.[10]

While the Paulistano hierarchy has thus succeeded in broadening the range of Catholic religious products available in São Paulo, this pluralization has also forced open a hitherto close-knit symbolic fabric. Clearly the recommissioning of Paulistano prelates such as Dom Angélico Sándalo Bernardino and the retirement of Dom Paulo Evaristo Arns, personalities whose names were synonymous with the liberationist struggle, facilitated this symbolic opening.[11] As a result, the liberationist project has been left without a distinct symbolic backdrop endorsed by and embodied in the local hierarchy. Furthermore, a new generation of liberationists has had to readjust liberationism to the social and cultural specificities of democratic Brazil.

In the Brasilândia region, the readjustment was placed in the hands of Father Konrado, a committed liberationist of German descent who has been working at the grass roots for twenty-five years. During an interview in August 2000, Pe. Konrado conveyed a glimpse of the envisaged changes and continuities that might shape the liberationist symbolic universe under his administration.[12] Committed to continuing the work of Dom Angélico, Pe. Konrado has been looking for a way to make the liberationist project more viable. Thirty years of liberationist activism in the region have saturated local culture with liberationist themes.

Concepts like the people, the struggle, authenticity, and popular culture as well as narratives of liberation have become part of the underlying, taken-for-granted cultural fabric of the neighborhoods: Whereas for Pe. Konrado the concept of the people still points at the poor periphery, he readily concedes that the concept has lost its radical meaning. Today, he explains, the concept of the people signals an opposition between organized associations and disorganized, anomic groups. For liberationists, Pe. Konrado claims, the people of God still are the bearers of the Light of Faith (*Luz da Fé*). The poor who have become agents of liberation are those who live Christian faith most authentically. Although this concept is currently being challenged, he thinks it is still valid. The problem remains how this agent can be mobilized, how the concept can be made to work. This question is especially pertinent at a time when the poor are seeking individual salvation in Pentecostal temples. For Pe. Konrado, mobilization is still possible, but only when the agents are faced with direct conflict and opposition. The struggle, Pe. Konrado agrees with Dom Fernando, had suffered a similar conceptual degeneration: "Today everything is *luta*. Today, *luta* is simply the struggle for daily survival." Authenticity, however, he thinks, was never a particularly important concept. Yet, he immediately revises this statement when defining popular culture. "Popular culture is trying to revive itself, but there is no longer a homogeneous [authentic?] popular culture."

Pe. Konrado is reluctant to read the symbolic dissolution of liberationist core images that come to the fore in the above interview in terms of a profound crisis. He prefers to frame the problem in terms of "a time during which old weapons have become blunt, have lost their bite." Nevertheless, his answers reveal an awareness that Brazil's pluralizing democratic culture at the turn of the millennium calls for a different liberationist response. To date, such a response has been but cursory indeed.

Given the current directive of the hierarchy to separate politics and faith and to tie Catholic communities closer to episcopal centers, strategies to harness grass-roots participation through the politicization of everyday life appear unlikely options. And while the success of the Charismatic model and its centrality to the new evangelization provide an obvious point of departure in the search for a new response, such an approach carries the risk that social problems will be increasingly solved or dissolved by way of mystifying ritual. Clearly, this would undermine the very core of the liberationist project.

How, then, can the liberationist project be transformed into a depoliticized but highly relevant movement without discarding any of its core assumptions? To me it looked as if Pe. Konrado was in serious trouble and would have preferred to look for a way to alter the context, to recreate instances of direct confrontation, in order to successfully redeploy liberationist conceptual tools. However, by ruling out the possibility of greater autonomy at the grass roots, the hierarchy has essentially truncated the liberationist movement's ability to recreate itself without significantly changing its character. Given these rather limited choices, liberationists such as Pe. Konrado have looked toward the successful mobilization efforts of the Charismatics for inspiration. Currently, a synthesis with the Charismatic movement—a movement that tends to divert authority away from the Church hierarchy by promoting a truth located in an unmediated Holy Spirit rather than a silent God whose will must be interpreted by the Church (Lehmann 1996, 42)—is at least contemplated.

For liberationists, the current pluralization of the Catholic doctrine in São Paulo creates a need for resolution and the construction of a new overarching synthesis potentially grounding the liberationist doctrine. "Religion needs interpretation," Pe. Konrado claims, "and Brazilian Catholicism suffers from a lack of interpretation." This statement hones in on an unresolved debate initiated by a Charismatic return to pre–Vatican II rituals and spirituality: while the progressives would like to interpret salvation in communal terms, conservatives hold on to an individualistic interpretation. For Pe. Konrado, lack of episcopal resolve in this debate gives rise to an untenable subjectivism and seems to stand in the way of a more lasting synthesis between the progressives and the Charismatic movement. However, according to Pe. Konrado, such a synthesis cannot be found in a return to a more mystical reading of the Bible. Clearly, as the case of the Charismatics demonstrates, an individualistic mystifying salvation carries much greater mobilizing capacity among Brazil's popular classes than the communal and more rationalistic approach (Mariz 1994) of the liberationists. Yet for liberationists, communal salvation forms the unshakeable foundation of a theology that associates religious salvation with a communal political participation in a movement toward a more just society. A move toward an individualistic eschatological project would, at least in theory, undermine the very basis of liberationism's this-worldly religious-political endeavor. While there can be no talk of resolving the profound differences that divide the two movements, cooperation is possible at the project level. The Charismatics in Santo Amaro, for instance, have initiated a number of popular education projects reminiscent of liberationist consciousness raising. Liberationists, at the same time, are at least talking about their failure to incorporate into their pastoral practice the latent popular yearnings for miracles.

INSTITUTIONAL RESTRUCTURING

As Gill (1998) points out, institutional restructuring forms a core strategy of the institutional Church to counter the Pentecostal encroachment. Much of the restructuring currently under way is geared toward reorganizing Church religious and social services in order to invest scarce resources more efficiently and to clear the way for a successful collaboration with the state, with NGOs, or with private-sector agencies (Gill 1998).

In the Brasilândia region, the departure of a well-established liberationist hierarchy has inspired a new generation of liberationists to question intensively the existing structures. Managerial discourse prevalent in contemporary NGOs and governmental social agencies is central to this review process. Terms such as *community ownership of projects* and *quantifiable outcomes* occupy a central place in the discourse of Pe. Konrado. He would like to hand responsibility and accountability back to communities and to encourage the construction of joint ventures (*parcerias*) with government agencies and NGOs. Achieving such goals means professionalizing services and phasing out projects or services that do not correspond to local needs.

With the departure of the old liberationist guard, Pe. Konrado claims, the structures that had emerged under their tutelage began to show their weaknesses. Whereas old-style personalist leadership structures of the previous liberationist administration fostered inefficient and unfocused initiatives, today communities need to take much more responsibility for their own activities. This, he believes, is a thoroughly positive feature. "For many community leaders or pastoral workers things have become harder and that is good. It demonstrates more clearly that their work is not directly related to the needs of the region." Pe. Konrado gave the example of the *pastorais* (pastoral services). According to Pe. Konrado, many of the services provided by the *pastorais* overlap, and some of them, such as the woman's pastoral (*pastoral da mulher*), do not correspond to local needs. For Pe. Konrado, this is evident when women make only very limited use of the service provided. Serious rethinking was necessary.

The introduction of a more rational approach to community management seems to stand in opposition to Pe. Konrado's commitment to democratic procedures within the diocese, where communities decide together how they want to interpret CNBB directives. However, this commitment to communal decisionmaking underlines the significantly weaker position of the much less personalist liberationist leadership of the Brasilândia diocese. Further, Dom Angélico's departure means that local communities are no longer shielded from the hostilities of Church politics (Hewitt 1998, 183). This arises not just from Pe. Konrado's liberationist ideals, but from necessity. As personalist liberationist leadership from bishops like Dom Angélico is no longer available in Brasilândia, local progressive communities have to negotiate and cooperate among themselves to achieve strategic goals. At the same time, however, the opportunity for experimentation is set by the episcopal hierarchy. For instance, the feminist experiments outlined in chapter 6 enjoyed the passive support of Dom Angélico, even though this support was limited, given Dom Angélico's reluctance to commit resources to projects that targeted only women (Drogus 1999, 43). Yet in the Brasilândia region, Catholic feminist initiatives were possible mainly because of Dom Angélico's willingness to afford institutional space to new forms of mobilization. Without such mediation by the diocesan leader, CNBB directives to bring Catholic feminist ventures into line appear to have had much greater impact on the ground. For instance, Julie pointed out (see chapter 6) that her feminist activities are possible mainly because they remain within the relative privacy of the *bairros* and out of sight of the episcopal hierarchy. Ironically, while the popular Church was charged with a renovation and decentralization of power within the universal Church, initiatives rebuilding the liberationist project depend on institutional space afforded by a strong liberationist episcopacy.[13] The absence of such leadership may limit the movement's creativity and inspiration and with it its ability to renovate itself and to maintain its social and cultural relevance.

CHANGING FUNDING PATTERNS

A parceria é um caminho mais racional para a filantropia

A joint venture is a more rational approach to philanthropy

Dom Fernando Antônio Figueiredo, 8 April 2000

The withdrawal of the Catholic Church from the political realm during the 1990s has spelled important changes to the nature of liberationist activism. In regions of São Paulo that were no longer under the authority of the liberationist archdiocese after 1989, these changes took hold almost a decade before they were felt in the Brasilândia region. In such regions, observers have commented on a secularization and professionalization of movement support structures (Lehmann 1996, 92; Assies 1999). While in Brasilândia, movements were still able to draw on a support network consisting of Church-affiliated entities and activists (see chapters 4 and 5); in other regions, this support structure took on an increasingly secular character as militant religious people left the Church in order to continue their activism in NGOs (Lehmann 1996, 92). According to Assies, formation of the movement's leadership strategy development was left increasingly in the hands of NGO professionals and middle-class consultants (1999, 218–23).

Assies alerts us to the fact that such changes are by no means neutral and may lead to a profound reconfiguration of the relationship between the state and civil society. In fact, Assies argues that democratization and neoliberal policies have in some cases caused the breakdown of enfeebled interclass alliances as middle-class movement consultants become dependent on state finance. Drawing on a Chilean case study recorded by Veronica Schild, Assies claims, "Under the new constellation, feminist professionals have increasingly become involved in the implementation of social programs, whereas poor and working-class women tend to be marginalized and turned into clients of those programs" (1999, 223). Hence, the clearing away of *basista* obstacles for a successful collaboration with state, NGO, or private-sector agencies tends to remove popular control over local initiatives. The secularization and professionalization of movement support infrastructure in regions hitherto dominated by liberationist ideas may inadvertently lead to a disenfranchising of communities.

In Brasilândia, this secularization process has not been as profound as the one depicted by Assies. Leadership training is still carried out by the local clergy (Levy 2000). Nevertheless, changes in the nature of project funding have taken their toll and altered the nature of projects. Project sponsorship underwent significant changes over the past two decades. Consequently, liberationist initiatives once principally funded by Catholic associations in Europe, the United States, and Canada have come to rely increasingly on financial support from the municipal government and, more recently, on funding from NGOs and private-sector charitable organizations. Until 1986, according to Levy, liberationist projects in the Brasilândia region received support from foreign charities. This gradually diminished, coming to a halt in the 1990s (2000, 176). Subsequently, local community organizers sought funding and resources from the municipality, which the PT governed during the early 1990s. With the election of the conservative governments of Paulo Maluf (1993–1996; the *Partido Progressista Brasileiro*, Brazilian Progressive Party or PPB) and Celsor Pitta (1997–2000; the *Partido Trabalhista Nacional*, National Workers Party or PTN), most of the financial commitments of the city administration were drastically curtailed. As a result, local community development projects entered a severe funding crisis, and project administrators were feverishly trying to establish links with new funding bodies. During the second half of the 1990s, despite substantial efforts, the fruits of this endeavor were meager, and some priests were forced to shut down their programs. In fact, the funding crisis was somewhat aggravated by the fact that the financial administration of dioceses had been centralized, and individual dioceses had less control over their own finances. In August 2000, Pe. Konrado mentioned that project funding continues to pose grave problems and that available resources were just enough to sustain the current level of activities.

During my last visit to the Brasilândia region in August 2000, I encountered two notable exceptions to the funding crisis. One was a project emerging from the workshop in Jd. Recanto (see chapter 5) that had reduced its dependence on the local Church; the other was designed by Pe. Pedro. These projects were able to establish joint ventures involving NGO or private-sector funding. Both proposals carried a strong vocational flavor, focusing on employment generation and training for local youth. Entrepreneurial in character, the projects align well with funding criteria currently prevalent in NGOs and private-sector charitable organizations. Both referred to major local needs, and vacancies in both projects are highly sought after and waiting lists are long, especially for Pe. Pedro's communication course. The Jd. Recanto initiative is based on a successful niche-marketing approach and establishes a space in which local young people can acquire skills in a safe environment. Pe. Pedro's vocational training course proposes to introduce students to the principles of communication and tries to integrate local youth into the job market by offering training and traineeship opportunities. Although both projects feature

political education and leadership training elements, their political and cate-
chetical content is left implicit. Hence, in both projects a vocational training
component comes first, and any political or religious consciousness raising is
secondary.

With this, liberationist community activism in Brasilândia has taken a
course reminiscent of the more overtly enculturation-focused approach of the
charismatic diocese of Santo Amaro.[14] This approach offers social services to
the needy, while focusing on the development of popular spirituality under
the aegis of the Church. For example, during our meeting Dom Fernando
pointed out that, alongside more traditional charity-oriented projects, the diocese placed great emphasis on education and vocational training programs,
such as computer education, graphic design, mechanical training, bread and
pastry-making workshops, and telecommunications courses.[15] Moreover, according to the bishop, all of these courses enjoyed the support of NGOs or
government organizations such as *Instituto de Estudos de Apoio Comunitário*
(Institute for Communitarian Assistance Studies, IBEAC) and *Servício Brasileiro
de Apoio às Micro e Pequenas Empresas* (Brazilian Assistance Service to Micro and
Small Business, SEBRAE). For Dom Fernando, cooperation with NGOs enabled the Charismatic Church to contribute to the betterment of the situation
of the masses (*o povo*), a term that stands within the Charismatic Movement
for the masses of the unhappy—the unemployed, excluded, and downtrodden.
Driven by their unhappiness as well as by a hunger for existence and a hunger
for God, the masses would arrive at the most fulfilling of all mysteries: the
love of God. For Dom Fernando, the Church is there to help them reach that
destination.

Community development programs, like those to which Dom Fernando
refers, respond to the enormous needs of a population starved of social services. Still, the question arises whether liberationist objectives are not lost in the
preoccupation with a new evangelization that seeks to give a Catholic inflec-
tion to highly individualistic and ritualistic popular spirituality—enculturation.
To be sure, the leadership-enhancing liberationist projects in the Brasilândia
region detailed in this chapter continue to have features that foster greater
civic dispositions and contribute to a strengthening of civil society. Moreover,
as Pe. Konrado and liberationist colleagues reluctantly admit, faith has a political dimension even in Santo Amaro, a diocese they otherwise charge with
the recasting of social questions in terms encouraging a search for individual

solutions in the ritual experience of unity with God. Liberationists have had to concede that their popular church overlooked the themes and movements in popular religion to which the Charismatics so successfully respond (Nagle 1997, 159). Whereas this response to people's latent mystical desires has not been ideal, Pe. Konrado claims, the success of the Charismatic venture has demonstrated to liberationists the mobilizing power of a sanitized, hyper-emotional, individual relationship with God, turned into a media spectacle.

Institutional restructuring in the form of combining pastoral projects, together with a weakening of liberationist leadership at the episcopal level, has brought institutional pressure to bear on local communities. This in conjunction with recent shifts in program finance has altered the character of newly emerging liberationist projects. Inasmuch as institutional interests and current funding guidelines preclude a politicization of issues relevant to *bairro* communities, the options available to reinvigorate an ailing liberationist movement are limited. Within this new configuration, liberationist activists are likely to turn into community development agents focusing on vocational issues. This dilution of liberationism within the Paulistano Catholic Church raises questions about the future of Brazilian democracy. Liberationism provided the moral focal point for secular oppositional politics during much of the previous two decades (Serbin 2000a, 150; Hochstetler 2000), so it is difficult to underestimate the importance of the decline of the liberationist symbolic universe. Will another master frame, as Hochstetler (2000) calls it, arise in democratic Brazilian oppositional politics? Will new forms of liberationism, relatively free of ecclesiastical control, emerge? Alternatively, are we seeing already the politics of postmodernity, in which cultural fragmentation leads to a politics of diversion, a politics of the spectacle, where constant pluralization dissolves alliances, and political agendas give way to sensationalist and entertaining slogans? The latter seems just as likely a scenario as a consolidation of an oppositional political force including and representing the interests of client groups from a silent and poor majority.

SECULAR CONTINUITY

There can be little doubt that throughout Latin America the popular Church is facing a profound crisis. Commentators have pointed to the lack of resonance with the expressed needs and aspirations of the popular classes that seems to undermine liberationist mobilization attempts of the 1990s (Lehmann 1996; Berryman 1996; Nagle 1997; Vasquez 1998; Drogus 1997; Gomes 1999, 64). Analyses of this crisis encompass a wide range of issues, but default into two basic positions: (1) liberationist symbols ceased to adequately depict reality due to the fundamental incorrigible flaw that they were time-bound to the political and economic realities of the 1970s and early 1980s; (2) liberationist symbols have lost their mobilizing capacity due to hierarchical pressure for discretion and, within the movement, dogmatism and a penchant for excluding segments of the population (see chapter 4 or Burdick 1993). In the light of much evidence for both of these positions, the question must be asked: Does the liberationist imagery still enjoy any purchase at all at the Brazilian grass roots?

Most analysts are skeptical. For Vásquez, lack of resonance stems from popular disenchantment with the teleological view of history at the core of liberationism. When, after thirty years of exhaustive struggle, the people find themselves not an inch closer to a this-worldly realization of God's Kingdom on earth and are hardly able to keep abject poverty at bay, the very promise of liberation theology has lost its credibility (Vásquez 1998, 125). Berryman puts forward a similar argument, but adds factors such as the end of a heroic era that fueled popular enthusiasm for the struggle (Berryman 1996). Nagle frames this disenchantment in terms of an undue politicization, which erased the boundaries between secular and sacred at the expense of mystery, ritual, and history that is central to popular religiosity (Nagle 1997, 116, 159). Lehmann, however, argues that the crisis stems from a dogmatic adherence to a masculinist discourse that emerged during the 1970s, a time of direct confrontations between the nascent union struggle and the military regime. Thirty years later, and deploying a discourse that is only marginally altered, the liberationist clergy is attempting to mobilize women, predominantly, in a pluralistic democratic environment in which direct clashes have become rare (Lehmann 1996, 114). Hence, liberationists have not been able to adapt their project and methods to the changing political reality of postdictatorial Brazil.[16]

These claims ring true with the case studies presented in previous chapters. In the neighborhoods, albeit at different points during the liberationist movement cycle, factors such as satisfaction of material demands, institutional pressures, disappointment with the broken promise of liberation theology, a dogmatic clinging to a masculinist *obreirismo*,[17] cycles of urban violence, the funding crisis of liberationist projects, the fragmentation and disarticulation of the Left in the face of neoliberalism, the changing nature of conflicts, and the melting of liberationist concepts into everyday language all play a decisive role. Given this array of factors detrimental to the viability of liberationist endeavors, avenues for successful revitalization seem limited. While chapter 6 offers a glimpse of a novel possible liberationist synthesis, the case study does not tell us much about the actual mobilizing power of reframed liberationist images.

In order to test and reveal the degree to which liberationist symbols still manage to capture the imagination of people, I propose an excursion into contemporary popular youth culture. A focus on secular associations will allow us to gauge the impact of a liberationist imaginary on contemporary politics, culture, and civil society. Moreover, such a focus will reveal that liberationist weapons, seemingly blunt in the Brasilândia region, still cut deep in popular culture. After three decades of consciousness raising, many of the features of critical popular Catholicism have been taken on board by a variety of secular movements and groups, lending unimagined and generally missed continuity to liberationist thought. Many of the concepts intrinsic to liberation theology have been privatized and cast off from Church moorings and control. To render visible the transfer of liberationist concepts into popular culture and to highlight the role of these concepts within a different context, the following section ventures into the world of rap and hip-hop in São Paulo.

My first close contact with Paulistano rap occurred during fieldwork in 1996. Over the course of several months, it became increasingly obvious that attributes of global hip-hop culture concealed a distinctly local framework of meaning. Two years later I found the opportunity to explore these local elements in greater depth. The case of Paulistano hip-hop is particularly interesting, as it reveals the heritage of three decades of progressive Catholic Church–inspired politics as well as a secularization of liberationist thought. In fact, São Paulo's hip-hop culture contains a multitude of re-elaborated popular religious symbols and modes of collective action used during the decades of liberationist mobilization.

In the United States, hip-hop is often mythologized in terms of a distant ancestral past involving the Griot, a gifted storyteller in African societies. The evocation of this myth of origin helps to turn rappers into an authentic political force in the African Diaspora. Hip-hop turns into the political voice of African Americans stranded at the urban rust belt, abandoned by a postindustrial society (Rose 1994).[18] Endowed with an African-American identity, rap is turned into a spectacle of identity politics whose essentialist message tends to expel and alienate a wide range of other ethnicities (Flores 1994).[19]

In Brazil, however, Afro-Brazilian identity politics runs along very different lines (Herschmann 2000). Differing from the U.S. version, Brazilian hip-hop has race, ethnicity, and color in subordinate roles (Herschmann 2000, 68, 185).[20] In fact, the theme of ethnicity enters Brazilian hip-hop through the back door, forming an almost incidentally black subject: the *mano* (homeboy). This *mano* is primarily a resident of the urban periphery. Inasmuch as he is constructed within a *basista* tradition that espouses a simplistic Marxist structuralist analysis, he is a struggling victim of the system. Hence, the theme of a black community's refusal to integrate into white society, a theme that still holds some currency within U.S. hip-hop, is expressed predominantly in terms of a refusal to abide by the rules of the capitalist system. The following ideological statement, taken from a rap by Racionais, probably São Paulo's most famous rap band, clearly demonstrates this color nonspecific, antisystemic sentiment: *"Seu comercial de TV não me engana. Eu não preciso de status nem fama. Seu carro e sua grana já não me seduz . . . e nem a sua puta de olhos azuis. Eu sou apenas um rapaz latino americano apoiado por mais de 50.000 mano. Efeito colateral que o seu sitema fez."*[21]

The statement hints at a number of religious currents within contemporary Paulistano rap and hip-hop: a politicization of a purity rooted in glorified poverty—a central theme in popular Catholicism (Levy 2000)—strong *basista* sentiments, anticonsumerism, a rejection of the aesthetics of the rich Brazil, and a structuralist anticapitalism mirroring the stance of radical liberationists during the 1970s and 1980s.

These traces gain clarity in other modes of hip-hop expression. Lyrics, stage decoration, and album covers frequently refer to popular religious symbols fused with the core concepts of hip-hop. In this syncretic collage, religious symbols are often used to express the purity at the heart of hip-hop. The Racionais MCs (Masters of Ceremony) are particularly prone to this kind of symbolization. For instance, the entire cover of their CD *Sobrevidendo no Inferno* (1997) is a reference to the Bible. *"Refrigere minha alma e guia-me pelo caminho da justiça"* (Psalm 23: 3)[22] reads the front cover, and *"e mesmo que eu ande no Vale da sombra e da morte não temerei mal algum porque tu estás comigo"* (Psalm 23: 4)[23] is on the back cover. Such references recur throughout the lyrics, where

God endows the *mano* with the strength to lead a righteous life.[24] In public, the MCs assume the role of the soldiers of the periphery, the high priests of a sword-wielding brotherhood, calling for a crusade against the senseless violence generated by the system of a morally bankrupt Brazil, the system of the *playboyzinhos*. Hence, while on the surface such themes echo rap lyrics written by U.S. artists, it is hard to overlook that in São Paulo hip-hop contains a distinctly religious flavor with clear references to the symbolic universe of the progressive Catholic Church.

The success of this prophetic strategy is reflected in commercial figures. The Racionais are the top selling hip-hop band in Brazil. In 1997 their CD *Sobrevivendo no Inferno* sold approximately 200,000 copies during the first month of its release and a further 300,000 copies over the course of the following three months—without the clout of multinational advertising.[25] Over the past two years, the group's popularity has escalated. An MTV award nomination in 1998 and exposure to European and U.S. hip-hop markets contribute to the group's becoming a national hip-hop icon. As such, the Racionais are the focal point of the Paulistano rap and hip-hop scene.

Commercial success, prophetic stance, and *basista* tendencies transformed the Racionais into the voice of the voiceless adolescents of the urban periphery. Moreover, their articulation of culture and politics turned them into the precursor of a new politics. During the 1990s, the concept of cultural politics enjoyed increasing popularity within PT circles, and hip-hop was seen as a new medium to mobilize Brazil's politically passive youth. As a result, hip-hop bands were asked to perform at PT election events throughout the second half of the 1990s. Such a request, for example, led the Racionais to play a highly visible role in the mayoral election campaign of Luiza Erundina in 1996 and in the presidential election campaign of Lula (Ignácio da Silva) in 1998. In São Paulo, this growing political interest in hip-hop produced several joint ventures with local politicians. For instance, for Vincente Cândido, member of São Paulo's municipal council,[26] rap is a way to renew an old disintegrating Left. "Culture," he claims, "is the new pillar that will constitute a new way of organization. It is that pillar so far neglected by the PT. Culture and in particular youth culture has the power to organize the masses and to lift the image of the PT, turning the party into a party of the people again. Cultural politics is the politics of the future, if the Left wants to survive," he explains.

The rise of Brazilian hip-hop at a juncture of old and new Brazilian politics signals the crisis of a political paradigm. The late 1980s laid bare the fragmentation of a left reliant on trade unions, the progressive Catholic Church, and social movements. With the retreat of the Catholic Church from politics, the evisceration of unions, and the decline of social movements, the Brazilian political constellation changed dramatically. Not only had the left lost the moral support of a Church that had provided the focal point of its political agenda, but it also faced a crumbling of the constituencies it claimed to represent. Increasingly, the *basista* tendencies within the PT came under pressure by educated technocrats and civil servants. Faced with the rise of elite politics within their party, PT representatives committed to grass-roots politics feverishly searched for a new constituency—and, in Vincente Cândidos's case, found it in the hip-hop movement.

Brazilian hip-hop fuses the legacy of several decades of radical and often messianic local popular politics with the prophecy of an African-American Diaspora celebrating the coming of a new black nation and transforms it into a commercially successful spectacle. This spectacle retains some older authenticity claims propagated by the CEB-inspired social movements two decades earlier; authenticity claims rooted in the purity of underclass poverty and spiritually prescribed antimaterialism. In this sense, Brazilian hip-hop lends continuity to a theme propagated by liberationists during the 1970s and 1980s, a theme increasingly under pressure within a new political environment hostile to *basistas*. By politicizing the systemic exclusion of a poor underclass, the Racionais MCs rehearse the *grito dos excluidos* and invoke a direct clash with the establishment. Curiously, while this continuity of liberationist-inspired direct confrontation is extremely relevant to thousands of young people at the periphery, advocates of a new pluralistic Brazilian politics, such as Herschmann (2000) prefer to ignore it.

The endeavor of Brazilian hip-hop, admittedly simplistic and populist in many ways, nonetheless conveys the fact that a reframed, liberationist-inspired prophecy still manages to mobilize people.[27] When symbols are presented as fixed, they die, metaphors worn out by time. The popularity of the deeply moralistic stance of the Racionais, predicated on a structuralist critique and identity politics synthesized with contemporary popular youth culture, clearly illustrates that such a reframing is possible given enough interpretative freedom. The success of the Racionais expresses the fundamental need for reinterpretation and revitalization of liberationist symbols and narratives. However, liberationists do not necessarily see things this way. Pe. Konrado realizes the need to present the liberationist doctrine in new contexts, but he does not envisage any modifications of the doctrine per se, and it would be very difficult to do so, given the institutional pressures on him. When liberationists note that the core concepts of their doctrine have exhausted their signifying capacity, they are speaking in the restrictive institutional context that inhibits the revitalization of liberationist symbols within the Church. Hence, although invited to join a pluralistic front against a prolific neo-Pentecostalism, the popular Church has been asked to transform itself fundamentally by leaving its old-fashioned *basismo* behind.

LIBERATIONISM AT THE CROSSROADS

What would become of the liberationist movement if it were to extinguish the *basismo* at its core? Liberationists such as Pe. Konrado seem lost for words. While it is too early to answer this question conclusively, the interviews reported above seem to indicate that the liberationist movement will play a subordinate role relative to the politics of pluralization of Church and state in the future. Current attempts to find common ground with the Charismatics have led to cautious exchanges. Given current directives to separate politics and faith, it seems unlikely that a future incorporation of Charismatic ritual life in liberationist base communities will result in a new politicization of the life of the popular classes. And more recent examples of joint ventures with NGOs, state agencies, and private-sector actors in the Brasilândia region seem to indicate that only an attenuated liberationism, focusing on politically neutral community-development work, will survive, at least in so far as liberationism is bound to the Catholic Church.

Liberationists committed to political mobilization are being dislodged from Church structures and seek to lend continuity to their projects in the secular realm. However, here too *basista* ventures, to the extent that they are aimed toward empowering the popular classes, are viewed by politicians and academic observers—even former liberationist activists—as a thing of the past. Whereas the liberationist agenda of the 1980s and 1990s still informs the political aims of the NGOs and secular movements observed by Hochstetler (2000), the popular classes have turned into clients of well-educated and well-connected middle-class NGO professionals. While these professionals may still refer to the moral economy shaped by *basista* liberationism, such references are increasingly rhetorical in character. At least in the cases stated by Assies (1999), the decline of *basista* ideals seems to usher in a return to representative clientelism, where popular interests are mediated by middle-class professionals well versed in *basista* rhetoric. Liberationism emptied of its radical propositions has become the moral backdrop of a new oppositional elite politics, a politics of pluralistic debate conducted exclusively within institutional boundaries.

In this new political scenario, liberation theology–inspired movements such as the MST that radically question Brazilian society, culture, and politics are historical fossils. Although widely endorsed by the public, such movements, refusing to insert themselves into institutional politics, symbolize a mode of action associated with a bygone political era. Increasingly it seems to be the case that a radical politicization of the rift dividing popular from affluent Brazil conjures up an association with a predemocratic political climate in which popular opinion had to be expressed outside state boundaries. The protagonists of a new Brazilian politics contend that with Brazil's return to democracy, this is no longer the case, and that democratic structures are now strong enough to serve as forums capable of mediating such differences. Ironically, the case of Brazilian hip-hop suggests that this opinion is not necessarily shared by a new disenfranchised generation that grows up in popular neighborhoods at the urban periphery. Paulistano hip-hop-fan communities hang on to a liberationism that has become the underlying taken-for-granted cultural fabric in many a *bairro* at the periphery. Hip-hop militants revitalize a liberationist mode of action that has become part of the repertoire of secular popular dissent.

Yet the case of hip-hop also points at another trend in Brazilian politics: a postmodern current gravitating toward a politics of diversion or, as some would see it, a ludic antipolitics. For hip-hop activists, radical politics is as much a marketing tool as the economy of the spectacle offers the means to broadcast the hip-hop prophecy. This close association between fan communities and market forces makes for a fairly fluid and ephemeral mix. When popular dissent is staged and performed by new, culturally hybrid movements that attach liberationist images and messages to new cultural commodities, political content dances in tune with fashion. Joint ventures rapidly unravel when markets move, the mood shifts, and popular taste embraces a new fad.

These ever-more pluralizing and precariously ephemeral political formations seem ill suited to serve as vehicles carrying a project for long-term structural change through the struggle for a more just society. Their pluralizing forces are likely to propel them to a point where aims and aspirations are dissolved in a music industry–driven movement of popular music, a politically empty vessel. Nonetheless, in Brazil spectacle politics, with its often frivolous and populist connotations, forms part of a new political constellation predicated on the consciousness-raising campaigns of liberationist activists during the 1970s and 1980s.

In the liberationist *bairros* of Brasilândia, *basista* projects, such as the feminist movement (see chapter 6), have suffered significant setbacks. For one, the radio station, the primary outlet for liberationist messages in the *bairros,* has suspended its broadcasts. As a result, the impact of the Catholic feminists is reduced to the confines of community meetings that attract only a small crowd of courageous women. The difficulties of the feminists are compounded by a thinning of leadership. Plagued by health problems, Julia finds it increasingly difficult to leave her house to make necessary contacts and to carry her project further. Irmã Rachel, one of the more important personalities of the movement in Jd. Recanto, was recalled by her order and left the neighborhoods. These losses, together with the mounting pressure of the CNBB to bring Catholic feminists into line, made the expansion of the movement difficult. Unable to attract a larger following, the gatherings of the Catholic feminists began to fade into the background of new liberationist activities in the *bairros.*

However, within the current pluralistic institutional climate, not yet pluralistic enough to confer space on liberated Catholic women, this fading into the background of institutional politics may safeguard the survival of *basista* liberationism. Their rejection of an overarching religious discourse, a rejection that should not be mistaken for a loss of words, may yet prepare the Church for a truly pluralistic embracing of faith and politics.

APPENDIX: SURVEY DATA

DEMOGRAPHIC DATA

Category	Number	Percentage
People captured by the survey	1,038	100
Households (HH) surveyed	233	8
Women interviewed	151	64.8
Men interviewed	82	35.2
Average age of interviewees	35.89	n.a.
Average years of residency in neighborhood	10.74	n.a.
Male-headed households	145	62.2
Female-headed households	44	18.8
Catholic households	176	75.5
Pentecostal households	33	14.2

ORIGIN

	Number	Percentage
São Paulo	60	25.8
Bahia	47	20.2
Pernambuco	42	18
Cêará	22	9.4
Minas Gerais	21	9
Alagoas	7	3
Paraíba	7	3
Sergipe	3	1.3
Santa Catarina	2	0.9

SOCIOECONOMIC DATA

	Number	Percentage
Formally employed (excluding retired)	124	53.3
Informally employed	93	39.9
Unemployed	11	4.7
Average salary (R$ = 1996)	549.8	—

SOCIOECONOMIC DATA

Category	Number	Percentage
Social Security coverage	147	63.1
Homeowners	176	75.5
Tenants	57	24.5
Car owners	62	26.6
TV owners	219	94
Hi-fi system owners	213	91.4
CD system owners	107	45.9
Phone (or extension) owners	52	22.3
Parabolic antenna owners	21	9
Average household expenditure (R$ = 1996)	240.8	—
Average household debt (R$ = 1996)	74.3	—
Students not attending school	15	6.4

HEALTH AND CRIME DATA

Ill residents (incl. drug abuse)	47	—
Reported violent deaths 1990–1996	8	—
Violent incidents in surveyed HHs	59	25.3

CITIZENSHIP AND CIVIL SOCIETY DATA

Interviewees with knowledge of social movements (SMs)	123	52.8
SM or political party members	19	8.2
Interviewees who could identify some of the historical factors that led to the construction of urban infrastructure (eg., SMs)	141	60.5
Interviewees who thought of SMs as the way to have their opinions represented in politics	66	28.3
Interviewees who consider themselves "citizens"	214	91.8
Interviewees who could explain what they meant by "citizenship"	118	50.6
Interviewees who could name some constitutional rights	87	37.3
Interviewees who could identify their municipal representative (*vereador*)	10	4.3
Interviewees who knew of the "Consumer Codex"	119	51.1
Interviewees who knew of the existence of "Children's Rights"	129	55.4
Interviewees who knew how to access legal aid	112	48.1

VOTING INTENTIONS

Category	Number	Percentage
No opinion	69	29.6
Blank ballot (protest vote)	46	19.7
Erundina (PT in 1996)	65	27.9
Pitta (PMDB, winner of the municipal election in 1996)	15	6.4
People who thought "corrupt" was the term adequately describing Brazilian politics	133	57.1

WOMEN'S RIGHTS

Interviewees who thought women have more rights today	209	89.7
Interviewees who thought this was primarily due to greater personal liberties	137	58.8
Interviewees who thought women had a greater disposable income as a result	179	76.8

GENERAL ATTITUDE AND SELF-REPRESENTATION DATA

Interviewees who consider themselves "poor"	65	27.9
Interviewees who declared they have suffered from hunger	24	10.3

NOTES

CHAPTER 1

1. The local young people often jokingly mention that they live in the *Jardins* (Gardens), a term that usually denotes the leafy inner-city middle-class suburbs.

2. Key concepts referring to the liberationist symbolic universe are italicized at first reference. With the term *popular* that I use frequently throughout this text, I hope to evoke some of the meaning the term has acquired among Brazilian grassroots activists. For neighborhood activists, the term is heavily charged politically and, in the widest sense, stands for *the poor, the working class,* or *the people.* However, the term also evokes an image of the poor as the authentic producers of culture, as the guardians of time-honored traditions—an image that I will explain in greater detail in chapter 2. In this sense, the term functions as an epitaph for the virtues rooted in the poverty of the honest worker.

3. "Webs of meaning" is a term coined by Clifford Geertz (Geertz 1973, 5).

4. My use of the term *subject* is intended to capture the flavor of this discourse on *social movements.* Personally, I would refrain from such a characterization of local residents.

5. Interviews with various Catholic militants in the region revealed that these communities were not necessarily considered CEBs at a local level. In this sense, the label CEB appears to be a concept predominantly used by external observers and the Church hierarchy.

6. Various other studies, such as Teresa Pires de Rio Caldeira's article on "Women, Daily Life and Politics" in São Paulo, confirm this. Caldeira claims that the majority of community leaders in the neighborhoods that she observed between 1981 and 1983 maintained strong links with the Catholic Church (Caldeira 1990, 52).

7. The term "secular Left" may be misleading as even the secular Left often entertained strong links with Catholic radicals.

8. Pedro Jacobi (1993) entertains a different thesis, claiming that the secular Left was extremely important for the emergence of popular movements in the area. The data collected for this volume do not support Jacobi's view. Instead, militants of the progressive Catholic Church played a far more important role, reaching well into the administrative realm of popular movements. The importance of the role played by the secular Left in Jacobi's structural analysis of the local political economy seems not to be warranted.

9. Caldeira's article represents a case in point. She refuses to abide by what she regards as "general categories" (Caldeira 1990, 47). Her deconstruction of general categories is crucial to a fuller understanding of the transformative processes at play in *bairro* politics. However, an undesired side effect of this semantic reelaboration is that the entire symbolic backdrop to the *struggle* of these women has been lost. In Caldeira's account, the political engagement of these women is strangely instrumentalized. Institutions like the progressive Catholic Church and CEBs come into view on almost every page, but their real impact appears to be artificially removed. Concepts impregnated with liberationist symbolic meaning such as *community, the struggle,* and *the people* enter Caldeira's account only reluctantly. Evoked by her interview transcripts, they seem like lost signifiers with no real impact on action, and they lack an important dimension. Purged of its liberationist symbolic content, Caldeira's account of *bairro* politics cannot but depict a *struggle* without (liberationist) mobilization and mobilizers.

10. Much of the liberationist thought was reelaborated by academic observers in terms of a cultural and identity centeredness of new social movements.

11. This is already hinted at by Edison Nunes (1985).

12. Daniel Levine, citing Rowan Ireland's study *Kingdoms Come* (1991), urges us to consider an expansion of "our working notions of 'religion' and 'politics' [that would lead us] well beyond Church, state," and institutions (Levine 1995, 113).

13. It appears to me that Scott Mainwaring, in his work published during the 1980s, used a similar division. While dealing with the Church, he focuses almost exclusively on the political impact of the progressive Church at the expense of religious matters.

14. On religious specificity and popular culture see, for instance, Ortiz (1980, 10–11).

15. Melucci has been interpreting *social movements* as predominantly expressive, symbolic, and prophetic (Assies 1992, 25).

16. Sader claims that the great majority of texts dealing with CEBs has been written by those imbued with the values of communitarianism and who tend to confuse the conditions that "should be" with the conditions that "are."

17. For instance, Eder Sader makes this explicit when he asserts: "But everyday life cannot be thought of as a mythical place where the poor, in their purity, present themselves as they are, free of strange ideologies" (1988, 141). Sader wants to limit the influence of liberationist currents within an analysis of "social movements," an attempt that concurrently removes the religious backdrop of *bairro* politics. Despite these attempts, the people continue to struggle in Sader's account, which is rich in liberationist imagery. While Sader is able to extract the notion of authenticity, he is stuck with much of the language that ties his account inadvertently to the symbolic universe of liberationist Catholicism.

18. Sader (1988, 141) refers to such instances.

19. For Lehmann, *basismo* and the progressive Catholic Church are two overlapping categories.

20. Ton Salman's recent reports of popular culture in Chile evoke this image (Salman 1994a; 1994b; 1996).

21. I am not referring to liberation theology in a wider sense, but to that part of the theology that has been institutionalized. I do, for instance, regard Ivone Gebara's work as strongly influenced by liberation theology. Her interpretation of liberation theology, however, has incurred the rigorous censorship of the Church. In this sense, noninstitutionalized arguments brought forth by liberationist theologians are often silenced by the guardians of the doctrinal faith.

22. The emergence of a new liberationist project bearing many of the features ascribed by Lehmann (1996) to Pentecostalist groups tends to raise questions about his conclusion that the liberationist "struggle for the spirit" has come to an end. In the light of the reelaboration of liberationist thought (chapter 6), I posit that, contrary to Lehmann's claim, the liberationist symbolic universe is fluidly evolving and is currently inspiring the construction of new projects.

23. The scope of this work does not allow for an in-depth treatment of Unger's theoretical trajectory. For a treatment of the Catholic background in Unger's work see, for instance, Hittinger (1994). Hittinger's critique of Unger's key concept is definitely relevant for the case of liberation theology and the PT experiment in the municipal administration of São Paulo between 1989 and 1990. Hittinger claims that Unger's practical reason—in a vein *basismo* and liberationism is often charged with—is condemned to remain local in outlook as the concept was not able to give birth to universals.

24. Rorty responds to Unger with prose that is surprisingly enthusiastic for Rorty (Rorty 1991, 177–92).

25. Brasilândia is the contemporary name for this region on the northern fringe of São Paulo. During the 1970s it carried the name Vila Brasilândia.

26. In the *bairros*, the first significant settlement occurred during the mid-1960s.

27. Alba Zaluar, for instance, investigating the structure of violence in a Rio *favela*, found that "because being a very sensitive issue that touches the negative image of the locality, the honor and values of individuals, and their personal physical security the restricted response pattern inhibited the attempted interviews. The discourse obtained in these interviews was always rhetorical, denouncing the government and the world outside . . . ." Individuals often lied in the face of the interviewer who already knew of some of the background of the person (Zaluar 1994, 72). Zaluar further explains that the nature of the data obtained depends on the familiarity of interviewer with the individual and the subject matter. She claims that it is less likely for someone who already has an intricate knowledge of local events and local codes to fall for false information (1994, 73). This last claim by Zaluar does not, however, apply to the present case. Rather, in spite of the fact that most of the quantitative interviews were conducted by local residents, the gathered material is warped by the avowed inability of the interviewers to distinguish unequivocally between true and false responses.

28. A 1991 estimate of the population in Jd. Damasceno mentions 2,600 families (Lajolo 1991).

29. In the mid-1980s, Pedro Jacobi conducted a survey in the area, sampling 200 of 40,000 residents.

30. I am grateful to Márcia Iolanda Juvéncio for her unceasing support and Ana Lucia Ariani and Christiane der Matossian, who carried the project further.

31. I would like to express my deepest gratitude to Cilto Rosembach.

CHAPTER 2

1. In the 1930s, the Brazilian Church hierarchy decided in favor of a conservative reading of ACB advanced by Cardinal Leme. ACB formed part of a strategy aiming at directly influencing the Brazilian elite whose policies were supposed to draw the masses into the Church (Soares 1988, 206; Bruneau 1979, 38). Under Cardinal Leme, the Brazilian Catholic Church embarked on a campaign of Romanizing, Europeanizing, and mobilizing the apostolic Church, taking advantage of the space that sociopolitical organizations offered and encouraging the growth of a social assistentialist network furthering Church education, health, and social welfare (Soares 1988, 219). On a political front, the Brazilian hierarchy continued its conservative struggle against socialism, Protestants, masons, spiritists, and communists well into the 1970s (Benedetti 1988, 90). On an institutional level, the Church successfully cooperated with various governments and particularly with Getulio Vargas, and was able to reintroduce Catholicism as Brazil's official religion. Toward the end of the 1950s, however, a far more radical laity increasingly challenged this conservative stance of the Brazilian hierarchy. Much of this radical thought surfaced within the realm of the CEBs as well as CEB-like groups during the 1960s and 1970s.

2. For a theoretical elaboration justifying an analysis of the symbolic universe of the 1960s in order to make sense of the 1990s, see, for instance, Carlo Ginsburg's reading of the Warburg school (1989).

3. David Lehmann points out that the term *the people* constituted an important invocation in Brazilian culture and politics whose meaning was hotly contested. Moreover, Lehmann demonstrates that the quest for the *authentic* traditional ways of *the people* was already present in Mario de Andrade's (1893–1945) search for a national cultural identity during the 1920s and 1930s (Lehmann 1996, 7).

4. This transposition of *the masses* into *the people* in Church discourse bears similarities to a Marxist approach that constructed the categories of a class "in itself" and "for itself." Liberation theology resolved the enigma of how the transition of one category to another was to be achieved by introducing the concept of *authenticity*. By positioning *authenticity* with the popular classes, liberation theology eliminated the problem of tension between the two concepts.

5. In part, this trajectory is already clearly visible around 1910 when Padre (Pe.— Priest) Julio Maria tabled a strategic proposal for the Church to descend to *the people* and engage with the prevalent superstition and suffering of the popular classes

(Bruneau 1979, 38). The nature of this Catholicism has been documented in works of literature such as *Rebellion in the Backlands* by Euclides da Cunha and Ralph Della Cava's (1985) historical analysis of the miracle in Joaseiro (*Milagre em Joaseiro*). Soares, for instance, traces this tradition to a radical split that divided official and popular Catholicism. While official Catholicism was formed by the colonial Church hierarchy, popular Catholicism was in many ways a popular rereading and reinterpretation of official Catholicism (Soares 1988,149). Manuel Vásquez refers to Brazilian traditional folk Catholicism as comprising a blend of pre-Trent (1545–1563) Portuguese Catholicism and native religious beliefs and practices (1998, 103).

6. According to Soares, the notion of popular Catholicism is necessarily empty, and in its most simple definition it denotes all practices outside the realm of official Catholicism. In this sense the term popular Catholicism is not value neutral. The term is predominantly used by the hierarchy and gives a negative image (Soares 1988, 220, n20). With Bruneau, quoting Pedro Ribeiro de Oliveira (1970) who has claimed that "popular Catholicism expresses a direct personal relation between mankind and the sacred, a relationship that evades the control of the Church as an institution" (cf. Bruneau 1979, 42), this negativity receives a strategic character.

7. As Della Cava demonstrates, this mysticism was not reserved for the lower ranks of the Church hierarchy, but was also present among members of the high clergy (Della Cava 1985).

8. This observation, intrinsic to the present volume, is taken from fieldwork interviews with Catholic militants. It coincides with the evidence gathered by other authors such as Soares (1988), Mainwaring (1986b, 132), and Lehmann (1996, 98).

9. For an elaboration of the impact of this developmentalist discourse on Brazil's Communist Party in the late 1950s see, for instance, Löwy (1992, 126). It is important to note that the ISB brought forward a multifaceted body of knowledge that ranged from contributions disenchanted with socialism to a capitalist national developmentalism and to the left populist nationalism promoted by Vieira Pinto who endowed 'the people' with an authentic consciousness (Navarro de Toledo 1998). However, it was Vieira Pinto's trajectory that turned hegemonic within ISEB circles shortly before closure of the institute by right-wing military forces in 1964 (Navarro de Toledo 1998, 129).

10. See de Kadt (1970) for an account of Church MEB connections to the ISEB.

11. During the late 1950s and 1960s, the boundaries between the secular and Catholic Left began to blur, and the new Left became increasingly influenced by the moral message of an emerging progressive Catholicism. For an analysis detailing the old and the new Left in Brazil, see, for instance, Löwy (1992).

12. Catholic Action, the basis of the ACB, emerged under Pius XI in the mid-1920s and was seen as a joint Catholic work with spiritual, apostolic, and social ends. It was largely conceived to fight against the common evils of socialism, the disaggregation of the Church, and the abuses of governments breaking their accords with the Holy See (Soares 1988, 65). After the late 1930s, under the tutelage of Cardinal Leme, the

ACB was turned into an antisocialist mobilization vehicle, aiming at deflating the growing labor struggle.

13. The MCP and, to a certain degree, the MEB movement distinguish themselves through their (supposedly) nonvanguardist stance and their promotion of a nondirective methodology.

14. The notion of *authenticity* in Brazilian Catholicism was also fueled during the 1950s by the arrival of European missionaries, whose social commitment had led them to draw close to the European working class (Riviere D'Arc 1999, 199).

15. Walter Salles's feature film *"Central do Brasil"* (Central Station—1998) celebrates this theme and carries it over into the late 1990s.

16. It is interesting to note that Paulo Freire, famous for his nondirective methodology, adopted this nondirectiveness only after his engagement with young Paulistano student militants during the mid-1960s (Soares 1988, 328).

17. The term *vanguardist* denotes practices of individuals who see themselves as agents of transformation.

18. It is important to remember that the term *secular* may be misleading because, within the university context of the time, Catholic and secular Left groups influenced each other mutually.

19. CPCs were groups who organized art events in popular neighborhoods with the aim of raising the consciousness of the masses by applying Paulo Freire's methodology to the performing and visual arts.

20. UNE, "Cultura Popular: Conceito e Articulação," *Movimento*, no. 4, Julho 1962.

21. Henrique Lima Vaz, a Jesuit priest, most influential in JUC, was famous for his Christian humanist stance (de Kadt 1970).

22. Freire's method distinguishes itself in many ways from the methods advanced by liberation theologists. Above all, Freire did not hold to the "see, judge, act" methodology, later made famous by liberation theologists.

23. I remind the reader that I am using gender explicit language. In this particular case I am trying to allude to the fact that women were not endowed with a specific militant status by the emerging progressive Church.

24. On the topic of ecclesiastical populism see, for instance, Alves (1979) and Romano (1979). Lehmann's (1996) notion of *basismo* serving as a catch-all concept for political groups and movements competing for the representation of *the people* tends to downplay such differences.

25. Chapter 3 will demonstrate how these two conceptualizations of consciousness raising have shaped *bairro* politics.

26. This prompts Lehmann to point out that *basismo* "is the construction of the people by those who do not consider themselves fully of them" (1996, 78).

27. Mainwaring is particularly concerned about the speed of the consciousness-raising process, slowed down by Church agents who insist on the importance of a natural rhythm.

28. Kowarick and Singer (1993) tell the story of the PT administration in São Paulo

which, after its first eighteen months in office, dropped much of its *basismo* and many of its claims to radical popular democracy.

29. Lehmann, in an attempt to demolish an idealized image of *basismo,* phrases this in more polemic terms. "Basista Catholicism," he claims, "depicts an idealized image of popular culture in the face of which its activists and theorists prostrate themselves in an almost reverential manner: the result is that they try very hard to take up the habits and idioms of this popular culture in order to bring the Catholic religion, as they see it, nearer to the people and also in order to reform Catholicism itself in the direction of the point of view of the poor" (Lehmann 1996, 18).

30. These two parties emerged after the more Left-leaning members of the PCB caused a split in 1962.

31. The Christian humanist influence of Padre Vaz, a Jesuit priest, remained important in the JUC during this period (Mainwaring 1986b, 64).

32. De Kadt (1970) adds that many JUC militants left the movement because they came to see *conscientização* as a failure.

33. The scope of this book does not allow fuller treatment of the ways in which these movements inspired the emergence of CEBs and the proliferation of the progressive Church in Brazil in general. However, many seminarians who completed their education in the 1960s were strongly influenced by these tendencies through their involvement in student politics.

34. For fuller analysis of this film see, for instance, Maria de Lourdes Beldi de Alcantara, *Cinema, Quantos Demonios—A Relação da Igreja com o Cinema* (Alcantara 1990, 160–66), produced by Verbo-Film, a Catholic film company. Dom Pedro Casaldáliga, the well-known liberationist, accepted the responsibility for the script, and Leonardo Boff appeared as narrator.

35. Virtually all saints important to popular Catholicism are reinterpreted in similar fashion. Due to the limited scope of this volume, I will pursue this line no further, offering instead a more general overview of this symbolic rearticulation.

36. Leonardo Boff left the Roman Catholic Church in 1995.

37. In one of his more polemical passages, Scott Mainwaring sums up the problem inherent in the discourse that deals with CEBs and the role of the progressive Catholic Church. He claims, "Although the Church lacks a development model, Church thought encourages reflection about the development process. Its emphasis on popular values, on participation, on democratic practices, on a just economic system, and on fraternity and community provides principles that should be observed in all societies" (Mainwaring 1986b, 235). This statement reveals Mainwaring's deep affinity toward liberationist Catholicism and the politics of the progressive Catholic Church during the 1970s and 1980s. However, it also reveals to what extent the political and the religious universes have merged within the space of the progressive Church. In the end, however, morals occupy center stage. Morals form the center of a transformative process that culminates in a juster society. This *is* the development model of the liberationist Church.

38. Scott Mainwaring has been arguing that one of the main differentiating features of the Catholic Left of the early 1960s and the popular Church during the 1970s was, in fact, a certain vanguardism of the Left. He believes the Catholic Left formed elite movements that were restricted in scope. The popular Church of the 1970s, however, gave rise to a mass movement based on antivanguardist principles (Mainwaring 1986b, 74). Equally, Mainwaring does not condone nonintervention, the opposite of vanguardism. This, according to the author, can easily lead to forms of anti-intellectualism or even mystical veneration of the popular ways (1986b, 213–15). What Mainwaring has in mind, then, is a certain sensitivity and dialogue that he sees in effective pastoral work of the popular Church. "Without listening, the pastoral agent cannot understand popular values and needs" (1986b, 208). The author reiterates the canon of the popular Church, which also emphasizes a strong respect for popular beliefs and practices, including popular religiosity (1986b, 209). While Mainwaring would like to see more effective change, a change that he sees stifled by an infatuation of the pastoral agent with popular culture, he believes change should still be administered in a sensitive fashion. His response to those who argue that "we must respect the slow process of consciousness raising" is that there exists no natural pace for this activity (1986b, 219), but he would still like to preserve a consciousness raising that listens and is sensitive to local needs. Besides the methodological tension contained by Paulo Freire's pedagogy that breaks into the open at this point, it seems as if Mainwaring overlooks the religious dimension of consciousness raising, with its moral rather than political implications.

39. A debate continues about the emergence of CEBs. Institutionalists claim that the Church hierarchy established the structures favoring the emergence of CEBs, while the liberationists claim that the CEBs grew out of the innovative practice of the grass roots.

40. Dom Paulo sold the episcopal palace in São Paulo, investing the funds in the struggle of the CEBs and the progressive Church.

41. Lehmann sees the creation of pastoral agencies such as the *Conselho Indigenista Missionario* (1972) and the *Pastoral da Terra* (1975) as a direct response to the hierarchy's loss of power over the ACB (1996, 63).

42. On this topic see, for instance, Macedo (1986).

CHAPTER 3

1. During the mid-1990s, only a handful of residents could be found who had lived in the region for twenty years or longer. My survey, for instance, shows that half of the households were established after the mid-1980s.

2. Mônica and Maria-Conceição are politically active members of the Catholic community and long-term residents of Jd. Damasceno.

3. Teresa Pires do Rio Caldeira writes about founding stories similar to those found in the *bairros* (Caldeira 1990, 52).

4. Julie has been active in the region for almost three decades. Her impressive work has encompassed many facets of community development and activism.

5. Maria da Glória, Edilene, and Cleide have been involved, along with others, In the struggle for day-care centers and in the women's movement. After the day-care centers were established in a joint venture with the municipality, these women installed themselves as head administrators of the facilities, positions that they occupied until mid-1990, when they were dismissed by the associations running the centers.

6. Claudia, arriving from Padua, Italy, through the mediation of the Catholic Church, established herself in Jd. Vista Alegre with the aim of engaging in community work. She administered basic health care in the *bairro* and got involved in almost every struggle during the time of her residency.

7. During my stay in the *bairros*, the Church very much managed the linkage with the Brazilian bureaucratic sphere. During the mid-1990s, priests and laypersons functioned as intermediaries, soliciting legal aid, social assistance, and psychological support. On the one hand they provided services that are normally furnished by the welfare state; on the other, they managed bureaucratic and legal procedures for local residents who did not have the skills to deal with the local bureaucracy.

8. Alexandra, a layperson in charge of the local radio station, also claims to have found material that points to a significant influence of JOC agents on the union struggles in the area, an influence that peaked during the late 1960s.

9. *Assistentialist* refers to state or Church assistance.

10. Interview, 27 June 1996.

11. *The cry of the excluded (o grito dos excluidos)* was given a central position in the pastoral guidelines drafted in 1995 by the archdiocese of São Paulo under the leadership of Dom Paulo Evaristo Arns. Rhetorical comments in the *bairros* often made direct reference to concepts and slogans published by the office of Dom Paulo.

12. Interview, 3 January 1998.

13. Interview, 3 January 1998.

14. Dom Paulo gave official support to *Custo de Vida* only in 1978.

15. Dom Paulo Evaristo Arns claims that he was not responsible for the construction of CEBs; they had already emerged by the time of his ordination in 1971 (Mainwaring 1986b, 104).

16. In this statement, the temporal frame may have collapsed, as *faith in politics* emerged officially only during the early 1980s. Nevertheless, a preoccupation with faith in politics between 1968 and 1970 is also evident in Berryman's work on religion in São Paulo (1996, 61). Within this militant climate, various political tendencies started to mix. CPC-inspired activists appeared in the *bairros*, aiming to awaken the authentic consciousness of *the people* through theater work; and student activists who had joined the MDB (Brazilian Democratic Movement) appeared in the region eager to add a

political direction to the nascent struggle of *the people*. Music had become an integral part of liberationist practices, and singing the suffering of *the people* was a liberationist tradition through the mid-1990s.

17. For a powerful account of Church-state relations during this period see, for instance, Kenneth P. Serbin (2000a).

18. Maria da Glória recalls that they were PUC (Catholic University) political science students.

19. As a consequence, in 1978, Dom Paulo paid a memorable visit to Jd. Vista Alegre on the invitation of militant communities who struggled for potable water and asphalt.

20. In a recent article, Rivière D'Arc outlines some of these confluences focusing on activism in the European Catholic Church during the 1950s and a Latin American Marxist version, by and large, developed in exile (Rivière D'Arc 1999, 199).

21. I do not mean to trivialize the importance of Brazilian priests or laypeople. The struggle for housing in Jd. Recanto, for instance, or the struggle for health services in the region was very much stimulated by Brazilian priests, though they are not remembered as key figures in *the struggle*. One possible explanation for this is that Brazilian priests and laypeople tend to change their place of activity more frequently than foreigners, who tend to stay for decades. This might account for the prominence in local memory of the foreigners. Sandra's case could lend weight to this hypothesis. Sandra, while never actually residing in the *bairros*, worked in the region for more than ten years. Her presence is still very much noted.

22. While the presence of middle-class professionals is frequently mentioned in case studies dealing with social movements in São Paulo, the importance of foreign community activists with strong links to the Church is generally overlooked.

23. Dealing with the region in question, Pedro Jacobi's (1993) account of popular movements in Vila Alta Brasilândia fails to mention this most important influence.

24. These Italian Catholic nuns were, at least in Claudia's case, not real nuns, as Claudia never joined an order. It was thought that this link to the Catholic Church would provide safety, respect, and, thus, greater cooperation from local residents. Maria da Glória was actually having a dig at the activists in this statement, because two of them married former priests. It should also be noted that they were not only organizing the struggle around the CJ, but were also heavily engaged in the struggle for water, electricity, health, education, and basic urban services, struggles overlooked by Maria da Glória. Furthermore, rather than visiting, Claudia lived and worked in Jd. Vista Alegre for almost a decade. By emphasizing the temporary character of this involvement, Maria da Glória underlined the existing class differences.

25. Sandra was contracted to work in Vista Alegre by *Orientao Socio-Educativa do Menor* (Socio-Educative Youth Orientation, OSEM) an organization connected with the Social Welfare Department (FABES). Her career as a community mobilizer in Vista Alegre can be regarded as classic. From a middle-class background, Sandra graduated from PUC in the mid-1970s. She joined the National Workers Front (FNT) and wanted to initiate consciousness-raising work at the periphery of São Paulo. During the mid-1980s she decided to enter party politics, joined the PT, and ran for deputy.

26. Two other local activists who fought in the movement for day-care centers.

27. According to Claudia, Padre Ivo left the *bairros* during the early 1990s.

28. I was told that Pe. Ivo used the damage caused by a thunderstorm as a pretext to close the school.

29. Jacobi (1993) documented this struggle with *Companhia de Saneamento Basico do Estado de São Paulo* (SABESP) in the Brasilândia region as part of his doctoral thesis.

30. Against the wishes of the hierarchy, many Catholic militants directly supported particular political parties of the Left. Elaborating this point, Carmen Macedo claims that the Church's option for the poor cannot be more than preferential, because otherwise it would destroy its universality (Macedo 1986, 48).

31. This is based on an interview with Maria da Glória and was confirmed by Claudia and Jd. Damasceno residents.

32. This persuaded me to use pseudonyms for all characters appearing in this volume.

33. PLAVEN (*Sociedade Civil de Planejamento e Vendas Ltda.*—Civil Society of Planning and Sales Ltd.), an entity also in charge of the land sales in Jd. Vista Alegre and Jd. Princesa.

34. Drogus argues that democratic governance has not resulted in a general increase in living standards. Hence, the picture of "upward mobility and religious complacency" does not apply to most (1999, 36). In like manner, Vásquez (1998) bases his argument on the premise that the declining resonance of liberation theology is the result not of a general disenchantment but of a teleological crisis in the project itself. Built on an image of a procession toward a better future (*a caminhada*), the project is facing the problem that the standard of living of the poor has, according to Vásquez, deteriorated. This contradiction turns a once appealing liberationist utopia into an "improbable dream" (1998, 207).

35. My survey did not reveal any absolute poverty. None of the 234 interviewees claimed to have suffered from hunger since living in Jd. Damasceno. This, however, may have been because interviewees would have been unlikely to admit to their own starvation when faced by fellow residents in the role of interviewers.

36. This imagery of a jungle that must be civilized appears in quite a number of accounts (see, for instance, Caldeira 1990, 52).

37. Irina has a very strong link with the Church and administers a mothers club in the region. She has been involved in struggles to legalize land titles for years and has successfully led resistance against seven evictions by standing in the way of approaching riot police.

38. It is difficult to overlook Irina's connection with the feminists featured in chapter 6.

39. Irina's account is strongly colored by a discourse that began to emerge during the late 1970s.

40. The violent nature of the *bairros* during the late 1970s is probably the only statement on which there was general agreement.

41. Zinha led the housing struggle in Jd. Recanto for much of the 1980s. In the

mid-1990s she assumed the leadership of the day-care center, closely connected with Irmã Maria's activities in the *bairro*.

42. It appears that many of the participants focused much more on obtaining improvements for their neighborhoods than the actual leadership (see also Caldeira 1990, 52).

43. When asked if they experience a sense of personal safety in the face of local violence, only 3 percent of interviewees responded that they feel secure in Jd. Damasceno. This percentage jumps to 48.7 percent when phrased more generally: "Do you feel safe?"

44. Caldeira offers a basic division between external agents, local leaders, and participants (1990, 52). In my study, which tries to cover a period of time rather than a point in time, such a division would not hold, as individual lives are fluid and participants have turned into leaders, changing their orientations on various occasions.

45. Chapter 6 offers a more detailed account of this gender division.

46. The rapid growth of the women's movement in the *bairros* during the early 1980s challenges the validity of this claim. Furthermore, during the mid-1990s, according to Francilene, the majority of local priests were still antagonistic toward feminist issues.

47. By the mid-1990s, the local priests were still critical toward attempts to mobilize women on an individualist platform. Such a politicization was seen to threaten the basis of family life and to contribute to the decay of the moral fabric.

48. Michael Löwy, in *The War of Gods*, points to the intrinsic tension between the core of the Catholic doctrine and modernity in general and the rationality of the market in particular. "The reified universe of capitalism offers finally no room for any charitable orientation. . . . Therefore, in a characteristic ambiguity, the clergy has always supported . . . patriarchalism against impersonal relations of dependence, although, on the other hand, prophecy breaks down patriarchal links" (Weber, cited in Löwy 1996, 21). Löwy cites Weber to elucidate "both the opposition of Latin American progressive Catholics to the cold and impersonal nature of capitalist relations and their struggle, in the name of prophetic justice, against traditional patriarchal domination over peasant communities" (Löwy 1996, 21).

49. The MDB activists tried to encourage locals to participate in the movements for redemocratization that surfaced between 1975 and 1982.

50. This posture is reminiscent of the approach of the CPCs of the UNE, outlined in chapter 2.

51. It should be noted that Claudia, unlike Maria de Lourdes and Sandra, was not greatly interested in feminist issues. The critique of the Left may have helped her decision not to participate in this increasingly gender-focused forum.

52. Löwy, for instance, suggests another reason for their disappearance from local memory: the effect of the *basismo*—a localism and rejection of outsiders—practiced by pastoral agents (1996, 89). Given the youthful appearance and academic background of the MDB militants, it is possible that they were identified as yet another

batch of researchers studying poverty. During the 1970s, it was quite common for students to spend some months as *estagiarios* (apprentices) or philanthropic helpers at the periphery. *Bairro* residents, however, did not get on too well with this brand of philanthropism. As early as 1974, Claudia was questioned about whether she had come just to do research or use the locals in some other way.

53. I am alluding here to the liberationist *listening* process, described in chapter 2.

54. The movement for day care (*Movimento de Lutas por Creches*) was initiated in São Paulo in 1979. It drew largely on the organization of women who participated in Catholic communities and was strongly influenced by the feminist movement (*Movimento Feminista*), founded in 1975, and by the Amnesty Movement (*Movimento da Anistia*), launched in 1976. This movement lost its radicalism after it had been integrated into the corporatist state.

55. Life-cycle issues have an important bearing on these developments.

56. All of the in-depth interviews with politically active women reinforced the point that these women saw themselves as *liberated*.

57. For Maria da Glória, the tendency of women to emphasize their own independence in individual terms already bordered on a form of egotism that left negative marks on children and on families. While claiming that it is increasingly common for women to leave husbands and children to pursue their own lives, she is very critical of this behavior.

58. See also Sonia Alvarez, who claims that the participation in mothers club–like organizations "empowered many women activists, sometimes leading them to question gender power imbalances within their marriages, their families, their communities, and even their parishes" (1994, 16).

59. With some reservations, Maria da Glória may be taken as an example of this. In many ways a radical exception to *bairro* standards, Maria da Glória expelled her husband from their family home in 1997, justifying this action with a discourse strongly colored by women's rights.

60. Hewitt's account supports this claim (1991, 88).

61. See also Hewitt (1991, 88).

62. This has also been confirmed by Alvarez (1994, 30).

63. Sandra herself, a member of the *Frente National dos Trabalhadores* (National Workers Front, FNT), joined the PT in the early 1980s.

64. This is very clear in Alvarez's account, which deals with the feminist movement in São Paulo (Alvarez 1994). See also Robin Nagle's account detailing similar events in Recife (1997, 155).

65. As early as the late 1970s, leading liberationists such as Frei Betto argued in favor of a withdrawal of the pastoral from the political scene in order to concentrate on the clerical roles (Doimo 1986, 111).

66. In this respect see also Hewitt (1991, 55).

67. According to Julie, this expulsion never occurred in a formal sense. Individuals were simply no longer contacted.

68. According to Vásquez, this consolidation of the progressive Church resulted from an increasingly powerful conservative critique within the universal Church that shook the institutional foundations of the Paulistano Church (1998, 108).

69. This represents one of the facets of the fragmentation of *social movements* that is usually overlooked.

70. Jacobi's (1990) account details some of the disaffection. MDB militants appear disappointed when faced by the fact that *bairro* residents responded in a far less radical manner than anticipated.

71. Clearly, life-cycle issues, underemphasized in the above account, play a great role in Sandra's disenchantment with the popular struggle.

72. In the mid-1980s Claudia shifted her activities to another *bairro* at the southern periphery of São Paulo.

73. As a result, the political initiatives that surfaced in the mid-1980s—such as the movement for direct elections (*Movimento Diretas Já* in 1984)—found only limited support within their communities.

74. The archdiocese of São Paulo was reduced by half, creating four new dioceses henceforth headed by conservative bishops.

CHAPTER 4

1. While the facilitation of urban services alleviated the burden of women in terms of household tasks, it actually increased their work as they were given the opportunity to enter the labor market.

2. Irina, for instance, sold her Vista Alegre home to buy a house in a better *bairro* closer to the urban center.

3. While all interviewees in Jd. Damasceno claimed to hold legal title to their land, the whole area of Jd. Damasceno is featured as "irregular subdivision" in the *Plano Diretor de São Paulo*—something like an urban master plan—elaborated under the Erundina administration in 1992.

4. While the settlement of Jd. Damasceno reaches back as far as the 1930s (*Folha* 28 February 1991, sec. 4, p. 2), the main settlement of the *bairros* occurred in three waves. The first wave took place at the end of the 1960s and early 1970s and resulted in the illegal subdivision of the land. According to the responses obtained by my questionnaire, the second wave was during the early and mid-1980s, a time of profound economic crisis in Brazil. The third wave occurred under the municipal administration of the PT, led by Luiza Erundina (1989–1992). During this administration, various *favelas* (slums) that emerged in high-risk areas were relocated onto empty public spaces such as the football ground of Jd. Recanto. This increase in population density since the late 1970s is dramatic; residents have frequently commented on it.

5. All four *bairros*, Jd. Damasceno, Jd. Princesa, Jd. Vista Alegre, and Jd. Recanto, had by the 1990s reached their maximum density. Virtually every possible piece of soil

was occupied. According to health post registers, at least 40,000 people lived in the *bairros* in the early 1990s. An estimate for a number of households in Jd. Damasceno indicates around 2,800 during the same point in time (*Folha* 28 February 1991. sec. 4, p. 2).

6. For residents of Jd. Damasceno, for instance, whose living standards are popularly reported to be slightly below those of the bourgeois *bairros* further down the valley, the survey shows that 94 percent of the households have a TV, 91 percent a sound system, 46 percent a CD player, 44 percent a video player, 27 percent a car, and 9 percent a parabolic antenna. Only 14 families of the 234 sampled live in wood or wood-compound constructed houses, while the rest enjoy the relative comfort of a masonry home.

7. According to my survey, 4.7 percent of the active workforce of Jd. Damasceno was unemployed, and 39.7 percent worked informally (*fazer bico*) in 1996. The average self-declared household income was R$549.84 a month during the same year.

8. In 1967, the average family wage in metropolitan São Paulo was Cr$21.767. Ten years later it reached Cr$35.077 to drop to Cr$21.641 in 1987 (Sempla 1990, 8).

9. In 1996, an irregularly constructed brick house consisting of a single room and in an unfavorable location—at the bottom of a steep hill, without road access and, thus, without secure car-port—was traded for as much as R$4,500. For a cheap and extremely dingy room in a wooden shack as much as R$150 per month was extracted, while a small dry concrete house could fetch around R$250 per month. In 1996, according to my survey, the average worker earned between two and three minimum incomes—between R$220 and R$330 in the *bairros*.

10. In 1983, the *Movimento de Desempregados em S. Paulo* (Movement of the Unemployed) was founded, signaling the deteriorating social conditions.

11. The land occupations that occurred between 1995 and 1997 drew strongly on this constituency of young, newlywed, underemployed couples.

12. The continuing settlement of high-risk areas in Jardim Damasceno, even after landslides had occurred, bears witness to this problem (*Suplemento* of the *Diário Oficial do Município de São Paulo*, 24 December 1992, 11).

13. Erminia Maricato ties the massive land invasions that occurred after the early 1980s to the deteriorating economic conditions (1988, 183). While this is certainly important, other factors also play a significant role: an increasing political permissiveness or even paralysis of the administration in the face of these land occupations; the increasing levels of militant organization; the Federal Law No. 6766 of 1979 that curtailed the offer of popular lots; the collapse of the Financial Housing System; and the politicization of housing by the liberationist Left.

14. During the second half of the 1980s, the universal Church embraced an increasingly conservative line, leading it away from social commitment to the grass roots. Emphasizing the renewed separation of the sacred and the profane, political matters were left to the formal political sphere (Hewitt 1991). In this context, the events in the Brasilândia region represent an exceptional episcopal radicalism that produced friction within all levels of the Church hierarchy, including the Vatican.

15. Dom Angélico Sándalo, placed in charge of the Brasilândia region in 1989, encouraged a politicization of ecclesiastical work that led him into conflict with the Church hierarchy. As a result, Pope John Paul II called him to take up a posting in Rome, where he served closer to the center of ecclesiastical power. The tension between John Paul II and Dom Angélico was only officially resolved during the Pope's visit to Rio de Janeiro in 1997.

16. The Union of Eastern District Movements of São Paulo (*União dos Movimentos da Zona Leste de São Paulo*) in many ways represented a response to the movements that emerged under secular tutelage during the first half of the 1980s (Gohn 1995, 137).

17. Certainly, a host of other mobilization attempts was carried into the *bairros*. These included attempts to mobilize the residents along the lines of a black and a women's consciousness. These movements, however, were relatively quickly swallowed up by political parties such as the PT. Furthermore, according to Irmã Maria, a Canadian Catholic militant who has lived in Jd. Recanto since 1986, the movements focusing on day care, electricity, water, and asphalt, lost much of their militancy during the mid-1980s.

18. Zinha is a local resident-militant who led this group, together with her husband, for more than a decade. Zinha represents in many ways an exception, as she participated in the struggle of both decades.

19. After the first successful land occupations, individual groups founded the Church-sponsored *Associação dos Moradores* (Residents Association) that administered the public housing and the *mutirão* (cooperative civil construction works) projects on the obtained land. According to Zinha, the last great struggle guided by this association united all the groups that fought for popular housing in the region. This struggle lasted for five years, and yielded 3,000 residential units. However, Zinha complains that of these 3,000 units, only 50 were distributed among the struggling families, as most other units went to outsiders and to friends and families of politicians involved. The association never recovered from the ensuing disappointment.

20. An incident that produced much publicity was the occupation of an extremely steep slope in Jd. Damasceno. This high-risk building site was buried by a mudslide in 1985, killing several people. When another slide occurred in 1992, all of the affected residents were evacuated and placed in state-sponsored public housing units. According to Damasceno residents, many of the evacuated residents sold their public housing apartments and moved back into the high-risk area.

21. I will not deal with these occupations in great detail as they were largely sponsored by a local populist politician—Viviane Ferraz—who was not highly respected by local militants with Church/PT links.

22. Sonia Alvarez indicates that this dissipation of *bairro* politics issues also from the decline of North-South aid, which provided important resources for local community projects (Alvarez 1994, 15).

23. These tendencies have also been noted in a recent article by Vàsquez, who describes the case of a progressive French priest who was replaced by a much more conservative Irish one (Vàsquez 1997).

24. Gradually long-term Catholic and secular militants withdrew from *bairro* activism. They were replaced by students and academics, who, according to locals, were mainly interested in furthering their own academic or political careers. Their temporal commitment to the *bairros* hardly exceeded a limited number of afternoons over the space of some three to six months. Such an involvement, however, could hardly match the much more extensive commitment of the militants during the previous decade. This absence of secular militants limited the diversity of the symbolic horizon in the *bairros* and restricted the available ideas and experiences. As pointed out by authors such as Levine and Mainwaring (1989, 220), these changes resulted in a loss of input for the development of local activism.

25. Evolving from an SAB rather than a CEB framework, Zinha maintained political connections with the Brazilian Social Democratic Party (PSDB) and later the Party of the Workers (PDT). In spite of a political network that led her outside the realm of the progressive Church and the Catholic Left, she preserved significant ties with this political and spiritual camp.

26. This brought her into contact with Irmã Maria, who had set up an education workshop addressing the idea of cooperativism.

27. As Adriana was the single most important active militant in the region between 1995 and 1998, this account focuses heavily on her practices.

28. According to Adriana and Julie, quite a number of local priests used their control over project funding to enhance their central position within their communities. These claims coincide with my observations.

29. Chapter 5 will pay closer attention to this point. Funding decisions were closely tied to the liberationist character of the proposed project. Attempts to venture outside this frame of reference simply did not attract the resources necessary to realize the project.

30. The consequent critique of these practices, issuing from community organizers such as Julie and Irmã Maria, and from established local leaders such as Maria da Glória, Zinha, and Adriana, for instance, remained largely unheard.

31. With the exception of Zinha, who began her political involvement in an SAB (Friends of the Neighborhood Association) and who has substantially widened her access to information by investing in her education, most local militants gained their political and spiritual orientation predominantly through education programs directed by Catholic clergy. Together with her husband, Zinha finished high school and enrolled in a social work course at PUC/SP.

32. Roberto died during the early 1990s. Statements about his activities were obtained from his mother and from fellow militants and friends. Sándra, who had worked with Roberto in a video production about everyday life in the *bairros,* still suffered from the circumstances surrounding Roberto's death. In many ways, Sándra felt responsible for the choice he made to live as a poor activist, a choice that took him to the existential edge.

33. This also led to intrafamily tensions as João, Adriana's oldest son, urged her to reduce her involvement with the local Church. On one particular occasion he aired

his frustration and claimed that: "They [the priests] don't take you seriously, they only use you in a game called [religious] conversion."

34. The film *"Pé na Caminhada,"* discussed in chapter 2, represents well the orientation of this consolidated progressive Church.

35. I agree with Vásquez when he argues, "To say that CEB members at the base simply mimic the reductive stance of pastoral agents is to deny the power of the laity to appropriate institutional messages according to their own experience" (1998, 124). Nonetheless, this appropriation process requires substantial educational resources and an ability to distance oneself from institutional dogma. The previous generation of liberationists is far better prepared to consciously choose a direction that leads beyond the dominant interpretation of religious practice (see chapter 6).

36. In mid-1996 Erundina was still using an explicitly liberationist terminology during her election campaign in Jd. Elisa Maria.

37. More seriously, however, many of these local groups had centralized much of the local political power and functioned as a political platform in the *bairros*. In Jd. Vista Alegre, for instance, Maria da Glória, Edilene, Cleide, and Adriana represent such a platform. Once they were connected with the formal political realm, most of the contacts would flow through the existing channels. Representing the nodes of these channels, these individuals exerted enormous control over the flow of information and resources. Shifting this local political power grid would have required much time and resources that were not available. During the 1996 municipal election campaign in the *bairros*, the PT still used the same channels that had been developed through the struggle of the 1980s. However, because only an almost insignificant proportion of these popular *bairro* residents participated in such an organized group, the overwhelming majority of *the people* remained beyond the scope of PT attention. In the *bairros* residents were extremely sensitized to a field of privilege that seemed to be open to only a few. For the vast majority not directly connected with PT politics, the Erundina administration seemed to make little difference. When measured against the improvements that the struggle of the late 1970s and early 1980s had brought to the *bairros*, the PT administration hardly made a difference. In many respects, the PT administration increased the competition for urban services in the *bairros*. The administration resettled a wave of new immigrants there, counterbalancing the benefits of the marginal improvements to urban services. Hence, the incorporation of locals into the administrative hierarchy had the disadvantage of creating power disparities in the *bairro* that conjured up images of clientelist practices.

38. Cecília Loreto Mariz notes, "People like to identify themselves as hard workers, and CEB members define themselves as people who like to work. All these people began their working lives very early, and they are proud of this fact" (Mariz 1994, 123).

39. This popular rejection of the formal political realm also emerged from my survey: 68 percent of the respondents judged the formal political system to be corrupt.

40. Berryman comments on this sublime and heroic angle of the struggle during the 1970s (1996).

41. Pe. Pedro's theological practices underwent some significant changes during mid-1997. His subsequent work was very much influenced by the success of the charismatic religious groups whose practices he tried to combine with the historical materialism at the basis of liberation theology (see chapter 6).

42. Striking in respect to Pedro's community radio project was the fact that program structure and content were reminiscent of Catholic radio transmissions during the late 1950s and 1960s (Soares 1988, 255 fn). Despite the mixture of liberationist, freedom of speech, and community-focused discourses that officially underpinned the project, the programs included conservative catechism courses, alphabetization, consciousness-raising blocks, religious instruction, and Bible readings with relatively traditional or conservative content. While musical styles may have altered and some messages may have acquired a distinctly liberationist flavor, the core of the program differed only marginally from its 1960s counterpart. Thus the term community radio somewhat disguised the fact that the station was aimed principally at a Catholic community. Above all else, it served as an outpost that tried to reinforce a religiously conservative and politically liberationist symbolic universe in the *bairros*.

43. This section is based on participant observation and personal interviews with Adriana, Gilberto, and other leaders and participants. I accompanied the occupation for almost one year and for several weeks resided in the area.

44. Due to the limited scope of the present volume I will not engage with the discourse on growing Evangelization in Brazil. For elaboration of this theme see, for instance, Burdick (1993), Mariz (1994), and Lehmann (1996).

45. The meeting had forty-three participants (mainly female), including three organizers; it was held on 31 March 1996 at the local school in Jd. Vista Alegre.

46. Adriana maintained a very troubled relationship with the local parish, whose priest she defined as incompetent, conservative, and bourgeois.

47. This also occurred in the case of a meeting (9 May 1996) organized by Dom Angélico, Bishop of the Brasilândia region, between the occupation leadership and their consultants and Mario Covas, then head of the State of São Paulo. The support team consisted of Padre Claudio and Padre Guilherme; Hélen, a lawyer of the Center of Human Rights Action affiliated with the metropolitan curiae; Paulo Teixera, a PT deputy with strong Church links; and some of the area representatives.

48. Adriana, dissatisfied with the services of these lawyers, mobilized other legal resources through her Catholic network.

49. To be considered a worker, I was told, one had to have a signed union membership card or, at least, full-time employment.

50. In this sense, unemployment undermined another strong local identity: that of the responsible family father. The discussion that ensued on that same night tried to make the case that the occasional illegal activity of those men present was their only possibility of supporting their families adequately. Unanimously, those present agreed that having to depend financially on their wives was an extremely unsatisfying condition, as it dramatically undermined their position within the family. Particularly de-

grading, they agreed, was being forced to ask their wives for money for their own leisure time. Consequently, their occasional illicit act was only to the benefit of everybody within the family.

51. The fact that within a formal political forum liberationist concepts have, in spite of the inroads of neoliberal policies, retained some of their validity could indicate that the liberationist crisis arises predominantly from the grass roots rather than from the formal political sphere.

52. This section is based on highly emotionally charged accounts of the occupation leadership and participants. As I only witnessed isolated incidents of the events depicted in this section, it relies heavily on fear-driven representations difficult to distinguish from gossip. Nonetheless, the section conveys a vivid image of how the perception of violence acquired a strong dynamic that began to dominate discussions and processes.

53. Interestingly, the argument that the occupation had caused some significant environmental damage was also taken very seriously by both parties.

54. As a relatively uninvolved outsider, I was often called on to conduct these sessions.

55. This figure is an estimate of Adriana, confirmed by Gilberto.

56. At stake was the administration of financial and material resources for which the association was responsible. Direct control over these resources would increase the chances for personal gain and a possible political career.

57. In this sense, subjects like Adriana have certainly matured politically and learned from past experiences.

58. Her deteriorating health also played an important part in her decision to withdraw from the occupation.

59. In spite of the dramatic liberationist collapse, even after the original leaders had been forced from office, they remained largely positive about what they had learned during the occupation. The women in particular declared that the occupation had given them an experience that expanded their horizons and gave them more self-confidence. As Sonia Alvarez (1994) pointed out, the experiences gained during the struggle are passed on during events like this land occupation and shape the identities of participants significantly. For instance, all the women participating in the leadership declared that they were prepared to become more actively involved in *bairro* politics in the future. Furthermore, they were prepared to assume a leadership role on other occasions. Nevertheless, this widened experience base needs an outside catalyst that is able to draw together the constantly changing tendencies in the *bairros* and construct a new synthesis on this basis (see chapter 6).

60. Many left out of fear or were driven away by the lack of comfort encountered in the area.

61. An attempt to gather survey data in that particular area revealed that this label was often applied unjustly and without any factual basis.

62. After this initial crisis, a more structured m̲u̲r̲a̲l̲i̲z̲a̲t̲ion took place during 1997 and 1998. Alexandra played an important role in these later attempts to defend the position of the occupants.

63. Documents of the Brazilian Left, presented by Michael Löwy (1992), show that the identity of the honest worker has a rich history, reaching back to the early Vargas era.

CHAPTER 5

1. This was the working definition of *popular cooperatives* given by Adriana.

2. As described and explained by Michael Löwy (1996, ch. 2).

3. See also Doimo (1995, 80).

4. SEADE.

5. All interviewed residents who had experienced that era underlined this fact.

6. Monthly FIESP/CIESP/DEPEA statistics, August 1996.

7. Adriana's accounts are particularly rich in violent encounters with local drug barons. Having almost lost her life as a result of one such encounter, she nearly abandoned her projects in the *bairro* and moved to another neighborhood. It took much priestly power of conviction to change Adriana's mind after this event.

8. Luiza Erundina forms part of a Catholic faction within the PT and has participated extensively in *the struggle*.

9. These policies focused largely on subsidized urban services.

10. The scope of this book does not allow for an investigation of the literature on popular cooperativism in Latin America. However, the attempts of these agencies replicated, by and large, the errors committed by similar initiatives during the 1970s and 1980s, as detailed by Martin Scurrah, for instance (Scurrah 1984a; 1984b; Scurrah and Podestá 1984).

11. According to Francilene, the CARITAS representative for the Brasilândia region, the municipality never fulfilled its financial promises to the local cooperatives.

12. Francilene, who functioned as the almost exclusive cooperative support person in the region, received funds to visit cooperatives once a month.

13. This account is based on interviews with cooperative members and administrators, priests, and a CARITAS representative in the area. A tendency to minimize the role played by CARITAS is evident. Adriana, for instance, minimized the role of a CARITAS-sponsored technical expert who held a one-week workshop in the area during which he introduced basic business principles. In fact, CARITAS offered some technical support, consisting of occasional workshops on weekends and one part-time social worker with the task of accompanying all the CARITAS-sponsored cooperatives in the area. Facets of this cooperativism are also visible in *São Paulo para todos* (1992, 38).

14. *Conviver*—to live together.

15. BANESPA is a major Brazilian bank.

16. A legal indictment focusing on the child-labor status of these adolescents contributed to this.

17. In the *bairro* of Vista Alegre, a worker in full-time employment earns on average around three minimum wages (R$330) per month.

18. Adriana complained in particular about certain priests who failed to forward cooperative resources because they used them for the construction of Church premises.

19. This emerged in particular from Adriana's attempt to attract the bank employees union of BANESPA to finance the education that would allow her to enter the market. This endeavor was unsuccessful, as the union president had doubts about the political direction of such a project.

20. In 1997, based on a model developed in Germany, CARITAS Brazil proposed a change of lending policies, adopting increasingly market-based criteria. In the future, CARITAS's services will resemble those of a credit union, drawing on pooled resources that will be available at near-market rates.

21. The forum was, for instance, housed in one of the premises belonging to the local Catholic Church. Furthermore, most of its support staff was associated with various Church agencies.

22. In her pursuit of this goal, she instructed me to take over the forum and to turn it into the basis of my activities in the region. She reckoned that under my permanent supervision—the supervision of an educated white European—the forum would turn into an entity that would lift local cooperatives politically and economically to the desired levels of success.

23. While the BANESPA Bank Employees Union, tied to the Catholic Left, did not approve of my directives, the State Welfare Secretary, who tried to capture votes for the PSDB, appeared interested in a political alliance that, as I was told, would prove extremely beneficial to my project.

24. Adriana envisaged the foundation of an independent financial body that could facilitate the credit requirements of popular cooperatives.

25. Certainly, the Catholic faction of the PT, led by Luiza Erundina, had discarded ideas of a grass-roots democracy in 1990 (see chapter 4).

26. *Arrastão (arrastar*—to drag a large net), was made famous by youths from Rio's *favelas,* who swept along local beaches snatching valuables from sunbathers.

27. The presence of local Church people created all sorts of problems that extend beyond the scope of this book. Geraldo, Adriana's oldest son, for instance, left the coop because he hated the gossip and sabotage attempts by Catholic Church members.

28. The workers consequently felt that their rights had been infringed and threatened to take Adriana to court, demanding a payoff entailing two monthly salaries.

29. Certainly, political loyalty also played into this decision.

30. Later, she justified her decision by arguing that the deal represented an opportunity to learn the skills necessary to manufacture larger orders.

31. A subsequent deal with the MST entailed a renegotiation of terms. In this in-

stance, the MST proved flexible and understanding with regard to the needs of the co-operative.

32. This same incident gave rise to Adriana's critique of the PT discussed earlier in this chapter.

CHAPTER 6

1. I use the word feminist here with great hesitation, as its connotations fail to depict the project of local women in the *bairros*. These women prefer the word feminine to represent their own activities. Given that the intellectual-theological trajectory of this feminism is strongly influenced by Sister Ivone Gebara, one of the leading Latin American feminist theologians, the term eco-anthropological feminism would be more accurate to describe the orientation of Catholic militants such as Julie. However, in order to reduce this complexity, I will use the terms feminine or femininity to refer to *bairro*-derived currents and simply feminism or feminist to denote the more academic theological position.

2. As a result of these episcopal initiatives, a plan emerged to unite and focus the activities of local *popular* groups and communities and to harness the ensuing political-religious energy by means of an overarching body—the *Fórum da Cidadania em Defesa da Região Noroeste* (The Forum of Citizenship in the Defense of the North Eastern Region). Combining a multitude of local neighborhood associations, CEBs, and branches of the Catholic Left, as well as other ecclesiastical and episcopal institutions, the forum set out to defend the gains and achievements of previous movements. As outlined in the forum manifesto, the main emphasis of this struggle would rest on health, housing, urban infrastructure, transport, children and adolescents, education, environment, unemployment, corruption, and social discrimination (*desrespeito*). By including most aspects of the liberationist struggle of the previous two decades, it was expected that the forum would generate mobilizing power. The manifesto was signed by the Assoc. Amigos do Parque Pedroso; Soc. União dos Amigos de Itaberaba; Soc. Amigos de Vila Cristo Rei; Assoc. de Moradia de Vila Erminia; Movimento Defesa da Moradia da População da Região Noroeste, Assoc. de Moradia do Jd. Damasceno; Assoc. de Amigos do *Bairro* Nossa Senhora Aparecida; Assoc. de Moradores do Jd. Recanto; Gr. de Movimentação e Discussão dos Problemas da Região; Central de Compras e Organização da Região Noroeste; Cáritas da Região Episcopal Brasilândia; Fórum de Educação da Região Noroeste; União dos Movimentos de Moradia da Região Noroeste; Assoc. Cantareira; Obras Sociais de Vista Alegre; PCdoB—Breguesia do ó; and the PT—Freguesia do ó.

3. This initiative was supported by the Association of North American Bishops and administered by the curia Brasilândia (24 August–9 November 1997).

4. During September and October 1997, Aldaíza made public the conflict between Zinha's day-care center in Jd. Recanto and the municipal administration, undermin-

ing local attempts to secure funding for the project. This event provoked the end of Aldaíza's popularity in *bairro* politics.

5. *Elas* relied heavily on the radio in order the reach women in the *bairros* who were not disposed to participate in the group in person but were open to its message.

6. See, for instance, a special report dealing with Julie's activism in the *Voz da Esperança*, vol. 3, no. 33, September 1997.

7. After more than thirty years in the *bairros*, Julie still refers to *the people* as "they" —never as "us."

8. A complaint frequently leveled at local priests is that their religious posture prohibits them from encountering locals on a more intimate level.

9. This entailed the advice to refuse to do the partner's laundry, ironing, cooking, etc.

10. This is based on the statements of Julie as well as those of other Catholic women in the *bairro*. Partners I interviewed in relation to this refused to discuss the topic.

11. Many of the reflections on Pentecostalism now focus on the practical feminism or even antiracism of Pentecostalist practice. This is often contrasted to the more political and historical projects of the CEBs. For an elaboration of this topic, see, for instance, Burdick (1993), Mariz (1994), and Lehmann (1996).

12. Although *elas* attracts only a limited number of regular group participants, its work with other feminist ventures in the region has given it an impressive cultural impact.

13. The workshop offers art classes and sewing courses to local women. During these activities, course organizers encourage the participants to critically elaborate their role in the *bairros*.

14. These include the above-mentioned radio programs of *elas*, the professionalization workshops at the cooperative in Jd. Recanto, the feminist spiritual guidance given by Julie and other Catholic militants, and the group discussions dealing with women's issues organized by Francilene.

15. According to Pe. Pedro and Alexandra, the response pattern and participation rates for *elas* are similar to most popular programs that focus on *música sertaneja* and *pagode*.

16. Many of the PT municipal election campaign videos in 1996 exemplified this carnivalesque touch, appealing to the electorate with catchy songs, colorful outfits, and an oversimplified, often meaningless message. In the *bairros*, liberationist priests often included a little raffle or bingo with colorful prizes to attract greater numbers of listeners.

17. Evidence of this global ecumenical integration of Catholic militant feminists such as Julie or Francilene can be taken from the fact that they attended a plenary session (2 August 1995) in defense of Sister Ivone Gebara, who was called to silence by the Vatican in mid-1995. This session, held at PUC in São Paulo, was sponsored by CE-HILA (Commission on Church Studies and History in Latin America) and united

more than 450 Roman Catholic and Protestant scholars from all over Latin America and the Caribbean, as well as academics and theologians from Europe and the United States. Sister Ivone Gebara, who has offered the main intellectual impetus to this feminism, was ordered to return to the convent of her order (Sisters of Saint Augustine) in Brussels.

18. Local feminine projects benefited financially from Francilene's coordinating and administering the CARITAS initiative in the region.

19. This proposal emerged as a result of an ecumenical encounter between women, reflecting on the question of what it is to be a woman in their denomination.

20. This information was volunteered by Francilene, active at the curia of Brasilândia and interviewed by *elas* during their weekly radio show (9 October 1997).

21. A lay seminarian, resident in Jd. Damasceno.

22. Interview with the author, 18 September 1997.

23. Sister Ivone Gebara, rejecting the notion of a positively interpreted spiritual poverty as well as that of an anthropological poverty (which accepts that women are poorer than men as a culturally given necessity), endorses the liberationist notion of an option for the poor. For Gebara, however, this option should address the fact that women are predominantly poorer than men. From this basis Gebara develops a trajectory that incorporates three previously separate movements: liberation theology, ecology, and feminism. For Gebara, the new people of God are "begotten in the woman who is the figure of the people." By reintroducing femininity into a patriarchal realm, Gebara aims at an extending of the spiritual and epistemological horizon. However, at the base of this analysis is a continuing belief in the living faith of this new people of God, who, as in the liberationist tradition, are poor, patient, and suffering (Thompson 1997). More recently, Gebara has rejected the vanguardist character read into CEBs by popular movement theorists and has questioned the dogmatic assertion of the popular Church that CEBs are the only vehicle leading to liberation (Vásquez 1998, 248).

24. In late 1997, Francilene eulogized the Erundina administration on community radio, while local traditional supporters of the PT, such as Alexandra, found it increasingly difficult to support any PT candidate, as most candidates would lose their credibility after a more detailed analysis of their political involvement in the *bairros*.

25. This proposal of a woman's ministry involved the establishment of a formal and institutionalized office held by Catholic women who would deal with questions specific to women.

26. The proposal of the Woman's Ministry is a case in point. While keeping the needs of Julie's group in mind, the project's main achievements were to create a basis on which financial assistance from the Catholic Church could be applied for, and it created a number of paid positions that could be passed on to allies in the cause.

27. In addition to the Woman's Ministry, two other issues form the agenda of the Catholic feminists: domestic violence and women's education.

28. For an elaboration of *basismo* in Brazil, see Lehmann (1996).

29. The most important problem for local women was their lack of access to education. In spite of this, intellectually oriented feminists such as Francilene were more excited about the possibility of constructing a woman's ministry. In this particular case, institutional concerns were diverting their attention from grass-roots issues.

30. On this topic see also Corcoran-Nantes (1990).

31. This paragraph is based on three discussions I had with Julie between 11 August 1997 and 15 August 1997.

32. Julie's impression was that western feminist discourses encouraged primarily the development of women and not necessarily the construction of a new cultural union.

33. Since the early 1990s, quite a number of priests have embraced the feminist current within their region (*Elas*, 9 October 1997).

34. Franco evokes here the words of Hector Aguer, auxiliary bishop of the Archdiocese of Buenos Aires, for whom the word gender "serves to provoke an ideological shift and to generate a new conception of the human person, of subjectivity, marriage, the family, and society" (Franco 1996, 1).

35. This was mainly achieved by keeping a low profile and by offering very little information to Church officials and researchers.

36. From a liberationist point of view, they could be seen to have constructed the ideal CEB.

37. This establishes an initial point of contact between the feminine currents in the *bairros* and the project of Catholic feminists. This connection has gained depth as a result of the proximity of Catholic militants to local women. At this point, femininity becomes an element that can enforce change within the institutions of the Catholic Church as well as in the cultural sphere of the *bairros*.

38. This emerged out of a discussion involving Julie, Francilene, Teresa, and others on 21 September 1997.

39. For a theological-anthropological background to this theme see Irmã Barbara P. Bucker, "O Feminino como Utopia na Igreja," *Vida Pastoral*, September-October 1997, vol. 38, no. 196, pp. 19–22.

40. Julie hopes that a movement based on a similar principle can be constructed among black communities.

41. This paragraph is based on an interview conducted by Elizangela Cordeiro, published in the *Voz da Esperança*, vol. 3, no. 33, September 1997.

42. This is essentially why I address Julie without referring to her religious title Irmã (Sister). Having always encountered Julie as woman and not as "nun," I felt it appropriate to address her as (Catholic) woman and not as a representative of the Catholic Church. According to Julie, "Priests are much more tied to their Catholic identity and find it much harder to establish an 'authentic' contact with 'the people.' Women [nuns] normally have a profession that can substitute for their Catholic identity. They find themselves much more capable of rejecting the role they play within a religious institution."

43. Julie herself referred me to Irmã Barbara Bucker in order to delineate the theological dimension of the Catholic feminist struggle in the region.

44. Interview, 16 December 1996.

45. Young women in the *bairros* often wish to get married quickly in order to leave their homes.

46. The difficulty in forming a secular PT, embodied by Eder Sader's (1988) project, underpins this. While the nascent PT was able to draw on substantial labor union support and enjoyed much secular intellectual input, the influence of the progressive Catholic universe that poured into the founding of the PT remains visible.

47. By no means should this be read in terms of constructing Adriana as the ignorant local leader whose practices are inferior to those of the much more enlightened, educated Catholic militants. In fact, the fate of Adriana's project is shared by many local militants in the region: Maria da Glória, Cleide, Edilene, and Zinha were equally unable to attach their day-care projects to other political projects. Similarly, Alexandra and Gilberto were not able to construct a lasting synthesis during their leadership roles in the land occupations referred to in earlier chapters.

CHAPTER 7

1. http://www.uol.com.br/folha/brasil/ult96u16851.shl.

2. This meeting took place on 10 August 2000.

3. John Paul II significantly curtailed the powers of the CNBB, the driving force behind the progressive stance of the Church during the 1970s and 1980s. In 1995, the conservative Dom Lucas Moreira Neves was elected president of the CNBB.

4. The term neo-Pentecostalism refers to a second generation of Pentecostal associations in Brazil. The first generation comprised those Pentecostal associations such as the Lutherans, who arrived with early European migrants in Brazil. In this sense, the second generation refers to comparatively newer associations such as the *Igreja Universal de Reino de Deus* (Universal Church of the Reign of God), *Igreja Deus é Amor* (God Is Love Church), and the *Assembleia de Deus* (Assembly of God).

5. Hochstetler (2000) notes that the theme of economic inclusion and exclusion underpins the citizenship frame, the symbolic framework that gave rise to NGO and pressure group mobilization during the 1990s. This master-frame, as Hochstetler calls it, stands in direct relation to discourse of the progressive Church during these years.

6. Dom Fernando is Bishop of the Diocese of Santo Amaro. Furthermore, Dom Fernando currently fulfills the function of the President of the Regional Sul 1 of the CNBB, Member of the Congregation of the Clergy at the Vatican and the Episcopal Council of the Doctrine at the CNBB.

7. For David Lehmann, "enculturation" denotes the attempts of the Catholic Church to assimilate other cultures, to draw them into itself (Lehmann 1996, 8).

8. In this sense, enculturation seems to go back to Paulo Freire's method of lis-

tening, a seemingly Habermasian ideal speech act that makes neutral cognitive exchanges possible.

9. To be sure, as noted by Vásquez (1998) and Nagle (1997), for instance, the reasons behind this drive to separate politics and faith are multifaceted and involve, alongside other contingencies, a pressure from the Church hierarchy as well as from *bairro* residents. For the politically active laypersons within the *bairros*, it had become imperative to clearly separate political from Church activities for the latter reason. Alexandra, for instance, who had taken on a position as campaign helper and later as a consultant of a member of the municipal council, emphasized that she took pains to make it clear to the local population when she acted as a political activist and when as a Church helper. Local residents, according to Alexandra, do not mind her involvement in local politics, but demand transparency. They fear that politicians might take advantage of their struggle without their knowledge. Consequently, they appreciate it when Alexandra clearly declares her activities as either politically or Catholic community focused.

10. Audiotapes featuring songs relating to distinct body movements promoted by Pe. Marecelo are among the more successful commercial ventures of the Charismatics.

11. Dom Angêlico Sándalo Bernardino was asked to head the newly created diocese of Blumenau (Santa Catarina), an office he officially took up on 24 June 2000.

12. The interview took place on 8 August 2000. During my last visit to the *bairros* during August 2000, Pe. Konrado had been in office for only five weeks, too short a period of time to draw conclusions about the actual impact of the change of leadership in the Brasilândia region.

13. This point echoes Vásquez's more general statement quoted in chapter 1 (Vásquez 1998, 108).

14. According to Dom Fernando, the development of community development programs formed one of the most important trajectories entertained by the Santo Amaro diocese.

15. These courses, according to Dom Fernando, involved some 5,000 people. However, the aim of the diocese was to increase that number to 100,000.

16. See also Gomes on other parts of Latin America (1999, 64).

17. *Obreirismo* denotes the celebration of the macho worker.

18. On the topic of homology in music see, for instance, Simon Frith, "Music and Identity," in *Questions of Cultural Identity*, edited by Stuart Hall and Paul Du Gay (London: Sage, 1996).

19. Stewart Hall argues that this essentialist tenor is being gradually superseded by a new approach more able to come to terms with difference (Hall and Du Gay 1996, 474).

20. Nevertheless, many of the rap and hip-hop fans I interviewed in Brazil defined themselves in terms of color. Moreover, rappers such as KLJ (Racionais) take their Afro-Brazilian heritage very seriously and, to some extent, replicate notions contained within African-American identity politics.

21. "Your TV commercial doesn't fool me. I don't need status or fame. Your car and your money already fail to seduce me . . . nor your blue-eyed whore. I am only a Latin American guy supported by more than 50,000 b-boys. Collateral effect that your system produced." (Racionais MCs, Sobrevivendo no Inferno chapter 4, verse 3)

22. "Calm my soul and lead me to the path of justice." Psalms, 23: 3.

23. ". . . and although I walk through the valley of shadows and death I do not fear evil because You are with me." Psalms, 23: 4. This biblical reference is widely quoted within pop culture. Quentin Tarantino, for instance, builds a whole scene around this psalm in his recent, widely acclaimed feature film "Pulp Fiction."

24. While such religious themes are particularly visible in the lyrics of the Racionais MCs, they form no exception. In fact, a wide range of Brazilian rap bands use religious images to tie notions of peace and justice to a higher principle.

25. The Racionais' "Raio X Brasil, Homem na Estrada" (1993) sold 250,000 copies, while "Sobrevivendo no Inferno" (1997) sold 500,000 copies in 1997 alone. Thaide and DJ Hum's best selling CDs "Humildade e Corgem são nossas armas para lutar" (1994) and "Preste Atenção" (1997) each sold 100,000 copies.

26. Vincente Cândido's own mandate was based on progressive Catholic support, a support that was increasingly drying up because of conservative currents within the Church hierarchy.

27. There are attempts to tie rap and hip-hop to the Church, but they are stifled by the staunch anti-institutionalism asserted by hip-hop artists.

REFERENCES

Adorno, S. 1992. "Criminal Violence in Modern Brazilian Society: The Case of the State of São Paulo." Paper given at Social Changes, Crime, and Police conference. Budapest 1-4 July.

Alcantara, M. L. B. de. 1990. "Cinema, ouantos demonios: a relação da igreja com o cinema." Master's thesis, PUC, São Paulo.

Alvarez, S. E. 1994. "The (Trans)formation of Feminism(s) and Gender Politics in Democratizing Brazil." In *The Women's Movement in Latin America: Participation and Democracy*, edited by Jane S. Jaquette. Boulder, Colo.: Westview Press.

Alvarez, S. E., E. Dagnino, and A. Escobar. 1996. "The Cultural and the Political in Latin American Social Movements." Paper presented at the conference *As culturas da política a política das culturas, revendo os movimentos sociais na America Latina*. São Paulo Unicamp, 20–22 March.

Alves, M. M. 1979. *A Igreja e a política no Brasil*. São Paulo: Brasiliense.

Assies, W. 1992. *To Get Out of the Mud: Neighbourhood Associationism in Recife 1964–1988*. Amsterdam: CEDLA, Latin American Studies 63.

———. 1999. "Theory, Practice and External Actors in the Making of New Urban Social Movements in Brazil." *Bulletin of Latin American Research* 18 (2): 211–26.

Baltar, P. E., C. S. Dedecca, and W. Henrique. 1996. "Mercado de Trabalho e Exclusão Social no Brasil." In *Crise e trabalho no Brasil: modernidade ou volta ao passado?* edited by C. A. B. de Oliveira and J. E. L. Mattoso. São Paulo: Pagina Aberta Ltda.

Barreira, I. 1986. "Incômodos hospedes? notas sobre a participação da Igreja e dos partidos politicos nos movimentos sociais urbanos." In *A igreja nas bases em tempo de transição (1974–85)*. São Paulo: Cedec.

Benedetti, L. R. 1988. "Templo, Praça, Coração: A Articulação do Campo Religioso Católico." Ph.D. dissertation defended at the Sociology Department, FFLCH, Faculty University of São Paulo. São Paulo: USP.

Beozzo, J. O. 1996. *A Igreja do Brasil: De João XXIII a João Paulo II, de Medellin a Santo Domingo*. 2nd ed. Petrópolis: Vozes.

Berning, K. 1987. *Pé na caminhada*. Verbo Filmes, São Paulo.

Berryman, P. 1996. *Religion in the Megacity: Catholic and Protestant Portraits from Latin America*. New York: Orbis Books.

———. 1999. "Churches as Winners and Losers in the Network Society." *Journal of Interamerican Studies and World Affairs* 41 (4): 21–34.

Betancur, J. 1988. "The Struggle for Settlement of the Urban Poor in Latin American Cities and its Impact on the Built Environment: a Discussion with Case Illustrations." *BISS* 10:165–75.

Beyer, P. F. 1990. "Privatization and the Public Influence of Religion in Global Society." In *Global Culture: Nationalism, Globalization, and Modernity*, edited by M. Featherstone. London: Sage.

Brandão Lopez, J., and A. Gottschalk. 1990. "Recessão, família e pobreza: a década mais do que perdida." *São Paulo em perspectiva* 4 (1): 100–09.

Bruneau, C. T. 1979. *Religião e politização no Brasil: a Igreja e o regime autoritário.* São Paulo: Loyola.

Bucker, B. P. 1997 "O Feminino como Utopia na Igreja." *Vida Pastoral* 38 (196): 19–22.

Burdick, J. 1993. *Looking for God in Brazil: The Progressive Catholic Church in Urban Brazil's Religious Arena.* Berkeley: University of California Press.

Caldeira, T. P. 1986. "Electoral Struggles in a Neighborhood on the Periphery of São Paulo." *Politics and Society* 15 (1): 43–65.

———. 1990. "Women, Daily Life, and Politics." In *Women and Social Change in Latin America*, edited by E. Jelin. London: Zed Books Ltd.

———. 1992. "City of Walls: Crime, Segregation, and Citizenship in São Paulo." Ph.D. dissertation, University of California at Berkley.

Camargo, C. P. F., et al. 1978. *São Paulo: Growth and Poverty.* London: Bowerdean Press.

Carmo, J. 1993 "O processo de terceirização e os abusos que estão sendo cometidos pelas empresas." *LTR—Revista de legislação do trabalho e previdencia social* 29 (7): 27–29.

Chesnut, A. R. 1998. "The Spirit of Brazil: The Pentecostalization of Christianity in the Largest Catholic Nation." Paper presented at the XXI International Congress of the Latin American Studies Association. September 24-26. Chicago, Ill.

Cohen, J. L., and A. Arato. 1992. *Civil Society and Political Theory.* Cambridge, Mass.: MIT Press.

Comblin, José. 1990. "Evangelização na atualidade." In *América Latina: 500 anos de evangelização.* São Paulo: Paulinas.

Corcoran-Nantes, Y. 1990. "Women and Popular Urban Social Movements in São Paulo, Brazil." *Bulletin of Latin American Research* 9 (2): 249–64.

De Kadt, E. 1970. *Catholic Radicals in Brazil.* London: Oxford University Press.

Della Cava, R. 1985. *Milagre em joaseiro.* São Paulo: Paz e Terra.

———. 1986 "A igreja e a abertura, 1974-1985." In *A igreja nas bases em tempo de transição (1974–85).* São Paulo: Cedec.

Doimo, A. M. 1986. "Os rumos dos movimentos sociais nos caminhos da religiosidade." In *A igreja nas bases em tempo de transição* (1974–85). São Paulo: Cedec.

———. 1995. *A vez e a voz do popular: Movimentos sociais e participação politica no Brazil.* Rio de Janeiro: Relume Dumará.

———. 1996. Paper presented at the conference *As culturas da política a política das culturas, revendo os movimentos sociais na America Latina.* São Paulo Unicamp, 20–22 March.

Drogus, C. A. 1997. *Women, Religion, and Social Change in Brazil's Popular Church.* Notre Dame: University of Notre Dame Press.

———. 1999. "No Land of Milk and Honey: Women CEB Activists in Post-transitional Brazil." *Journal of Interamerican Studies and World Affairs* 41 (4): 35–52.

Escobar, A., and S. Alvarez. 1992. *The Making of Social Movements in Latin America: Identity, Strategy, and Democracy.* Boulder, Colo.: Westview Press.

Flores, J. 1994. "Puerto Rican and Proud, Boyee!: Rap Roots and Amnesia." In *Microphone Fiends: Youth Music and Youth Culture,* edited by A. Ross and T. Rose. New York: Routledge.

Foweraker, J. 1995. *Theorizing Social Movements.* London: Pluto.

Franco, J. 1996. "The Great Gender War." Paper presented at the conference *As culturas da política a política das culturas, revendo os movimentos sociais na America Latina.* São Paulo Unicamp, 20–22 March.

Geertz, C. 1973. *The Interpretation of Cultures.* New York: Basic Books.

Gill, A. 1998. "The Struggle to Be Soul Provider: Catholic Responses to Protestant Growth in Latin America." Paper presented at the XXI International Congress of the Latin American Studies Association. Chicago, September 24–26.

Ginsburg, C. 1989. *Mitos, emblemas e sinais: morfologia e história.* São Paulo: Editora Schwarcz.

Gohn, G. M. 1991. *Movimentos sociais e luta pela moradia.* São Paulo: Edições Coyola.

———. 1995. *História dos movimentos e lutas sociais: a construção da cidadania dos brasileiros.* São Paulo: Loyola.

Gómes, I. 1999. "Religious and Social Participation in War-Torn Areas of El Salvador." *Journal of Interamerican Studies and World Affairs* 41 (4): 53–72.

Governo de São Paulo. 1993. *Direitos da criança e do adolescente.* São Paulo: Imprensa Official do Estado IMESP.

Greenblatt, S. 1996. *Possessões maravilhosas: o deslumbramento do novo mundo.* São Paulo: Edusp.

Gricoli, I. Z. 1996. *Igreja e camponeses: teologia da libertação e movimentos sociais no campo, Brasil e Peru 1964–1986.* São Paulo: Ed. Hucitec.

Hall, S., and P. Du Gay. 1996. *Questions of Cultural Identity.* London: Sage.

Herschmann, M. 2000. *O Funk e o Hip-Hop invadem a cena*. Rio de Janeiro: Editora UFRio de Janeiro.

Hewitt, W. E. 1991. *Base Christian Communities and Social Change in Brazil*. Lincoln: University of Nebraska Press.

———. 1998. "From Defenders of the People to Defenders of Faith: A 1984–1993 Retrospective of CEB Activity in São Paulo." *Latin American Perspectives* 25 (1): 170–91.

Hittinger, R. 1994. "Roberto Unger: Liberalism and 'Superliberalism.'" In *Liberalism at the Crossroads*, edited by C. Wolfe and J. Hittinger. London: Rowman and Littlefield.

Hochstetler, K. 2000. "Democratizing Pressures from Below? Social Movements in the New Brazilian Democracy." In *Democratic Brazil: Actors Institutions, and Processes*, edited by P. R. Kingstone and T. J. Power. Pittsburgh: University of Pittsburgh Press.

Ireland, R. 1986 "Communidades eclesiais de base, grupos espíritas, e a democratização no Brasil." In *A igreja nas bases em tempo de transição (1974–85)*. São Paulo: Cedec.

———. 1991. *Kingdoms Come: Religion and Politics in Brazil*. Pittsburgh: University of Pittsburgh Press.

———. 1997. "Pentecostalism, Conversions, and Politics in Brazil." In *Power, Politics, and Pentecostals in Latin America*, edited by E. L. Cleary and H. S. Gambino. Boulder, Colo.: Westview Press.

Jacobi, P. R. 1990. "Descentralização da gestão municipal: a inovação em debate." *Espaço e Debates* 30:89–90.

———. 1993. "Pobreza, educação, infância e adolescência: o retrato da desigualdade, exclusão e desestruturação social na metrópole de São Paulo." Cadernos CEDEC 30.

Kowarick, L., ed. 1988. *As lutas sociais e a cidade*. São Paulo: Paz e Terra.

Kowarick, L., and A. Singer. 1993. "A experiência do partido dos trabalhadores na Prefeitura de São Paulo." *Novos Estudos* 35:195–216.

Lamounier, B. 1996 "Brazil: The Hyperactive Paralysis Syndrome." In *Constructing Democratic Governance: Latin America and the Caribbean in the 1990s*, edited by J. I. Dominguez and A. F. Lowenthal. Baltimore: Johns Hopkins University Press.

Lajolo, T. 1991. "Areas de risco." *Folha de São Paulo*, 28 February.

Lehmann, D. 1990. *Democracy and Development in Latin America: Economics, Politics, and Religion in the Postwar Period*. Cambridge: Polity Press.

———. 1996. *Struggle for the Spirit: Religious Transformation and Popular Culture in Brazil and Latin America*. Cambridge: Polity Press.

Levine, D. 1992. *Popular Voices in Latin American Catholicism*. Princeton: Princeton University Press.

———. 1995. "Review Essay: On Premature Reports of the Death of Liberation Theology." *The Review of Politics* 57 (1):105–32.

Levine, D., and S. Mainwaring. 1989. "Religion and Popular Protest in Latin America: Contrasting Experiences." In *Power and Popular Protest: Latin American Social Movements*, edited by S. Eckstein. Berkeley: University of California Press.

Levy, C. 2000. "CEBs in Crisis: Leadership Structures in the São Paulo Area." In *The Church at the Grassroots in Latin America: Perspectives on Thirty Years of Activism*, edited by J. Burdick and W. E. Hewitt. Westport and London: Praeger.

Löwy, M. 1992. *Marxism in Latin America from 1909 to the Present: An Anthology*. London: Humanities Press.

———. 1996. *The War of Gods: Religion and Politics in Latin America*. London: Verso.

Macedo, C. C. 1986. *Tempo de gênesis: o povo das comunidades eclesiais de base*. São Paulo: Brasiliense.

Mainwaring, S. 1986a. "A Igreja Católica e o movimento popular: Nova Iguaçu— 1974–85." In *A igreja nas bases em tempo de transição* (1974–85). São Paulo: Cedec.

———. 1986b. *The Catholic Church and Politics in Brazil 1916–1985*. Stanford, Calif.: Stanford University Press.

Maricato, E. 1985. "Housing Policy in Brazil—The Space of Accumulation and the Space of Poverty." *BISS* 7:275–78.

———. 1988. "The Urban Crisis in Brazil in the 80s and the Popular Movement for Urban Reform." *BISS* 10:179–84.

Mariz, C. L. 1994. *Coping with Poverty: Pentecostals and Christian Base Communities in Brazil*. Philadelphia: Temple University Press.

Martin, D. 1990. *Tongues of Fire: The Explosion of Protestantism in Latin America*. Oxford: Blackwell.

———. 1998. "From Pre- to Postmodernity in Latin America: The Case of Pentecostalism." In *Religion, Modernity, and Postmodernity*, edited by P. Heelas, D. Martin, and P. Morris. Oxford: Blackwell.

Martins Filho, J. R. 1998 "Students and Politics in Brazil, 1962–1992." *Latin American Perspectives* 25 (1): 156–69.

Melucci, A. 1985. "The Symbolic Challenge of Contemporary Movements." *Social Research* 54 (4): 789–816.

———. 1989. *Nomads of the Present*. London: Century Hutchinson.

Nagle, R. 1997. *Claiming the Virgin: The Broken Promise of Liberation Theology in Brazil*. New York and London: Routledge.

Navarro de Toledo, C. 1998. "ISEB Intellectuals, the Left, and Marxism." *Latin American Perspectives* 25 (1): 109–25.

Nunes, E. 1985. "Carências urbanas e reivindicações populares." Mimeo, CEDEC.

Oliveira, P. 1970. *Catolicismo Popular no Brasil*. Rio de Janeiro: Cris.

Ortiz, R. 1980. *A consiência fragmentada: Ensaios de culture popular e religião*. Rio de Janeiro: Paz e Terra.

————. 1985. *Cultura Brasileira e identidade nacional*. São Paulo: Brasiliense.

————. 1988. *A moderna tradição Brasileira: cultura Brasileira e indústria cultural*. São Paulo: Brasiliense.

Papadakis, E. "Interventions in New Social Movements." In *The Politics of Field Research*. London: Sage, 1989.

Pinheiro, P. S. 1992. "São Paulo: People on the Margin and Civil Society." Paper presented at the Place and Right Conference, Ardem Homestead, New York, September 11–13.

Procópio, C. F. *Igreja e desenvolvimento*. CEBRAP. Sao Paulo: Editora Brasileira de Ciências Ltda, 1971.

Riviere D´Arc, H. 1999. "Has Basismo Disappeared?" *Bulletin of Latin American Research* 18 (2): 199–209.

Romano, R. 1979. *Brasil: Igreja contra Estado*. São Paulo: Kairós.

Rorty, R. 1984. "Habermas and Lyotard on Postmodernity." *Praxis International* 4.

————. 1991. *Essays on Heidegger and Others. Philosophical Papers*, vol. 2. Cambridge: Cambridge University Press.

Rose, T. 1994. "A Style Nobody Can Deal With: Politics, Style, and the Postindustrial City in Hip-Hop." In *Microphone Fiends: Youth Music and Youth Culture*, edited by A. Ross and T. Rose. New York: Routledge.

Rowe, W., and V. Schelling. 1991. *Memory and Modernity: Popular Culture in Latin America*. New York: Verso.

Sader, E. 1988. *Quando novos personagens entram em cena: experiências e lutas dos trabalhadores da Grande São Paulo, 1970–1980*. São Paulo: Paz e Terra.

Salman, T. 1994a. "The Diffident Movement: Generation and Gender in the Vicissitudes of Chilean Shantytown Organizations, 1973–1990." *Latin American Perspectives* 21 (3): 8–31.

————. 1994b. "Challenging the City, Joining the City: The Chilean pobladores between Social Movement and Social Integration." *Bulletin of Latin American Research* 13 (1): 79–90.

————. 1996. "Culture and Politics in Chile: Political Demands in an 'Apolitical' Society." In *The Legacy of the Disinherited in Latin America: Modernity, Globalisation, Popular Culture, Hybridity, and Authenticity*, edited by T. Salman et al. Amsterdam: CEDLA.

São Paulo para todos: Relatório final do governo. 1992. Prefeitura do município de São Paulo. December.

Scurrah, M. J. 1984a. "The Sector and Firm in Self-Management: I. Institutional Models, Economic and Industrial Democracy." *SAGE* 5:325–40.

————. 1984b. "The Sector and Firm in Self-Management: II. Lessons from the Peruvian and Chilean Experiences." *SAGE* 5:421–43.

Scurrah, M. J., and B. Podestá. 1984. "The Experience of Worker Self-Management in Peru and Chile." *Grassroots Development* 8 (1): 12–23.

Serbin, K. P. 2000a. *Secret Dialogues: Church-State Relations, Torture, and Social Justice in Authoritarian Brazil*. Pittsburgh: University of Pittsburgh Press.

———. 2000b. "The Catholic Church, Religious Pluralism and Democracy in Brazil." In *Democratic Brazil: Actors Institutions, and Processes*, edited by P. R. Kingstone and T. J. Power. Pittsburgh: University of Pittsburgh Press.

Slater, D. 1996. "Spatial Politics/Social Movements: Questions of (B)orders and Resistance in Global Times." Paper presented at the conference *As culturas da política a política das culturas, revendo os movimentos sociais na America Latina*. São Paulo Unicamp, 20–22 March.

Smith, C. 1991. *The Emergence of Liberation Theology: Radical Religion and Social Movement Theory*. Chicago: University of Chicago Press.

Soares, I. 1988. *Do santo oficio à libertação: o discurso e a prática do vaticano e da Igreja Católica no Brasil sobre a communicação social*. São Paulo: Paulinas.

Steil, C. A. 1998. "A Igreja dos Pobres: Da Secularização à Mística." *Religião e Sociedade* 19 (2): 61–76.

Stewart-Gambino, H. W. and E. Wilson. 1997. "Latin American Pentecostals: Old Stereotypes and New Challenges." In *Power, Politics, and Pentecostals in Latin America*, edited by E. L. Cleary and H. W. Stewart-Gambino. Boulder, Colo.: Westview.

Telles, V. S. 1986. "Anos 70: experiencias e praticas cotidianas." In *A Igreja nas bases em tempo de transição (1974–85)*. São Paulo: Cedec.

———. 1996. Paper presented at the conference *As culturas da política a política das culturas, revendo os movimentos sociais na America Latina*. São Paulo Unicamp, 20–22 March.

Thompson, T. A., I. Gebara, and M. C. Bingemer. 1989. *Maryknoll*. Orbis Books. http://www.udayton.edu/mary/brevfour.html, 1997.

Todorov, T. 1993. *Nós e os outros: a reflexão francesa sobre a diversidade humana 1*. Rio de Janeiro: Jorge Zahar.

Unger, R. M. 1975. *Knowledge and Politics*. New York: Free Press.

———. 1987. *Social Theory: Its Situation and its Task*. Cambridge: Cambridge University Press.

Unger, R., and C. Gómes. 1996. *O proximo passo: uma alternativa pratica ao neoliberalismo*. Rio de Janeiro: Topbooks.

Vásquez, M. A. 1997. "Structural Obstacles to Grassroots Pastoral Practice: The Case of a Base Community in Urban Brazil." *Sociology of Religion* 58 (1): 53–68.

———. 1998. *The Brazilian Popular Church and the Crisis of Modernity*. Cambridge: Cambridge University Press.

———. 1999. "Toward a new agenda for the Study of Religion in the Americas." *Journal of Interamerican Studies and World Affairs* 41 (4): 1–20.

Weffort, F. 1984. *Por que democracia?* São Paulo: Brasiliense.

Zald, M. N. 1996. "Culture, Ideology, and Strategic Framing." In *Comparative Perspectives on Social Movements: Political Opportunities, Mobilizing Structures, and Cultural Framings*, edited by D. McAdam, J. D. McCarthy, and M. N. Zald. Cambridge: Cambridge University Press.

Zaluar, A. 1990. "Teleguiados e chefes: juventude e crime." *Religão e Sociedade* 15 (1).

———. 1994. *Condomínio do diabo*. Rio de Janeiro: Revan: Ed. UFRJ (Universidade Federal de Rio de Janeiro).

———. 1996. *Da revolta ao crime S.A.* São Paulo: Edora Moderna.

INDEX

abortion, 71, 139
AC. *See* Catholic Action
ACB. *See* Brazilian Catholic Action
Afro spiritism, 11
agency 5, 11
antiassistentialism, 38
Arns, Dom Paulo Evaristo, 12, 18, 44, 53, 54, 82, 160, 169
arrastão, 123, 206n26
assistentialism, 121–22, 132–33, 157

BANESPA, 116, 119, 206n15
Base Education Movement (*Movimento Educacional de Base*—MEB), 28–30, 38
basismo, 4, 15, 29, 36, 55, 56; contradictions in, 4; as defined by David Lehmann, 4; eccentric, 57–58; liberationism without, 159, 178; political opposition of, 14; postmodern, 159; radical, 109, 123, 124, 132, 133, 163; strategic, 150
Bernadino, Dom Angélico Sândalo, 18, 83, 87, 144, 149, 152, 160, 164, 168
Betinho (Herberto da Souza), 116
Boff, Leonardo, 10, 39
Brazilian Catholic Action (*Ação Católica Brasileira*—ACB), 25, 28, 30, 33, 38
Brazilian Communist Party (PCB), 37
Brazilian Democratic Movement (*Movimento Democrático Brasileiro*—MDB), 51, 54, 57, 68, 69, 70
Brazilian Popular Party (*Partido Popular Brasileiro*—PPB), 104–6, 170
Buenos Aires, 149

Câmera, Dom Helder, 25
Cândido, Vincente, 176

career politics, 80, 132
Caritas, 112, 115, 119
catechist groups, 76, 91, 108, 118
Catholic Action (*Ação Católica*—AC), 25, 38
Catholic Agrarian Workers Youth (*Juventude Agrária Católica*—JAC), 30, 38
Catholic Charismatic Renewal Movement (CCRM), 160, 162, 164, 166, 171–72, 178
Catholic Student Youth (*Juventude Estudantil Católica*—JEC), 30, 38
Catholic University (*Pontifício Universitário Católico*—PUC), 31, 33, 70, 88
Catholic University Youth (*Juventude Universitária Católica*—JUC) 30, 33, 37, 38
Catholic Workers Youth (*Juventude Operária Católica*—JOC), 30, 38
Catholicism, popular, 28, 174–75. *See also* church, popular
CDHU. *See* State Public Housing Commission
CEBs. *See* Ecclesiastical Base Communities
CELAM. *See* Latin American Bishops Conference
charismatics. *See* Catholic Charismatic Renewal Movement
Children's Pastoral, 89, 119
Chilean case study (Veronica Schild), 169
Christian humanism, 27, 31, 32, 53
church, popular, 7, 12, 15, 18, 73, 83, 160, 162, 168, 172, 178. *See also* Catholicism, popular
Cintra, Benedito, 70
civil society: condemnation by, 74; effects of liberationism in, 162, 171, 174; project to construct a secular, 7–9; rela-

tionship between the state and, 94, 169
clientelism, 94, 108, 120, 179
CNBB. *See* National Conference of
  Brazilian Bishops
collective action, 2, 8, 54, 174
collective identity, 1, 98
collective mobilization, 6, 69
collective subjects, 5, 7, 8
Communist Party of Brazil (PCdoB), 37
conscientização (consciousness raising), 34;
  authenticity and, 35, 37
cooperatives, 110–12, 115, 118, 120, 126, 128
cost of housing, 84
cost-of-living movement (*Movimento do
  Custo da Vida*), 52
CPCs (Popular Centres of Culture),
  29–32; directive elements in, 141; liberation theology and, 141, 167, 171, 174;
  popular movements and, 52, 75, 81
cultural politics, 176
currency stabilization plan (*Plano Real*), 113
CUT. *See* workers' union

da Silva, Ignácio (Lula), 176
Democratic Workers Party (PDT), 17, 112
discourse analysis, 21, 112
Dom Aloisio. *See* Lorscheider, Dom
  Aloisio
Dom Angélico. *See* Bernadino, Dom
  Angélico Sândalo
Dom Carmelo. *See* Motta, Dom Carmelo
  Vasconcello
Dom Eugênio. *See* Sales, Dom Eugênio
Dom Fernando. *See* Figueiredo, Dom
  Fernando Antônio
Dom Helder. *See* Câmera, Dom Helder
Dom Luis. *See* Fernandes, Dom Luis
Dom Paulo. *See* Arns, Dom Paulo
  Evaristo
domestic violence: as beyond the
  Church's focus; and *elas*, 137–40; and
  the feminist left, 71; during land occu-
  pation, 103, as reason for participation
  in Catholic communities, 63–66; un-
  dermining collective action; 2, 15

Ecclesiastical Base Communities (CEBs),
  6; academic writing on, 9, 10, 43, 75;
  Catholic Church and, 44, 45, 53, 60, 82,
  162, 177; democratizing effect of, 13,
  14, 17, 35, 38, 48; institutionalization of,
  12; politicization of, 12, 43; popular
  movements and, 11, 162; proliferation
  of, 83; PT and, 144; socioeconomic ad-
  vancement and, 14
economy, popular, 122, 123
education, popular, 33, 37, 167
El Salvador, 89
elas (the shes), 136–41
enculturation, 163, 171
enlightenment, 52–53
Erundina, Luiza, 116; *basismo* and, 93, 144;
  election campaign of, 127, 130–32, 176;
  employment and, 114, 115; mobilization and, 142
Evangelical Politics, 43

feminism, 35, 149; academic-theological,
  145, 146; applied, 139; Catholic, 143,
  145–51, 155, 156, 168; ecumenical, 142,
  143, 153; liberationist, 71, 150; pastoral,
  143, 145, 150, 152. *See also* feminist
  Catholic movement; gender issues;
  gender roles
feminist Catholic movement, 138, 139, 144,
  150, 152, 180; and liberationist methodology, 138; and liberationist synthesis,
  73, 143, 149–51, 153, workshops of, 71,
  80. *See also* feminism; gender issues;
  gender roles
Fernandes, Dom Luis, 44
Figueiredo, Dom Fernando Antônio,
  161–63, 165, 168, 171
film. *See Pé na Caminhada*
FNT. *See* National Workers Front
food riots, 86
Freire, Paulo, 30, 34, 35, 46; Catholic Left
  and, 68; Christian Humanism and, 32;
  methodology, 29, 35, 36, 46; pedagogy,
  34, 35; teaching, 36; thought, 31, 35, 80,
  123, 138; work of, 31

Friends of the Neighborhood Association (*Sociedade Amigos de Bairro*—SABs), 87

Gebara, Ivone, 144, 146, 147, 151
gender issues, 66–67, 71–72, 136, 139, 141–42
gender roles, 14, 73, 136, 155
Gramsci, Antonio, 10, 34
grass-roots activism, 2, 18
grass-roots democracy, 76, 92–93

Higher Institute of Brazilian Studies (*Instituto Superior de Estudos Brasileiros*—ISEB), 29–34
hip-hop, 174–79
Holy Spirit, 166
Housing Pastoral, 88–89, 100, 107, 115, 119, 135
housing, popular, 85, 89, 91
Human Rights Pastoral, 100
human rights, 27, 53, 93
humanist enlightenment. *See* enlightenment
Hummes, Cláudio, 160, 161

imaginary, popular, 46
ISEB. *See* Higher Institute of Brazilian Studies

JAC. *See* Catholic Agrarian Workers Youth
JEC. *See* Catholic Student Youth
JOC. *See* Catholic Workers Youth
John Paul II, 59
John XXIII, 27, 55
joint venture (*parceria*), 167–68

Konrado, Father, 164–68, 170, 172, 178–79

Latin American Bishops Conference (CELAM), 42, 52
Leme, Cardinal, 25
liberation theology: applied, 91; break with, 152; consolidation of, 25, 26, 36, 39; crisis of, 10, 87; development

finance and, 119; disenchantment with, 10, 15, 173; faith and, 148; gender and, 66, 141, 152; historical background of, 96; influence of, 56, 179; institutional impact of, 17; institutionalization of, 16; political differences and, 51, 111; program of, 59; project of, 9, 13; PT and, 93; symbolic framework of, 38, 48, 102, 125, 164, 174; tension within, 44; values within, 61, 110. *See also* liberationism; liberationist thought
liberationism: attempted revival of, 86, 96; *basismo* and, 92, 117, 179, 180; conceptual basis of, 26, 173, 166; definition of, 2; disenchantment with, 83; dogmatism in, 129, 131; faith and, 148; feminism and, 71; flexible, 148; future directions in, 159–61, 164, 172, 178; impediment to, 4; influence on academic writing of, 10, 11, 13; lack of resonance of, 14; paradox in, 12; politics and, 172; redefinition of, 81; traditional, 142, 144. *See also* liberationist theology; liberationist thought
liberationist thought, 4, 16; consolidation of, 111; continuity in, 174; disenchantment with, 15; dogmatism in; 91; influence of, 10, 126; practice and, 2; reformation of, 148; secularization of, 175; subjectivity and, 109, 129, 137. *See also* liberation theology; liberationism
living conditions, deteriorating: and consciousness-raising, 79; and disenchantment with liberationist Catholicism, 14; and organized land occupations, 86–87; and political Left, 11; state agencies' attempts to improve, 115
Lorscheider, Dom Aloisio, 53
Lula. *See* da Silva, Ignácio

Maluf, Paulo, 74, 131, 170
Marcelo, Father, 164
Marx, Karl, 34. *See also* Marxism
Marxism, 10, 33; and class analysis, 38; and humanism, 37; and structuralism, 175

MCP. See Popular Culture Movement
MDB. See Brazilian Democratic Movement
MEB. See Base Education Movement
Medical Missionaries of Mary, 50
Mercadante, Aloísio, 131
military dictatorship, 6, 7, 9, 14, 162
Motta, Dom Carmelo Vasconcello, 43
Movement of the Landless (Movimento
    Sem Terra—MST), 111, 116, 128–29, 161,
    163, 179
MST. See Movement of the Landless

Natal Movement (Movimento de Natal), 31
National Conference of Brazilian Bishops
    (CNBB), 53, 161, 168, 180
national development, 29, 33
National Student Union (União Nacional
    dos Estudantes—UNE) 30–33, 37
National Workers Front (Frente National
    do Trabalhadores—FNT), 99, 100, 116,
    118
neighborhoods, 2, 4, 7, 61, 179
neo-Pentecostalism. See Pentecostalism
neoliberalism: and Catholic theology, 110;
    in mid-1990s, 1; and policymaking, 94;
    and reforms, 14; ; and revitalization,
    173–74; secularization of, 169
neo-Nietzschean revisionism, 20
new evangelization, 159, 163, 164, 166, 171
new social movements. See social movements

obreirismo, 173, 212n17

Pastoral Housing Agency. See Housing
    Pastoral
Pastoral Woman's Agency. See Woman's
    Pastoral
Pastoral Workers' Agency. See Workers'
    Pastoral
pastoral: agencies, 45; agents, 12, 18, 42,
    45, 88–89, 108, 113, 119, 122, 124; femi-
    nism, 143, 145, 150, 151, 152; initiatives,
    12, 51, 148, 150; organization, 50; plan,
53, 60, 63, 84, 87; practices, 2, 167; proj-
    ects, 172; publications, 66; reforms, 43;
    researcher, 89; services, 167; theme,
    161; workers, 42, 167. See also Housing
    Pastoral; Woman's Pastoral; Workers'
    Pastoral
Paul VI, 27
Paulista Women's Congress (1979), 67, 71
PCdoB. See Communist Party of Brazil
PCB. See Brazilian Communist Party
PDT. See Democratic Workers Party
Pé na Caminhada, 39, 40–42, 99
peasant organizations, 37
Pentecostalism 98, 159, 161, 164, 178
Pius XII, 27
political parties, 71, 74–78, 105, 109, 112,
    145–46, 162–63. See also specific names of
    parties
politics, popular, 2–6, 17, 19, 31, 58, 87, 94,
    96, 108, 134–35, 153, 177
Popular Action (Ação Popular—AP), 37–38
Popular Centres of Culture (Centro Popu-
    lar de Cultura—CPCs), 30–33
popular communities, 28, 174, 175
Popular Culture Movement (Movimento
    da Cultura Popular—MCP), 30. See also
    popular culture
popular culture, 32, 33, 39, 46, 96; authen-
    tic, 28 32–36, 57, 80, 83, 95, 108, 122–24,
    151; elite, 30, 163; as key symbol, 4, 26,
    162, 165, 174; non-capitalist principles
    and, 132; reframing of, 40; idealized,
    57–58
popular movements, 5–6, 54; activism, 18,
    20; approach, 127; Catholic communi-
    ties and, 11, 38; Dom Angélico Sândalo
    Bernadino and, 87; liberation theology
    and, 89; MDB and, 68; participation
    in, 59; politics of, 87; religious themes
    in, 9; struggle of, 89
popular struggles, 13, 19, 96
popular wisdom, 7, 137
populism, 29, 34
PPB. See Brazilian Popular Party
practical reason, 17

pragmatism, 5, 17, 19, 81, 95, 158
preferential option for the poor, 6
Protestantism, 4, 10. *See also* Pentecostal-
ism
PT. *See* Workers Party
PUC. *See* Catholic University

Racionais MCs (Masters of Ceremony),
175–78
Radio Cantareira, 96, 136, 140, 142, 145
Ramos, Guerreiro, 29
rap. *See* hip-hop
real wages, 86, 113
recession of 1982 and 1983, 74
religiosity, 41, 172–75
Rorty, Richard, 17

SABs. *See* Friends of the Neighborhood
Association
Sales, Dom Eugênio, 30
Santo Amaro, diocese of, 166, 171
Santo Domingo, 159. *See also* Latin American Bishops Conference
sexuality, 66–67, 71
social movements, 5; autonomous, 163;
Catholic Church and, 75; CEBs and,
162; decline of, 177; foreign influences
in, 55; gender issues in, 65, 72; identity
formation in, 9; international meeting
of, 89; Left and, 177; liberationist values and, 13; popular culture and, 177;
popular participation in, 49; secular
reading of, 6, 8, 9, 13; student movements, 26, 31, 37, 45, 69, 79, 97, 146
solidarity, popular, 106
Sposati, Aldaíza, 130, 135
State Public Housing Commission
(CDHU),104

underemployment. *See* unemployment

UNE. *See* National Student Union
unemployment, 75, 84, 86–87, 92, 108, 110,
113, 115, 130, 132
union movement, 5
United Nations (UN), 115
universal truth, 91, 125, 131

Vatican, 4, 12, 18, 27, 28, 60
Vatican II Council, 27–28, 166

Welfare Department (*Secretaria do Bem
Estar Social*), 115
welfare: bureaucracy, 113; handouts, 94;
mentality, 94
Woman's Pastoral, 143
women's movement, 71, 76, 97
women's rights, 66, 71
workers' movement, 51. *See also* Workers
Party; Workers' Pastoral; workers'
union
Workers Party (PT), 6–7; Catholic
Church and, 22, 74, 77; Catholic factions in, 36, 87–88, 100, 111, 144, 161;
cultural politics of, 132–33, 176–77;
Ignácio da Silva (Lula) and, 176; employment generation and, 94, 95, 131;
Luiza Erundina and, 114, 127, 130, 131,
170; favoritism and, 94; grass-roots
democracy and, 93; market capitalism
and 115; political conflicts involving,
104; popular participation and, 77, 80;
popular support for, 60, 105, 112, 116,
118–19, 131; Aldaíza Sposati and, 130,
135
Workers' Pastoral, 51
workers' union (*Central Unica dos Trabal-
hadore—CUT*), 87, 161
World War II, 26, 27

youth culture, 174, 177. *See also* hip-hop